Educator's Guide

SCHOLASTIC INC.

New York • Toronto • London • Auckland • Sydney
Mexico City • New Delhi • Hong Kong • Buenos Aires

Published by Scholastic Inc.

Printed in the U.S.A.

ISBN 0-439-74213-7

2 3 4 5 6 7 8 9 10 10 13 12 11 10 09 08

Table of Contents

Welcome to *SRI*

Getting Started

The *SRI* Student Program

Table of Contents

The Scholastic Achievement Manager

Welcome to *SRI*

Are your students making progress in reading? *Scholastic Reading Inventory*™ (*SRI*) is designed specifically to help you answer that question. More and more, teachers are being asked to use ongoing assessments of reading comprehension in the classroom to track student literacy skills, monitor students' reading progress, establish attainable goals, encourage accountability, and gauge the effectiveness of their reading programs. *SRI* will not only help fulfill these needs but will also provide information for teachers to work more efficiently by fostering improved planning for instruction as well as the ability to better match students to appropriately leveled text, encouraging growth and success.

SRI is an interactive reading comprehension test that provides an assessment of student reading levels, reported in Lexile® measures. The teacher component of *SRI* is the Scholastic Achievement Manager (SAM). *SRI* test results are automatically calculated and sent to SAM, which generates a variety of reports that help teachers monitor student progress and make data-driven decisions.

SRI . . .

- provides ongoing assessment.
- encourages accountability.
- is based on the Lexile Framework® for Reading.
- is computer-adaptive.
- generates actionable reports.
- matches readers to text.

NOTE FOR ADMINISTRATORS: *SRI* includes a number of features—including administrator-only reports—that leaders on both the district and school levels can use to monitor and guide the program. See pp. 129–131 for more details.

See Also...

For a detailed explanation of the Lexile Framework for Reading and Lexile scores, see pp. 135–140.

The Student Test

SRI has an item bank of over 4,500 questions and is based exclusively on passages from authentic children's literature, both fiction and nonfiction, as well as excerpts from young adult and classic literature, newspapers, magazines, and periodicals. Results are reported in both criterion-referenced and norm-referenced terms, indicating students' reading ability on the Lexile scale and how their test results compare to those of other students.

Upon completing the test, students receive Lexile scores, which are used to find the range of texts with which they are most likely to succeed. Students can also print customized reading lists with recommendations based on their determined reading level, interests, and developmental level.

Teacher/Administrator Management

The teacher component of *SRI,* the Scholastic Achievement Manager (SAM), is designed to make it easy for you to set up your Scholastic software and monitor student progress. Through SAM's easy-to-use interface, you can generate a variety of meaningful reports, and identify students who need special attention. SAM also enables you to customize the program to meet the needs of all your students.

SRI Reports

Key to making the most of *SRI* is to make full use of the reports that are generated by the Scholastic Achievement Manager. The reports will help you monitor progress, make instructional decisions, foster the school-home relationship, and administer the program. For more on reports, see the reports section of *Teaching With SRI,* beginning on page 127.

About This Guide

The Educator's Guide features easy-to-use, practical instructions for setting up and using *SRI* as well as instructional information on how to interpret and make the best use of test results. The first part of the guide is devoted primarily to instructions on using the software, and the second part primarily comprises instructional information.

In the first sections of the Educator's Guide, you will find information on how the Scholastic Achievement Manager can help you use the tools and menus for all of the features in *SRI*. You will learn how to set up, use, and customize the program to meet your students' needs and track their progress. The latter part of the guide contains instructional information on how to best administer and manage *SRI*, and use the test results in your classroom to help students succeed.

Program Information

- Getting Started (pp. 10–15) provides basic information on getting started on the Scholastic Achievement Manager.
- *SRI* Program Settings (pp. 16–25) provides a highlight on settings specific to *SRI*.
- *SRI* Student Program (pp. 26–32) walks you through the student *SRI* test-taking experience, including the generation of personalized Recommended Reading Reports.
- Scholastic Achievement Manager (pp. 33–126) leads you through this powerful and comprehensive program that will help you effectively run Scholastic programs; enroll students; import records; manage accounts; add students, classes, and groups; print reports; and customize student settings.

Instructional Information

- *Teaching With SRI* (pp. 127–194) provides suggestions for administering the test successfully, guidelines for interpreting student results, including summaries and examples of the *SRI* reports, and an overview of how *SRI* can be incorporated in a variety of instructional environments.
- *Reproducibles* (beginning on page 195, then numbered by reproducible) include parent letters, student reading log, a book recommendation form, and a number of other forms and worksheets you can use to build on and broaden the utility of the program for the teacher as well as students' *SRI* experience.

How *SRI* Works

Students

1. Students log on to the computer.

2. Students choose their reading interests (which are used to later prepare customized Recommended Reading Reports) and take the Practice Test, if required by the teacher.

3. The test begins. (Tests generally take 20–30 minutes to complete.)

4. The test ends when the student has answered enough questions for the test to accurately calculate a Lexile score for the student.

5. Students may view and print their Recommended Reading Reports.

Teachers

1. Test results, converted into Lexile scores, are automatically entered into a complete series of actionable reports in the Scholastic Achievement Manager.

2. Teachers review the reports to evaluate student reading levels and to monitor student progress. Test results help guide instruction and identify students who require intervention.

3. Teachers encourage students to read books on their Recommended Reading Reports, as well as other literature that is matched to the students' reading levels.

Why *SRI* Works

Authentic Text Passages

- Test items include fiction, nonfiction, and high-interest low-readability passages from high-quality trade books and informational materials.
- Authentic text passages increase test validity as well as student interest and motivation.
- Passages require students to make inferences, draw conclusions, and demonstrate use of vocabulary knowledge in context, among other higher-level thinking skills.

Computer Adaptive Testing

- The test adapts to students' responses. Students start the test; the test steps up or down according to their performance; and when the computer has enough information to generate a Lexile measure, the test stops.
- Adaptive testing shortens test-taking time and increases testing accuracy. (There are generally between 20 to 25 questions per test; never more than 30 questions will appear.)
- Lower-achieving students experience less test-taking anxiety because questions are at their level.
- With an item bank of more than 4,500 questions, students receive a unique test on each administration, with no two tests alike.

Actionable

- Test results measure students' reading comprehension levels, enabling teachers to assess their students' reading ability and plan instruction accordingly, and monitor their students' reading progress.
- Teachers can match students to appropriate reading materials according to both their Lexile level and interests, thereby encouraging reading success.
- Other tests and instructional programs are linked to the Lexile Framework, making it possible to share measures for text and readers across instructional and assessment options.

Accountable

- *SRI* provides teachers with an accurate measure of students' changing reading levels over time.
- Students' test scores are automatically saved in SAM and can be viewed in over twenty reports generated for individual students, groups, or classes. Reports can be shared with administrators. Some reports are for administrators only.
- An alert report identifies students who do not complete a test, making teachers aware of situations possibly requiring intervention.
- Results are criterion- and norm-referenced, providing a snapshot of students' reading abilities on a scale of text difficulty and how their test results compare to other students.

Flexible

- The test can be administered at any computer station (Mac or PC) and on any number of computers.
- The test is appropriate for most students from Grades 1–12.
- Settings (see pp. 16–18 in the Getting Started section) can easily be adjusted to accommodate specific student needs.
- The SAM management system is easy to use and can be customized to meet the needs of your students.

Indicative

- The Lexile measure is linked to various assessments, including the North Carolina End-of-Grade Test, Stanford 9 (SAT9), Stanford Diagnostic Reading Test (SDRT), and other popular tests.
- Immediate feedback on *SRI* test results provides educators with an indication of future standardized test performance.

The Lexile Framework for Reading

- Test scores are based on the Lexile Framework, a scientifically accurate system that assesses reading comprehension levels and matches readers to text (see page 135).
- The Lexile Framework measures the reading level of both students and text, placing them on the same absolute scale.
- The framework enables teachers to target students to text, which motivates them to read more and allows them to practice comprehension skills, build vocabulary, and respond to text—strategies that are essential for reading growth.
- The Lexile Framework not only provides a measure of the level at which each student is reading, but also a context in which to compare students' performance (their rate of growth in reading skills) across the entire developmental continuum for reading skills (e.g., from recognizing letters to reading and interpreting high school texts).

Valid and Reliable

- The Lexile Framework was developed based on the analyses of the reading comprehension levels of over 400,000 students between Grades 1–12 over a period of 15 years.
- *SRI* has been administered to over three million students between Grades 1–12 over the past five years.
- The Lexile Framework, supported with grants from the National Institute of Child Health and Human Development (NICHD), is based on more than 40 years of research by various reading comprehension specialists. Thousands of students and hundreds of teachers have contributed to its development.

See Also...

The *SRI Technical Guide* (packaged with software) contains more information on *SRI* test validity and reliability.

See Also...

For detailed information about the Scholastic Achievement Manager, see the SAM section beginning on page 33.

If your students are not set up or enrolled, refer to "Setting Up Your Classroom" in the SAM section beginning on page 71.

For detailed information on installation procedures, refer to the *SRI Installation Guide.*

Getting Started

Installation

Scholastic Reading Inventory is designed to run on a system of networked computers, working in conjunction with the Scholastic Achievement Manager. Some of the *SRI* program software will live on the network's application server and some will live on a workstation. The *SRI* program software can accommodate a variety of equipment setups and classroom management scenarios.

First check that SAM and *SRI* have been installed on your district or school servers, and have been configured for your school, teachers, classes, and students. If not, then you may need to contact your school's Technical Coordinator to complete the installation and set up procedures, depending on your permissions setting.

SAM "client" software must be installed on the teacher workstation that you will use for administrative tasks related to *SRI*. This computer (which can be one of the student computers, if necessary) must be part of the school network, ideally be connected to a printer (preferably color) that you can access easily, and must have an Internet connection.

When SAM is installed, you will see the SAM icon on your teacher computer workstation desktop.

Once the software is installed on the server, the *SRI* "client" software should be installed on each student workstation in your classroom on which *SRI* will be used.

When *SRI* is installed, you will see the Scholastic Reading Inventory icon on your classroom computer desktops.

Permissions

For security purposes SAM includes a set of permissions based on user account type, which controls the information different users are permitted to view, add, edit, or delete.

There are four different types of user accounts in SAM: Teachers, School Administrators, District Administrators, and Technical Coordinators. SAM has created a standard set of permissions, but these can be customized to suit your own network installation and technical support needs.

You can view your permissions from any screen in SAM by clicking the My Profile link at the upper right corner of the screen, and then clicking the Permissions tab.

If you have a Teacher account, using the standard SAM permissions, you will be able to view and edit information on your students and classes, as well as your own profile. If you have a School Administrator account, you will not only be able to view and edit the same information as teachers, but for Grades and your School as well. If you are a District Administrator, you will additionally be able to view and edit information about your District. Technical Coordinators have total access to view and edit all information on the system.

See Also...

For detailed information on permissions, see the SAM section beginning on page 41.

Passwords

Like most computer software programs that contain sensitive information, SAM uses a password system to secure data.

When your District or School Technical Administrator installed SAM, part of the procedure was to create accounts for SAM users. To log in to your SAM accounts you will need to use your username and password; if you do not know your username and password, contact your Technical Administrator.

To ensure the security of your school's data, it is recommended that each SAM user change his or her password when he or she begins to use SAM. Further, it's advisable to change passwords regularly thereafter. Administrators may also set new passwords for any teachers who forget theirs.

Changing a Password:

1. Launch SAM (if it's not already open).
2. From anywhere in SAM, click the My Profile button on the upper right corner of the screen. The Edit Profile window will open.
3. Type your new password in the Password field.
4. Re-type the new password in the Confirm Password field.
5. Click the Save button to save your new password and close the Edit Profile window, or click Cancel to exit the window without saving changes.

Starting the Program and Logging In

When the Scholastic Achievement Manager and *Scholastic Reading Inventory* programs are installed, you will see icons for both SAM and *SRI* on your classroom computer desktops.

To perform classroom management activities such as adding students; changing student, group, or class information; grading; and running reports, launch SAM by double-clicking its icon.

Enter your Username and Password; verify the server name and click Login. This will open your SAM Home Page.

To launch *SRI* for student use, double-click the *SRI* icon.

> **TIP**
>
> The easiest way to access a profile screen is by double-clicking on a Student, Class, Teacher, or School name in the SmartBar.

Enrollment and Settings

Once SAM and *SRI* have been installed, you are ready to enroll your students in the program. You may also adjust the program settings for your students' particular needs.

There are three tabs on the *SRI* settings screen (each tab is explained in more detail in the sections below):

1. Enrollment
2. Settings
3. Advanced Settings

Enrolling Students Tab

If your school's Technical Coordinator has already enrolled students in *SRI*, skip to the next section, "*SRI* Program Settings," to customize the *SRI* program for your students.

To check that your students are enrolled in the Scholastic programs, in SAM:

1. Click My Classes to open your profile.
2. Look at the Usage Summary table to see the number of students that are enrolled in each Scholastic program.

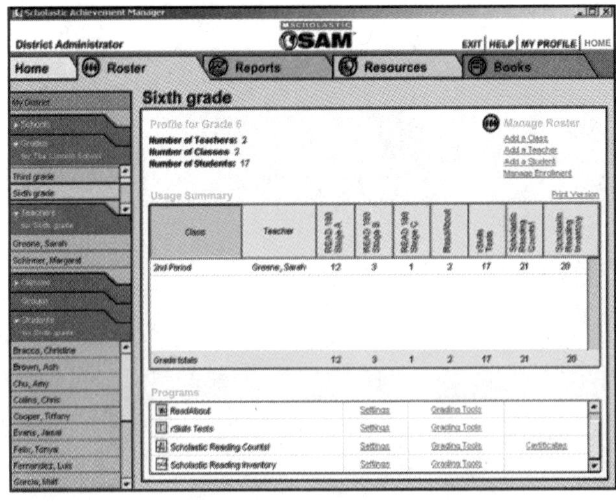

Enrolling Students *continued*

If you need to enroll students in *SRI*:

3. On the SmartBar, double-click the class name of the students you wish to enroll.
4. In the table called Programs, click Settings in the Scholastic Reading Inventory row. This will open the *SRI* settings window.
5. Click the Enrollment tab to display a list of students in the selected class.
6. To enroll all students in a class, click the box in the column header. To enroll specific students, check the boxes adjacent to individual names.
7. Click Save to save your changes and enroll another class. Or, click Save and Return to go back to the Roster screen. Click Cancel and Return to return to the Roster without making any enrollment changes.
8. To continue and enroll a different class in *SRI*, double-click another class name on the SmartBar. This will display the Enrollment tab for that class; follow the same procedure.

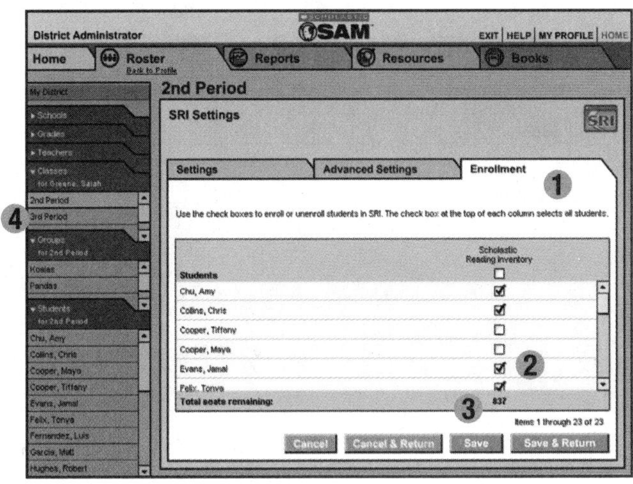

1. To enroll all students, click this box.
2. Use the check boxes to enroll specific students in *SRI*.
3. Click Save to save your changes.
4. Double-click another class name to see the Enrollment tab for that class.

SRI Program Settings

To individualize the *SRI* experience, you can adjust ***SRI* Program Settings** for your classes, groups, and students. Those with administrator permissions have additional options under the **Advanced Settings** window. You can use the settings to:

- set an estimated reading level before students take their first *SRI* test to obtain more accurate test results.
- set whether you want students to take a practice test.
- adjust the number of days between *SRI* tests.
- give your students the option to choose reading topics that interest them and see a list of recommended books based on their choices.
- allow your students to see their Lexile scores.
- determine the Lexile ranges for reading proficiency (administrators only.)
- enroll and unenroll students in *SRI.*

The ***SRI* Program Settings** window can be accessed from any Profile screen in SAM.

1 Double-click a **class, group,** or **student** name on the **SmartBar** for whom you would like to adjust settings.

2 Click Settings next to Scholastic Reading Inventory to open the ***SRI* Program Settings** menu. The ***SRI* Settings** screen will appear.

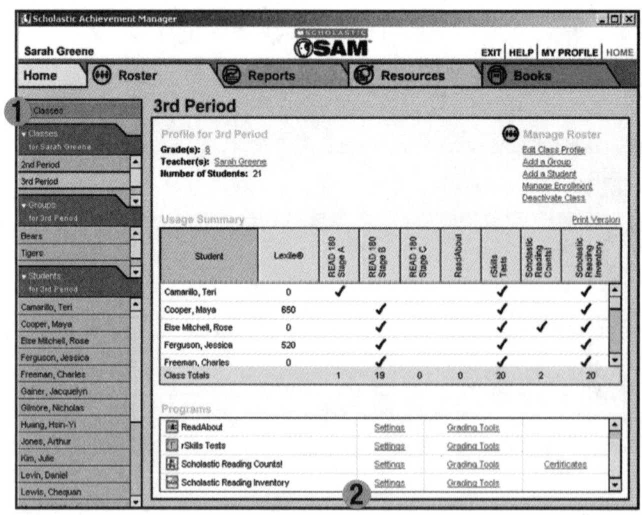

Changing Student Settings

Settings

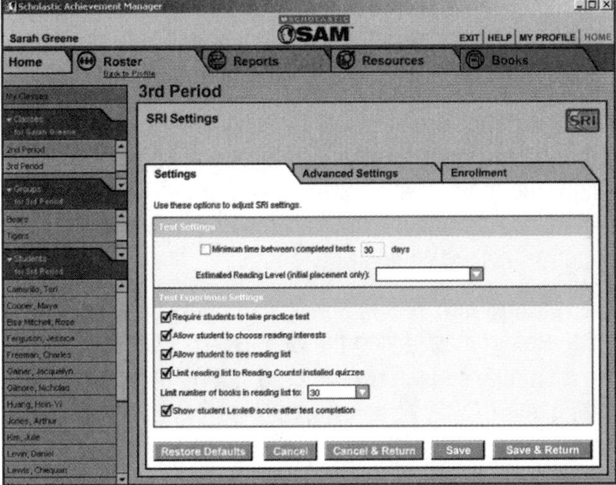

The following is a list of the program options for *SRI*. You can click the boxes to check or uncheck the items and use the pull-down menus to make your selections.

Student Settings

- **Minimum time between completed tests:** This lets you set the minimum number of days between *SRI* tests. Click the box to select this option and then enter the minimum number of days before students take another *SRI* test. The default is 30 days.
- **Estimated Reading Level:** You can select a reading level prior to a students taking the first *SRI* test. This option is not available after the first *SRI* test. Use the pull-down menu to choose undetermined, far below grade level, below grade level, on grade level, above grade level, or far above grade level based on previous test scores, teacher observations, or other data.

TIP

Remember that some settings might make sense for your whole class. You may want to change other settings for just one student. Use the SmartBar to adjust settings for the whole class or for individual students.

Student Settings *continued*

- **Require students to take practice test:** Choose this option to have the student take a practice test before the actual test each time *SRI* is administered. If this option is not selected, the student will take the practice test only the first time he or she takes *SRI*. The default setting is on.
- **Allow student to choose reading interests:** Students can choose the topics that interest them the most. The program uses students' self-reported reading interests in determining the Recommended Reading List. The default setting for this option is on.
- **Allow student to see reading list:** This option lets students view the Recommended Reading Report after taking the *SRI* test. This list of titles is selected from a database of approximately 10,000 appropriate titles. The default setting is on.
- **Limit reading list to SRC! installed quizzes:** Choose this option to create a Recommended Reading Report exclusively of titles for which you have *Scholastic Reading Counts!™* quizzes installed. The default setting is off. To turn the setting on, ensure that students are enrolled in *SRC!*
- **Limit number of books in reading list:** You can select the number of titles to include in the Recommended Reading Report. The default number of titles in the Reading Report is 30.
- **Show student Lexile score after test completion:** This option allows students to view their Lexile score at the end of the test. The default setting is on.

When you are finished making your selections, click Save and Return to go back to the Profile screen. Click Save if you wish to remain on the Settings screen. You may use the SmartBar to change the settings for another class, group, or student. Click Restore Defaults to return to the original *SRI* settings.

Changing Advanced Settings

Advanced Settings

The Advanced Settings window allows school or district administrators to customize the number, name, and Lexile range of proficiency bands for reporting *SRI* scores. Proficiency bands allow you to determine the level of performance students must demonstrate to meet certain reading performance standards.

Anyone using SAM may view the information in this tab. However, only those with administrator permissions may make changes. Any change will apply to the entire school or district selected on the SmartBar.

To change the number of proficiency bands:

1. Use the Number of Proficiency Bands pull-down menu to select the desired number of proficiency bands. The default setting is four.
2. Click OK when you have made your selection. The table will show the number of bands you selected. The upper limit scores for each band will appear blank.
3. Type the name for each proficiency band at the top of each column.
4. Type the Lexile score that will be the upper-limit cutoff for each band for each grade. SAM automatically fills in the lower score for the next range. The table must be filled in completely for SAM to save the new proficiency band settings.
5. Click Save and Return when you are finished to go back to the school or district Profile screen. Or, click Save to remain on the Advanced Settings window.

Click Restore Defaults to return to the default proficiency band settings for *SRI*.

Advanced Settings *continued*

1. Type in the fields to make any changes to default names.
2. Select the number of proficiency bands for your school or district.
3. Enter the upper-limit Lexile number for each grade.
4. The lower limit automatically fills in once you've entered the upper-limit numbers.
5. You can revert to the original program settings by clicking **Restore Defaults.**

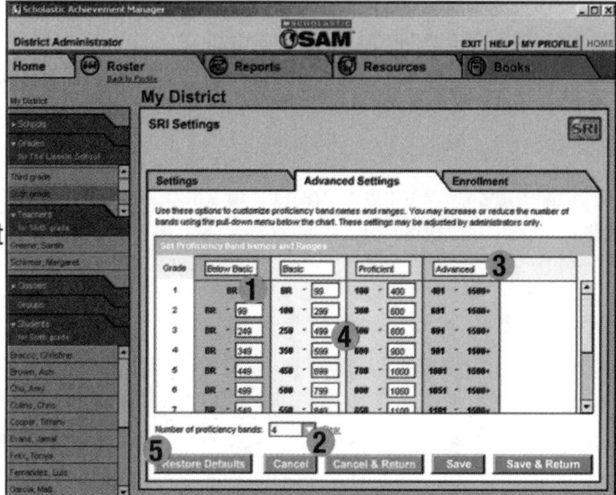

SRI Grading Tool

The ***SRI* Grading Tool** allows you to include results from the *SRI* print test in your students' records in the Scholastic Achievement Manager. The print test scores you enter into SAM are included in the data used to generate *SRI* reports that help you assess your students' performance and progress. You can also view your students' *SRI* computer test scores here to get a complete picture of your students' *SRI* testing history.

Viewing a Student's Test Results

You can see a list of all the test scores that have been recorded for a student—both *SRI* print tests as well as the *SRI* computer tests. To view this list:
Launch SAM.

1. Double-click a student's name on the SmartBar and click the yellow Roster tab to open the student's Profile screen.
2. In the Programs table at the bottom of the Profile screen, click the Grading Tools link in the *SRI* row. The *SRI* Grading Tool window will appear.

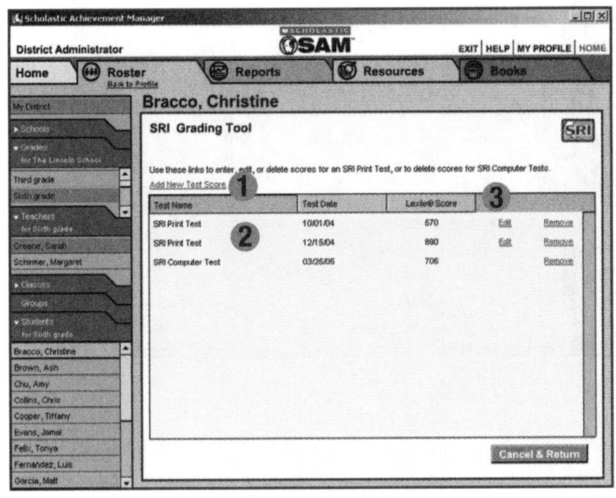

1 Add a new score by clicking here.

2 This table contains a list of all the tests recorded for this student.

3 Edit or delete any score here.

TIP

If you delete a test in error, you may immediately click Cancel on the *SRI* Tests window. The test will be restored the next time you see the window.

Adding, Editing, or Deleting a Student's Test Results

If your students take the *SRI* print test, you can add their scores into SAM to be included in the *SRI* reports. You may also edit those scores using the ***SRI* Grading Tool**.

To add, edit, or delete a print test score:

1. Launch SAM.
2. Double-click a student's name on the SmartBar and click the yellow Roster tab to open the student's Profile screen.
3. In the Programs table at the bottom of the Profile screen, click the Grading Tools link in the *SRI* row.
4. To add a test score: Click the Add a New Test Score link to open that window. This is where you can enter the test detail.

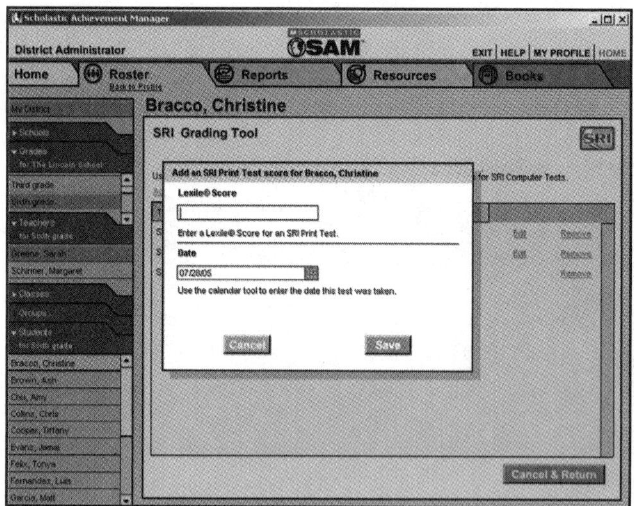

Adding, Editing, or Deleting a Student's Test Results *continued*

5. Enter the new Lexile score.
6. Use the calendar tool to select a different date. The date field will automatically show the current date.
7. Click Save to save the new test score and return to the *SRI* Grading Tool window, or Cancel to return to the window without saving the new information.
8. To edit a test score: Click the Edit link. A window opens for you to change the test information.
9. To delete a test score: Click the Remove link. The screen will refresh and the deleted test score will no longer appear on the list.

TIP

See the *SRI* reports section under *Teaching With SRI* for detailed information on using reports.

SRI Reports

Overview

The Scholastic Achievement Manager automatically saves the results of each student's work in *SRI*. You can access this information through the blue Reports button at the top of the main screen of SAM. Reports provide you with information on student, class, and group progress in a variety of formats, including charts, graphs, and narratives.

Each of the reports can be used for different purposes. For your convenience, the reports have been organized into the following types: Progress Monitoring, Instructional Planning, Alerts & Acknowledgments, School-to-Home, and Management. Some reports are available only to school administrators and principals.

Quick Steps for Running Reports

Here are a few *basic* steps to run a report:

1. Double-click the name of the teacher, student, class, group, grade, or school on the SmartBar for which you would like to run a report.
2. Click the blue Reports tab to show the Reports Index. The Reports Index lists the programs being used in your school and the recommended reports in each program for the SmartBar selection.
3. Click the *SRI* bar to show the list of *SRI* reports.
4. Click the circle next to the report name to select the *SRI* report you want to run.
5. Use the radio buttons if you wish to select different dates for the Time Period. SAM automatically fills this in with the current time period.
6. Click Run Report to see the report on your screen.

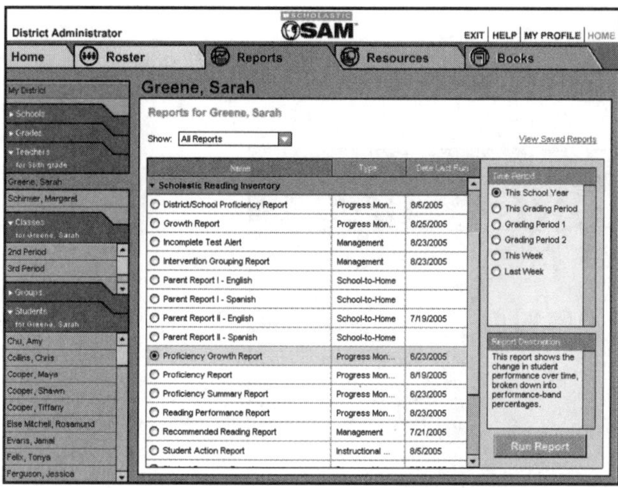

To print the report:

1. Click the Print Preview (PDF) link in the upper right part of the window. A new window will open with an Adobe Acrobat® (PDF) version of the report.
2. Click the Print button to print the report. Confirm your printer settings by clicking Page Setup to change the page orientation of a report, the printer you wish to print to, or the paper size.
3. Close the window running Adobe Acrobat and return to the SAM window when you are finished viewing and printing.

Use the Show pull-down menu at the top of the screen to quickly find a list of reports to run. The Show option allows you to filter the types of reports (multi-classroom, classroom, student, or all reports).

Click the column headers to sort by report name, date run, or by the category of reports (Progress Monitoring, Instructional Planning, Alerts & Acknowledgment, School-to-Home, and Management).

TIP

Before your students take the *SRI* test, you may wish to review some test-taking strategies with them. See the Test-Taking Strategies section on page 134.

See Also...

To change or find a student's password, use SAM to open and edit the student's profile. Refer to the SAM section of this guide for detailed instructions.

The *SRI* Student Program

Student Login

Once your students are enrolled in *Scholastic Reading Inventory* and the Scholastic Achievement Manager, they are ready to take the *SRI* test.

To log in to *SRI*, a student:

1. Double-clicks the *SRI* icon on the desktop. A login screen opens.
2. Types in his or her username and password.
3. Clicks Go or presses the Enter key.

Using the Book Interest Screen

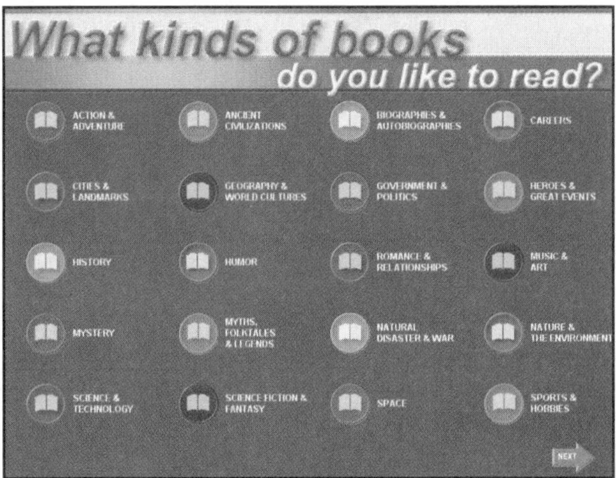

Before taking the *SRI* test, students are asked to indicate what types of books they like to read. Students can select up to three categories of books. The categories include topics such as "friends and family," "sports and fun," and "earth and space." These categories change based on grade level: K–2, 3–5, and 6–12.

The choices made by each student are used to create an individualized Recommended Reading Report at the completion of the test. The books on the Recommended Reading Report are chosen based on the student's reading interests and current Lexile score, ensuring that recommended books are engaging and at an appropriate reading level.

To select the three book interest categories:

1. The student clicks on the types of books he or she likes to read. The student can click again to deselect the choice.
2. The student then clicks the Next button.

TIP

If you do not wish to include students' interests in the Recommended Reading Report, you can turn off this feature on the *SRI* program settings window.

Taking the Practice Test

After logging in, a student is presented with the test directions. When he or she finishes reading or listening to the directions, he or she can click Next to begin the practice test.

The purpose of the practice test is to make sure that students understand the directions and how to use the computer to take the test. The practice test consists of three practice questions that are in the same format as the actual test questions. These questions are designed to be easier than the student's targeted reading level, and the student should be able to answer them correctly. The purpose is simply to assess whether the student understands the directions and the interface.

During the practice test, students will:

- read a paragraph of fiction or nonfiction;
- read a fill-in-the-blank question;
- read the four multiple-choice answers;
- select the best answer choice and click Next.

Practice Test questions do not count towards the student's final score. If a student answers a question incorrectly during the practice test, a Help window appears to suggest that the student approach the teacher for assistance. The student is then given a few additional questions to answer before completing the Practice Test.

After the practice test is completed, the actual test will begin. If a student does not have an Estimated Reading Level set in SAM, the first time he/she takes SRI, the practice questions are followed by 2 to 5 questions, depending on correct and incorrect responses. These questions determine an appropriate starting difficulty for the test.

Taking an *SRI* Test

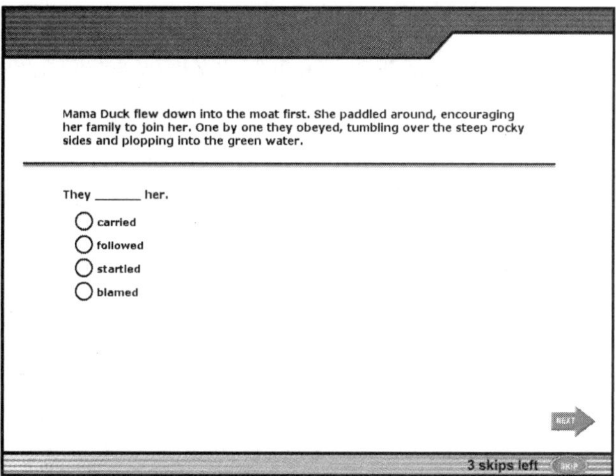

Mama Duck flew down into the moat first. She paddled around, encouraging her family to join her. One by one they obeyed, tumbling over the steep rocky sides and plopping into the green water.
They _____ her.
carried
followed
startled
blamed
NEXT
3 skips left
SKIP

An *SRI* test consists of brief selections of authentic fiction and nonfiction literature.

After reading each passage, the student is asked a question. The student selects the answer and clicks Next. To change an answer, the student selects another answer choice before clicking Next. Once the student clicks Next, he or she cannot return to the question.

Students can select answers by using either the mouse or the arrow keys on the keyboard.

To select an answer using the mouse:

1. The student clicks on the answer. The answer will be selected and the word or phrase will appear in the blank in the sentence.
2. To change an answer, the student clicks on the new answer.
3. The student clicks Next when he or she has completed the question.

To select an answer using the keyboard:

1. The student uses the up and down arrows to move through the choices.
2. The student presses the space bar to select an answer. The word or phrase will appear in the blank in the sentence.
3. To change an answer, the student uses the up and down arrow keys, and presses the space bar to select a new answer.
4. The student presses the Enter key when he or she has completed the question.

To change an answer, the student must select another choice before moving on to the next question. Once the student clicks Next or presses Enter, he or she cannot return to that question.

Throughout the SRI test, students can choose to skip up to three questions. To skip a question, students click on the Skip button in the lower right of any question screen. Skipped questions do not affect students' final scores.

To skip a question using the keyboard, students press the Tab key until the Skip button is highlighted, then press the space bar.

Exiting and Returning to an Incomplete *SRI* Test

Students may quit and save incomplete *SRI* tests to accommodate schedules for computer use or if they simply need more time. When they log in to *SRI* again, they will be automatically prompted to continue taking the test.

To *exit* the program, students press the <Esc> key. They will then be asked if they want to quit (click Yes) and if they want to save and return to the incomplete test later on (click Yes). If they click No, the test will be counted as incomplete and will not be saved.

To *return* to a test, students log in to *SRI*. They will be immediately taken to the question on which they previously exited the test.

A test might also be interrupted due to a computer crash or a power outage. If the testing session is going to take a long time, we recommend that you give your students small breaks, save the incomplete *SRI* tests during the breaks, and have your students return to the tests after their breaks.

Viewing the Recommended Reading Report

At the completion of the test, students can click View to see an individualized Recommended Reading Report based on the results from the *SRI* test and the types of books selected on the Book Interest screen. These are selected from a 10,000-title database of age-appropriate books. The Recommended Reading Report will also show which of the books have *Scholastic Reading Counts!* quizzes installed.

Printing the Reading Report

To print the customized Recommended Reading Report, students can click Print after clicking View. The Print window will open. Click OK to print the Recommended Reading Report.

Exiting *SRI*

To exit the program, the student simply clicks Quit once he or she is given the choice. The program will close.

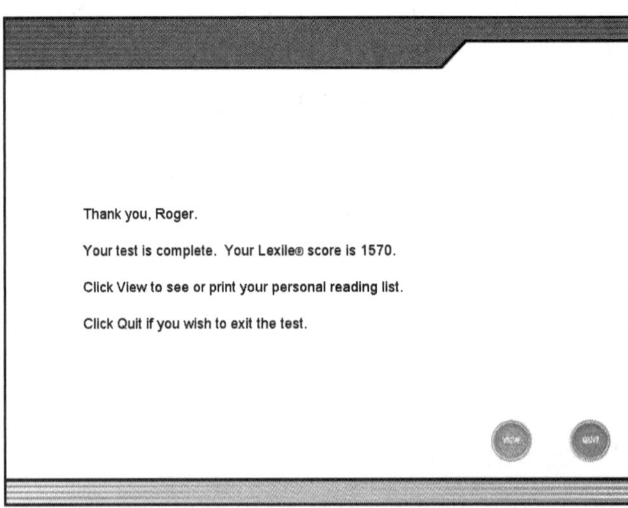

Thank you, Roger.
Your test is complete. Your Lexile® score is 1570.
Click View to see or print your personal reading list.
Click Quit if you wish to exit the test.

About SAM

The Scholastic Achievement Manager™ (SAM) is the learning management system for all Scholastic software programs, including *READ 180, Scholastic Reading Inventory, Scholastic Reading Counts!,* and *ReadAbout.* SAM collects and organizes performance data students generate while using Scholastic programs. SAM allows teachers and administrators to understand and implement data-driven instruction by providing easy-to-use tools for:

- Managing student rosters;
- Generating reports that capture student performance data at the student, classroom, school, and district levels;
- Locating helpful resources for classroom instruction.

SAM also supports teachers and administrators by:

- Including demographic information and enhanced data aggregation capabilities to generate reports that meet No Child Left Behind (NCLB) requirements;
- Aligning instruction to standards;
- Communicating student progress to parents, teachers, and administrators;
- Facilitating the import/export of data to/from a Student Information System (SIS) and/or a data warehouse.

A Note About Installation

Your school or district Technical Coordinator should have installed and set up SAM and the Scholastic programs that your school has purchased.

For detailed information about the installation process, consult the *SRI Installation Guide.*

For more information on setting up Profiles in SAM, refer to page 46.

Signing In and Signing Out

Signing In

In order to sign in to SAM you will need to have a Username and Password. Your Technical Administrator may have set these up during the installation and setup process. Contact your school technical coordinator if you are unsure about your Username and Password.

To sign in once you have a Username and a Password:

1. Double-click the SAM icon on your computer to launch SAM and open the sign-in screen.
2. Type your Username and your Password.
3. Click the check box to select **Remember my Username, Password and settings** if you are the only person to use this computer on a regular basis to speed up future sign-ins.
4. Click the **Password Hint** link if you can't remember your password to display your preselected password hint. If you do not see a hint, contact your Technical Administrator.
5. Select the server (network address) where SAM was installed on your school's network. The address that was most recently used will be displayed. If you need to change server locations, use the pull-down menu to select a different server.
6. Click **Add Servers** to create a new server connection. Contact your administrator for more information about available servers.
7. Click **Sign In** to begin work on SAM.

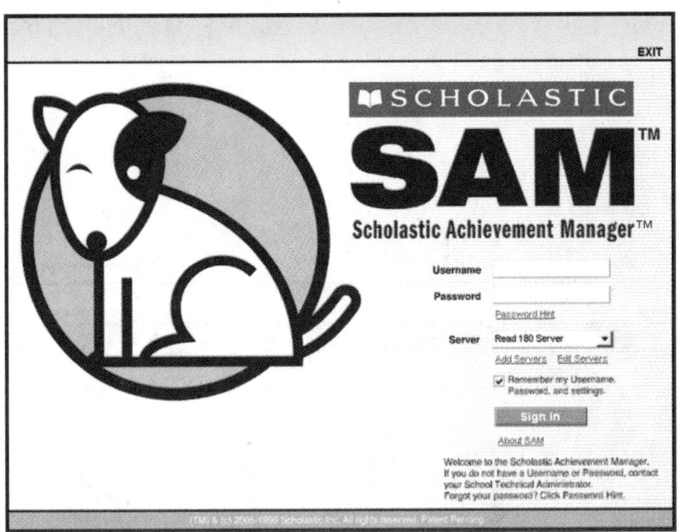

Changing Your Password

The first time you sign in to SAM as a teacher or administrator, you will use the password assigned to you by your Technical Administrator. We recommend for future use that you change your password. To change your password:

1. Click the **My Profile** link in the Quick Links of any SAM screen to open your **"Edit Profile"** window.
2. Type your new password in the **Password** field, then retype it in the **Confirm Password** field.
3. Click **Save** to change your password.

Signing Out

To sign out of SAM, click **Exit** in the Quick Links of any SAM screen. Click **Exit SAM** when you are asked to confirm your choice.

NOTES/TIP

Use the **Password Hint** field in the **"Edit Profile"** window to provide yourself a password reminder as you sign in to SAM in the future.

The Home Page

The Home Page gives you access to any part of SAM with just a few clicks. It has three main areas:

- Quick Links
- Main Display
- **SmartBar**

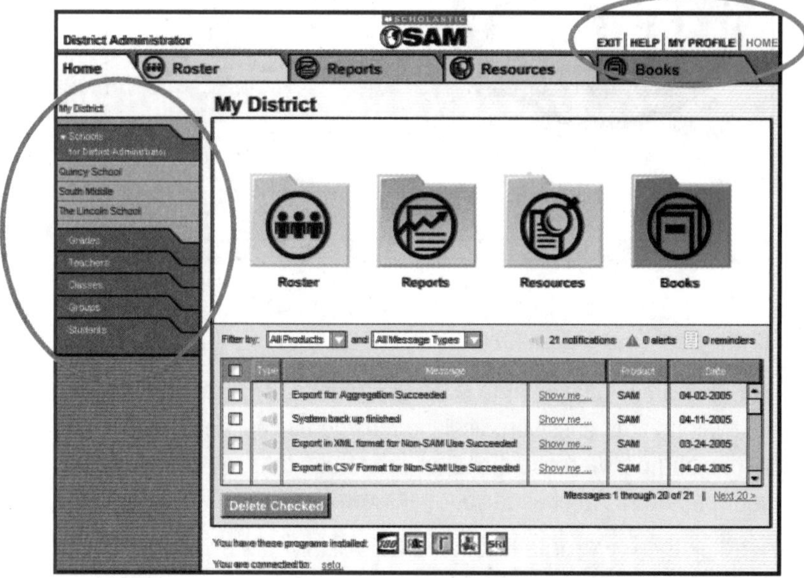

Quick Links

The Quick Links appear on the top right-hand side of every SAM screen so that you never get lost, and will always have an opportunity to:

- **Exit** SAM;
- Get **Help**;
- Go to your Profile screen;
- Return to the SAM Home Page.

The SmartBar

The **SmartBar** is the core of SAM navigation. It appears as the left hand column on every SAM screen and is the quickest route to displaying information about the schools and students that are using Scholastic programs. Your selection on the **SmartBar** will appear in the main display.

The **SmartBar** gets its "smarts" from the way it quickly sorts all Profile and reports information for any **School**, **Class**, **Group**, **Teacher**, or **Student** you select.

Your **SmartBar** choices will vary based on the level of permissions you have in SAM.

There are two types of permissions:

- **Administrative Accounts:** provide access to **Schools**, **Grades**, **Teachers**, **Classes**, **Groups**, and **Students** on the **SmartBar**.
- **Teacher Accounts:** provide access to your own **Classes**, **Groups**, and **Students** on the **SmartBar**.

See page 41 for more detailed information on permissions.

The **SmartBar** works using a "top-down system." All of the information in the **SmartBar** is related and the information contained in the tabbed lists beneath are dependent on the tabs above. Click any **SmartBar** tab to expand each of the tabs separately.

If you select a class name on the **SmartBar**, the **Groups** and **Students** tabs underneath will list only those in that class.

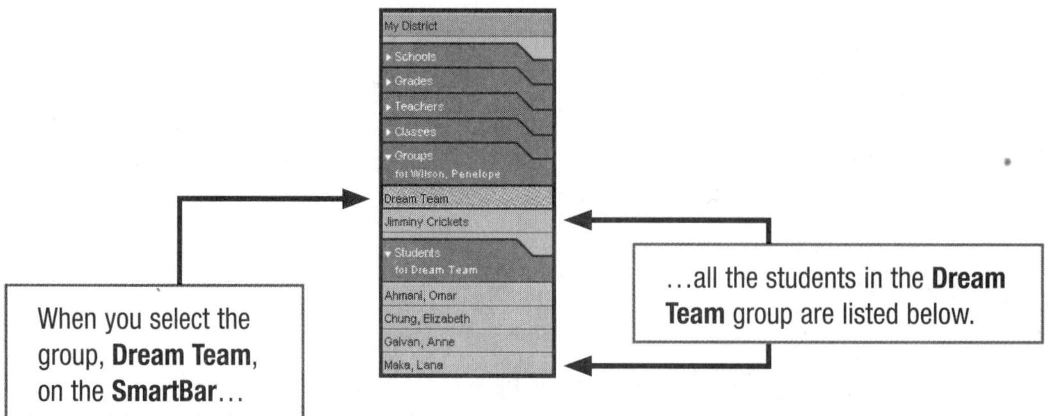

If you select a different class, then the **Groups** and **Students** tabs will list all the groups and students in the new class you just selected. In some cases, there may be too many names to display at once and a scroll bar will appear in the **SmartBar**.

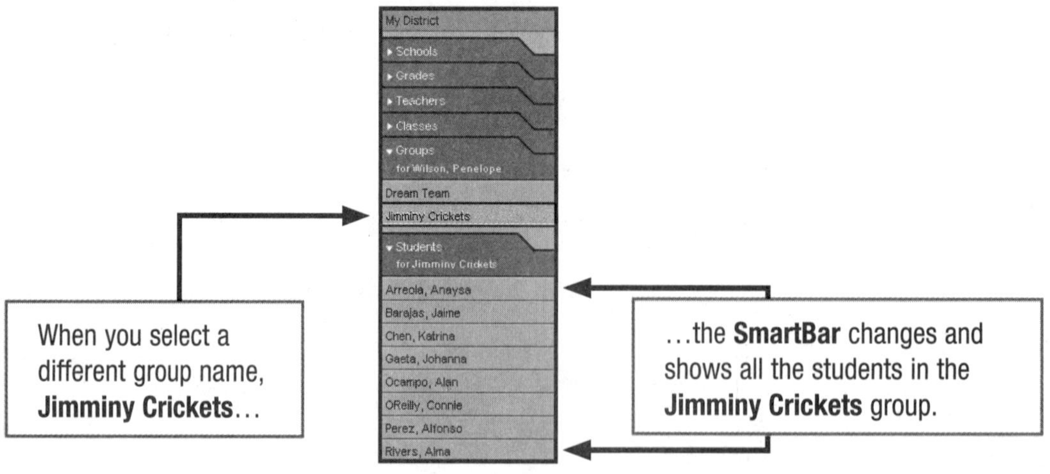

To navigate using the **SmartBar**:

1. Single-click either the **Schools**, **Classes**, **Groups**, or **Students** tab to reveal enrollments. Click the tab again to compress and hide the names on it.
2. Double-click any name on the **SmartBar** to select it. Use the tabs along the top of the main display to manage a Profile or generate reports for your selection.

Main Display

The Home Page main display shows:

- Four Home Page buttons: **Roster**, **Reports**, **Resources**, and **Books**
- **Message Center** and **Programs** tabs

Home Page Buttons

Roster

Reports

Resources

Books

NOTES/TIP

Use the **Password Hint** field in the **Edit Profile** window to provide yourself a password reminder as you sign in to SAM in the future.

Clicking one of these buttons (or tabs along the top of any SAM screen) will change the main display and take you to information on:

- **Rosters,** providing detailed information about your students, groups, classes, grades, teachers, and schools;
- **Reports** about your students' performance in the Scholastic programs;
- **Resources** for your students, classrooms, and professional development purposes, as well as related state standards;
- **Book Expert,** a database of book titles and quizzes to support your curriculum needs.

Message Center

SAM automatically keeps you updated on your students' program usage and progress by sending you periodic messages. Each message shows the type, the program it refers to, the date it was generated, and a short description. There are three types of messages:

- **Alerts & Acknowledgments** let you know about a student's performance or program usage. If you click an **Alert** link, you will generate an alert report.
- **Notifications** give you information about SAM system activity, such as file exports and system backups.
- **Report Reminders** prompt you to run a specific report based on our recommendations during a school year.

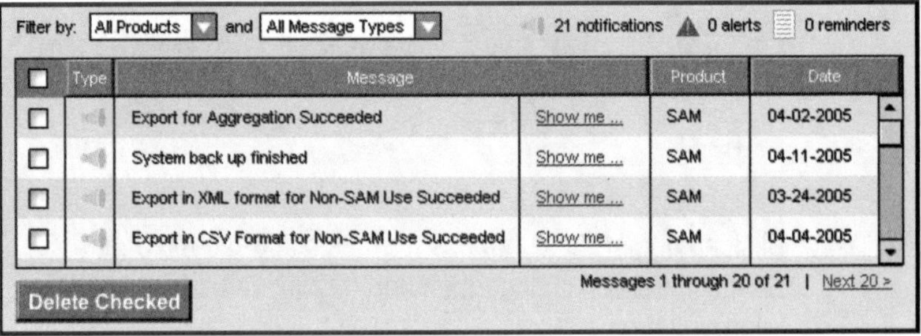

NOTES/TIP

To keep your Message Center updated, SAM automatically deletes messages from your message box on the first of each month.

To manage your messages:

1. Click any message name to display the message in a pop-up window.
2. Click any of the column headings to sort your messages by **Type**, **Message**, **Product**, or **Date**.
3. Use the **Filter by** menus at the top of the **Message** tab to search for specific messages by type.
4. Click the check box to the left of each message to select a message you want to delete, then click **Delete Checked** to clear them from the list.

Access to SAM and Permissions

For security purposes, SAM uses permissions to allow different levels of access to student information, settings, and performance data. Permissions are based on account type, which is assigned during the setup process. However, permissions can be changed to suit you or your particular school's needs. For example, you may be a teacher as well as the Technical Administrator in a building and need to have access to the administrative functions of SAM.

Account Types

There are four account types in SAM. Each school may choose different levels of access based on the technical setup.

The four account types are:

- Teachers: These accounts are for classroom-based educators, including teachers, teaching assistants, and reading coaches.
- School Administrators: These accounts have management or administrative responsibilities for multiple educators within a single school. These could include principals or reading coaches.
- District Administrators: These accounts have management or administrative responsibilities for multiple school administrators, and subsequently for a number of different schools.
- Technical Coordinators: These accounts are for the primary technical contacts for the school or district systems using Scholastic programs. Technical coordinators may be responsible for one school or several schools.

Setting Permissions

Permissions can be adjusted for any account to view or edit all functions in SAM. To view your permissions:

1. Click **My Profile** in the menu bar to open your profile window.
2. Click the **Permissions** tab. The default permissions for each account type are shown on the table on page 42.

NOTES/TIP

Use this table to determine which settings in SAM you can access with your permissions.

	SAM Features	Teacher	School Administrator	District Administrator	Technical Coordinator
Student Setting	• Student Profiles • Program Usage • Program Settings • Grading Tools • Student Reports • Resources & Standards	✔	✔	✔	✔
Class/Group Setting	• Class/Group Profiles & Rosters • Program Usage • Program Settings • Class/Group Reports • Resources & Standards	✔	✔	✔	✔
Teacher Setting	• Teacher Profile • Class/Group Assigned • Program Usage • License Availability • Resources & Standards	✔	✔	✔	✔
Grade Setting	• Grade Profile • Teacher Lists • Program Usage • License Availability • Resources & Standards	✔	✔	✔	✔
School Setting	• School Profile • Grade Lists • Program Usage • License Availability • Aggregated School Reports • Resources & Standards		✔	✔	✔
District Setting	• District Profile • School Lists • Program Usage • License Availability • Aggregated District Reports • Resources & Standards			✔	✔
Advanced Settings	• Manage Licenses • Manage Enrollment • Create/Delete Accounts • Import/Export Data			✔	✔

Using SAM in Your District or School

Scholastic programs share SAM as their common database, which facilitates administrative functions, including creating accounts for teachers and students, as well as data aggregation for reporting and analysis.

SAM installation should be completed by your district or school's Technical Administrator.

The installation process includes steps on how to set up certain accounts that will create Profiles for whole districts or schools, as well as for the school administrators and teachers at each school. You can locate details on this process in the *SRI Installation Guide*, provided with your software package.

Managing Accounts and Profiles

Everybody using SAM has an account that contains information about that person and how they will use SAM. Every district, school, grade, class, group, and student entered in SAM will have a Profile screen which includes:

- Basic information (will have name, title, etc.);
- Usage Summaries that provide at-a-glance views of enrollment and usage status;
- Links to add, edit, and manage accounts.

To open a Profile screen:

1. Click the yellow **Roster** tab along the top of the main display.
2. Double-click the **SmartBar** to highlight the name of a school, teacher, class, or student for which you would like to see a Profile.

   The **SmartBar** allows you to navigate to any grade, teacher, class, group, or student in your district that is enrolled in SAM.

NOTES/TIP

To see your own Profile at any time, click on the **My Profile** link in the Quick Links.

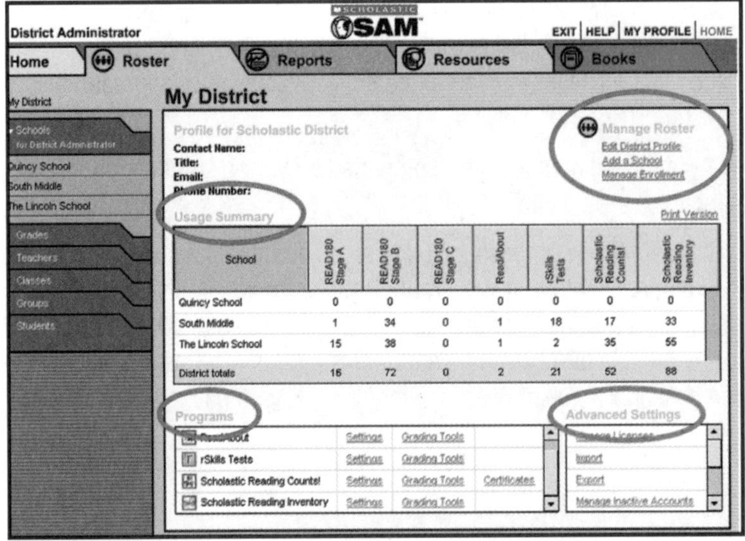

3. The Profile screen for your selected teacher, class, or student will appear in the main display.

   Each Profile contains basic contact information at the top of the page, as well as information that shows what schools, grades, and classes are assigned to that account. You can view and manage information from the following areas of the Profile screen:

   - **Usage Summary:** This table shows a summary of Scholastic programs already in use or available.
   - **Programs:** Provides selections that allow you to manage program settings, enrollment, and grading options in SRI.
   - **Advanced Settings:** Allows you to import, export, and back up data as well as track maintenance and manage inactive accounts.
   - **Manage Roster:** Allows you to add or remove Profiles for schools, teachers, students, groups, and manage licenses and enrollment in SRI.

Changing Account Permissions

As a District Administrator or Technical Administrator, you can change permissions to allow access to different parts of SAM. You can do this on the **Edit Profile** window, which you can access from any Profile screen.

To change permissions:

1. Double-click the **SmartBar** to select the Teacher or Administrator for whom you would like to change permissions.
2. Click the appropriate **Edit Profile** link under **Manage Roster** on the top right part of the screen.
3. Click the **Permissions** tab to view the current permissions settings.
4. Check the boxes to select (or deselect) the desired permissions.
5. Click **Save** when you are done to save the new settings and return to the Profile screen. Click **Cancel** to return to the Profile screen without saving your changes.

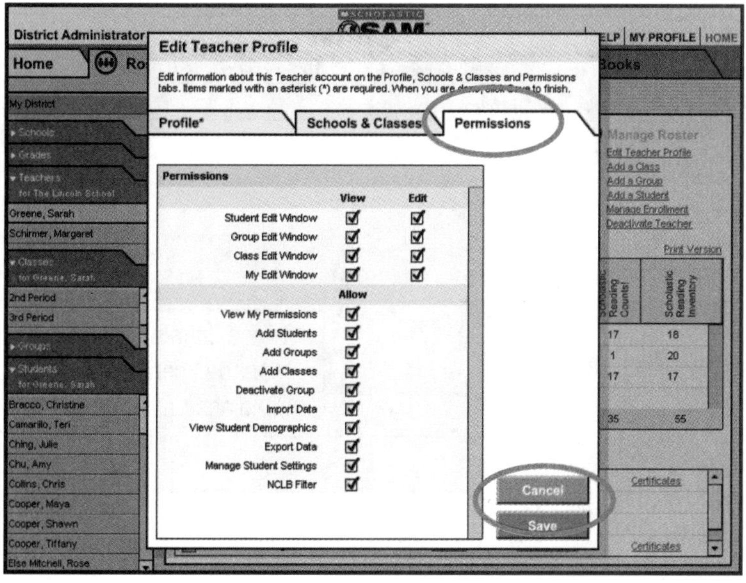

Editing, Viewing, and Creating Accounts

Editing Your Own Administrator Account

If your Profile was set up by your district or school's Technical Administrator, you will have access to the information in your Profile.

To view this information:

1. Click the **My Profile** link at the top right of any screen in SAM. This will open the **Manage Your Profile** window that displays all the information in your account.
2. To edit any field, highlight the text and type the new information.
3. Click **Save** to save all information when your edits are complete.
4. Click **Cancel** to close the window without saving any changes.

Editing a District Profile

As a District Administrator, you have access to view and edit a district Profile. To see this information, double-click **My District** at the top of the **SmartBar**.

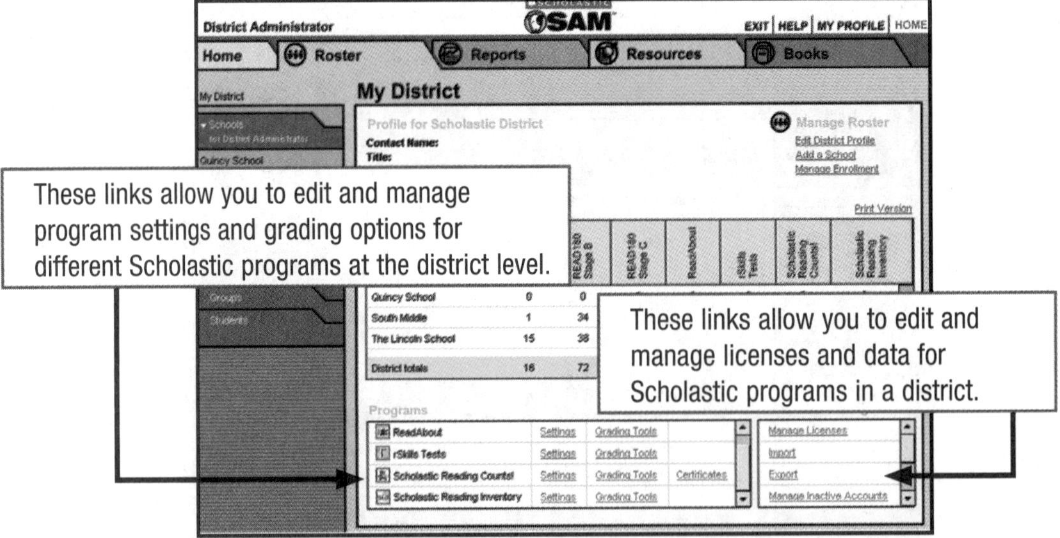

These links allow you to edit and manage program settings and grading options for different Scholastic programs at the district level.
These links allow you to edit and manage licenses and data for Scholastic programs in a district.

Viewing or Editing a School Profile

To view or edit a school's Profile, click **Schools** on the **SmartBar**, then double-click the school's name to access a school's Profile window.

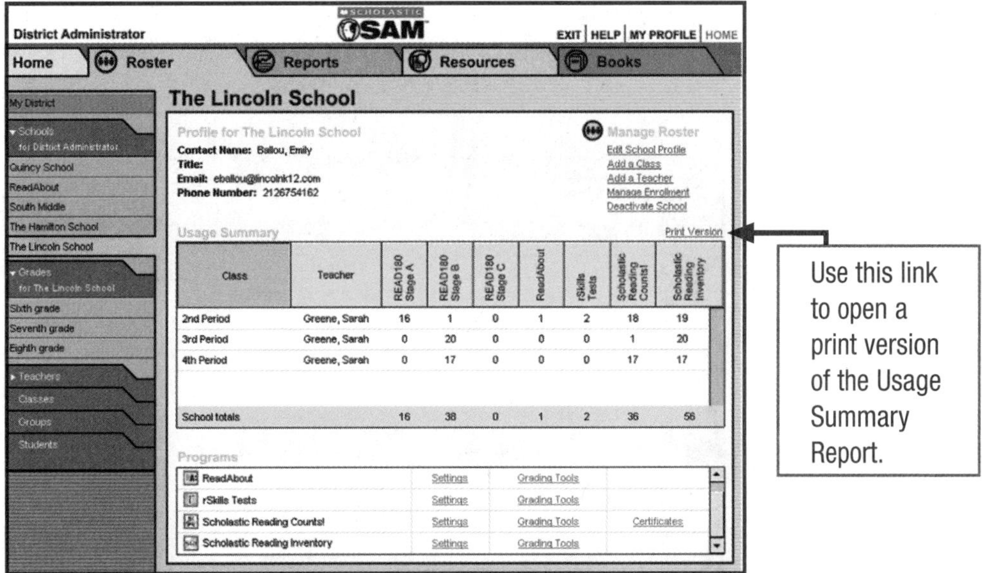

Adding and Editing New Profiles

As a District or School Administrator, you can create Profiles for schools, grades, teachers, classes, groups, or students. You can create these accounts from your Profile screen.

Create a School Profile first. Once a school has a profile, create class and group profiles for that school. Lastly, create Profiles for teachers and students and associate them with schools and classes.

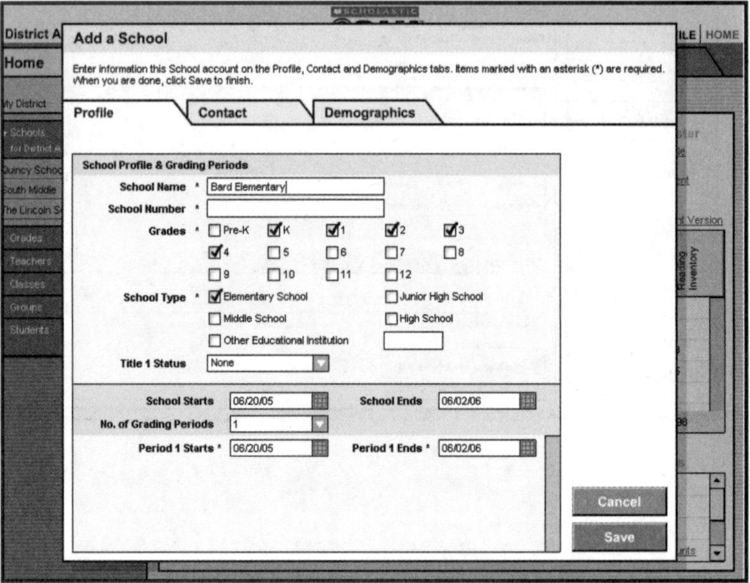

To add a School Profile to SAM:

1. Click the **Add a School** link under **Manage Roster** on upper right-hand of your **My District** Profile screen to open the **Add/Edit a School** window. Enter the requested information (information with an asterisk [*] is required).
2. Click **Save** to keep your changes and return to the Profile screen.

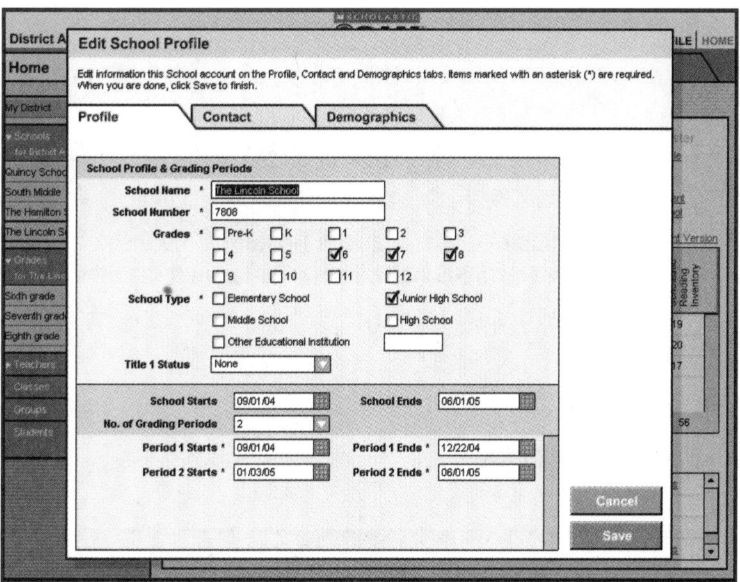

To edit an account Profile for a school:

1. Double-click a school name in the **SmartBar** to open the school's Profile screen.
2. Click the **Edit School Profile** link under **Manage Roster** on the upper right-hand of the screen to open the **Edit School Profile** window.
3. Use the check boxes and calendar tools on the Profile tab to associate grade levels and grading periods with the school.
4. Click **Save** to save your changes and return to the School Profile screen.
5. Click **Cancel** to close the window without saving changes.

Setting Up Schools in Your District

Adding a School Profile

Each school that has students that will be using Scholastic programs will need to have a SAM profile. To set up a school:

1. Login to SAM and click **My District** on top of the **SmartBar** to open the District Profile screen.
2. Click **Add a School** under **Manage Roster** on the District Profile screen to access the **Add a School** window. There are three tabs on the **Add a School** window:
   - **Profile**
   - **Contact**
   - **Demographics**

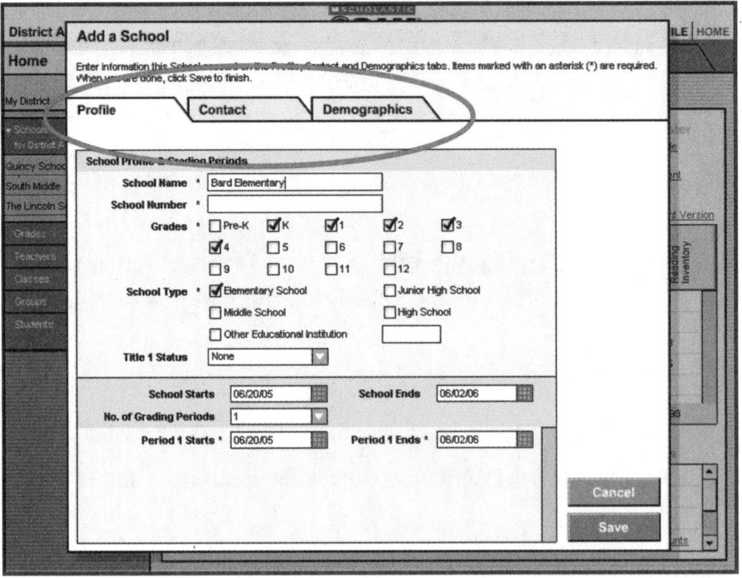

3. Use the **Profile** tab to add basic information about the school. This is the only tab that has required information. Enter the requested information, including:
    - School Name;
    - School Number;
    - Grades (use the check boxes to indicate what grades are at this school);
    - Title 1 Status (use the pull-down menu to identify your school's Title 1 status);
    - School Type (use the check boxes to indicate what type of school you are setting up);
    - School Calendar (use the pull-down menus to select the start and end dates for the school semester, as well as how many grading periods the school uses).
4. Click the **Contact** or **Demographics** tabs when you are finished to continue entering information (your changes are automatically saved). Or, click **Save** to save your entries and return to the District Profile screen. Click **Cancel** to exit without saving your changes.

Adding a School Contact from the Add a School Window

1. Use the **Contact** tab to add specific information (title, address, phone number, etc.) to the school's Profile. The information on this tab is not required.
2. Use the **Demographics** tab to choose AYP (Adequate Yearly Progress) information for reporting purposes. This allows anyone enrolling a new student to provide demographic and program information about them that will be used for reports or data export needs.

Adding School Demographics

You can add custom demographic groups to be associated with your school in the **Demographics** tab.To create custom demographic groups:

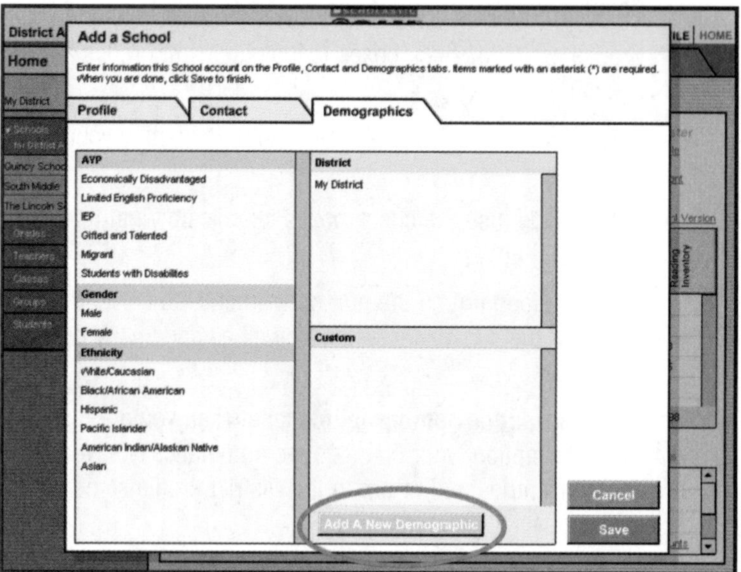

1. Click the **Add a New Demographic** button on the **Demographics** tab. A pop-up window will appear.
2. Enter the custom information in the fields. Click **Save** to add the information to SAM. Click **Cancel** to return to the **Demographics** tab.
3. Your additions will appear in the **Custom** menu on the **Demographics** tab. Use the **edit** and **delete** links next to your custom demographic to change or remove it from SAM.

Adding Class and Teacher Profiles

Adding Class Profiles

Once you have added a School Profile to SAM, you can then associate classes to your school. You can add Class Profiles and associate them to a school from the School Profile screen. To add classes:

1. Click the **Add a Class** link under **Manage Roster** on the School Profile screen to access the **Add a Class** window.
2. Enter the requested information in the **Profile** tab (information with an asterisk [*] is required). Use the check boxes to associate the class with Scholastic programs.
3. Click **Save** to add the class's information to SAM.

For detailed information about adding classes to SAM, see page 72.

Adding Teacher Profiles

Once you have added School and Class Profiles to SAM, then add Teacher Profiles and associate them with schools and classes from the School Profile screen. To add teachers:

1. Click the **Add a Teacher** link under **Manage Roster** on the School Profile screen to access the **Add a Teacher** window.
2. Enter the requested information in the **Profile** tab (information with an asterisk [*] is required).
3. Use the check boxes in the **Schools & Classes** tab to associate the teacher with schools and classes. Use the check boxes in the **Permissions** tab to assign permission levels to the teacher.
4. Click **Save** to add the teacher's information to SAM.

Running Reports

District or School Administrative Reports

One of the key functions that SAM provides administrators is the ability to monitor program usage, reading performance, and progress using reports. As an administrator, you can run reports for an entire district, or by school, grade, or class. You can also aggregate data using demographics information to facilitate district-wide reporting requirements.

Technical Administrator Reports

The administrative reports that can be created in SAM are:

- **Usage Summary Report,** which details the school name, program name and installation date, the number of licenses purchased, and the number of licenses still available. Access a printable PDF of this report by clicking the **Print Version** link at the top of the **Usage Summary** table on your Profile screen.
- **Maintenance Report,** which contains a log of when the Scholastic programs were backed up and by whom, or when any data was imported or exported. You can access these reports from the **Advanced Settings** menu on the **My District** Profile screen.

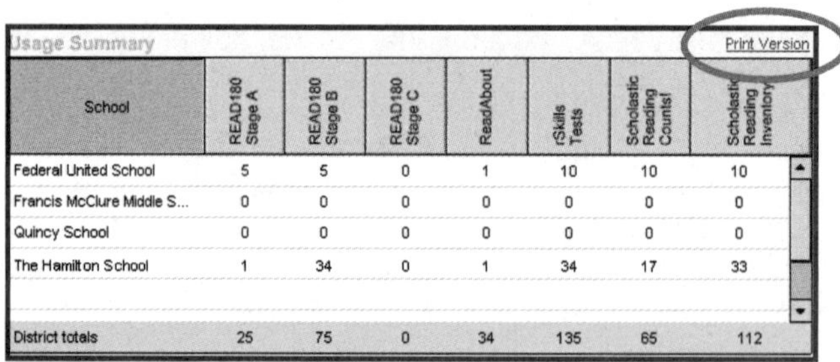

Usage Summary — Print Version

School	READ180 Stage A	READ180 Stage B	READ180 Stage C	ReadAbout	rSkills Tests	Scholastic Reading Counts!	Scholastic Reading Inventory
Federal United School	5	5	0	1	10	10	10
Francis McClure Middle S...	0	0	0	0	0	0	0
Quincy School	0	0	0	0	0	0	0
The Hamilton School	1	34	0	1	34	17	33
District totals	25	75	0	34	135	65	112

See the Reports section beginning on page 97 for instructions on how to run, view, print, and save SAM reports.

Advanced Settings

These features are available only to those with administrative permissions to maintain school technology systems and SAM databases. The activities include:

- Managing licenses (page 55);
- Managing enrollment (page 57);
- Deactivating accounts (page 59);
- Backing up/restoring the database (page 61);
- Importing/exporting student data (page 63).

Managing Licenses

Licenses allow teachers and students to use Scholastic programs purchased by your district or school. Any time SAM is installed, whether on a district-wide basis or for individual schools, you will also purchase licenses for each of the different Scholastic programs. Licenses are transferable from student to student.

NOTES/TIP

You must have a license for every student enrolled in a Scholastic program.

To manage licenses, sign in to SAM then:

1. Double-click **My District** or **My School** at the top of the **SmartBar** to open the District or School Profile screen.
2. Double-click the **Manage Licenses** link in the **Advanced Settings** menu on the lower right of the screen to open the Licensing tab. Here you can review the installed Scholastic programs and verify the number of seats (licenses) allocated, used, and available. This will help you determine if you need to purchase additional licenses to meet current needs.

3. Call Scholastic Customer Service at 1-877-268-6871 to purchase additional licenses for *SRI*. Provide the customer service representative with the installation code (you can find this code at the top of the **Licensing** tab), as well as a purchase order number or a method of payment.

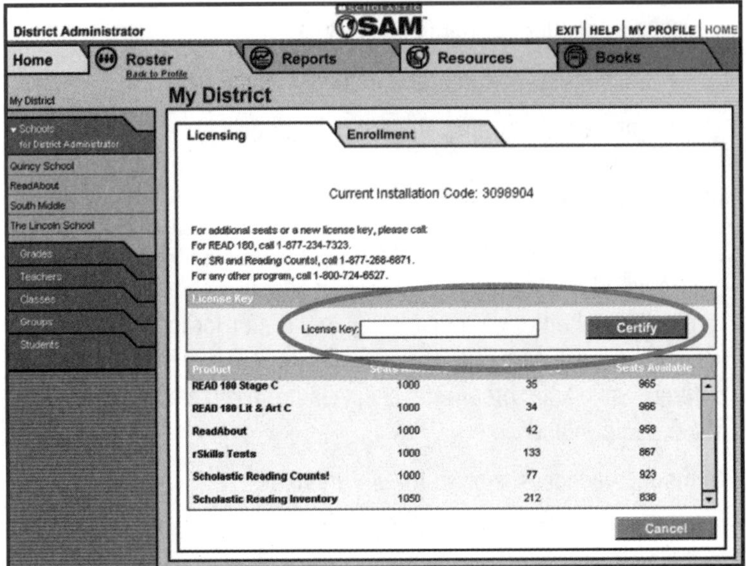

4. Type the license key in the **License Key** box and click **Certify**. SAM will verify the license key so you can enroll additional students in Scholastic programs following the procedure outlined in the next section.

Managing Enrollment

The **Enrollment** tab is where you can enroll and un-enroll students in Scholastic programs. You can also access this screen by clicking the **Manage Enrollment** link under **Manage Roster** on the District Profile screen.

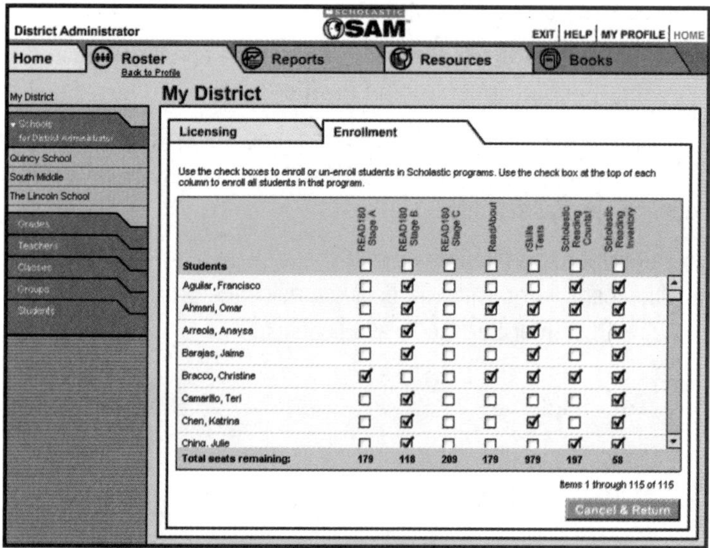

Students who are enrolled in a Scholastic program will have a check in each program box that follows their name. Clicking a box to remove the check will un-enroll that student in that program.

If you wish to enroll or un-enroll all students in a given program, use the check box under the appropriate program name to change the enrollment status of all students in the school, grade, class, or group that you have selected.

To make changes in enrollment for licensed students from the District or School Profile screen:

1. Double-click the **Manage Enrollment** link under Manage Roster in the top right of your Profile screen to open the **Enrollment** tab.
2. Use the check boxes to select or deselect students for enrollment in the appropriate Scholastic programs.
3. Click **Save & Return** when you finish to save enrollment changes and return to the **District** or **School Profile** screen.
4. Click **Save** to save changes and remain on the **Enrollment** tab. Double-click a different selection on the **SmartBar** to manage detalied enrollment options for that selection.

If you attempt to enroll more students in a given program than you have available licenses for, you will receive a message prompting you to contact Scholastic Customer Service to add licenses.

Deactivating Accounts

Technical Administrators may be responsible for deleting accounts or Profiles. This is necessary when students or teachers are no longer enrolled in Scholastic programs or may have left the school. Any teacher or student who has a Profile in SAM but is not using any program can be designated as an Inactive Account. Inactive Accounts do not appear in the **SmartBar**. However, information associated with Inactive Accounts still exists in the SAM database and can be accessed or reactivated if necessary.

The table below shows what defines each account type as Active or Inactive:

ACCOUNT TYPE	ACTIVE	INACTIVE
Student	Associated with at least one class	Not associated with any classes
Teacher	Associated with at least one class	Not associated with any classes
Class	Associated with at least one school	Not associated with any schools
School	Associated with at least one district	Not associated with any districts

Reactivating Inactive Accounts

As an administrator, you can reactivate accounts by clicking the **Manage Inactive Accounts** link, which is found in the **Advanced Settings** menu on the District or School Profile screen.

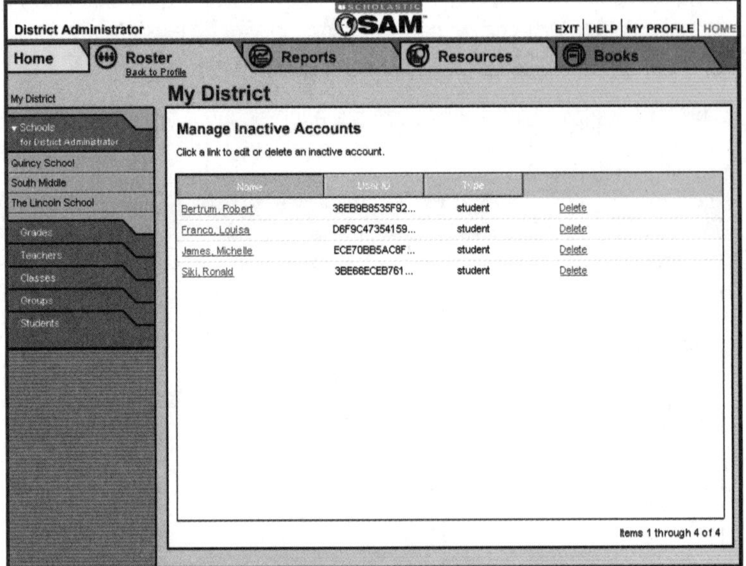

To manage Inactive Accounts:

1. From your District or School Profile screen, click the **Manage Inactive Accounts** link in the **Advanced Settings** menu.
2. Click on the link associated with the account name you wish to reactivate and use the pull-down menu on the **Reactivate This Student** window to select a school to which you would like to associate this account. This will open the account's Profile information.
3. Click **Proceed** to open the account's Profile information.
4. Click **Save** to reactivate the account.

Backing Up and Restoring the Database

SAM's database aggregates a large amount of information that ranges from district, school, and grade levels, all the way down to individual classes and the students enrolled in them. Depending on your district or school setup, the database resides on a central server. It is very important to keep the information on this server secure.

As with any database that contains information that is updated regularly, you should back up your files in case of a power outage or damage to the drive on which you save files.

The backup utility in SAM allows you to select a time each day when the system will perform the backup. However, it is not possible to perform a backup while the system is in use; this utility should be scheduled for after-school hours.

Backing Up the Database

1. Double-click **My District** at the top of the **SmartBar** to show your **District Profile** (if you are a District Administrator) or on **My School** to show your **School Profile** (if you are a School Administrator).
2. Select **Backup** from the **Advanced Settings** menu. the Backup Wizard will open in a separate screen. Choose **To Backup Data** and click Next to proceed.
3. Use the pull-down menus to enter the time at which the backup will begin. Backups can take several hours, and must be performed when no one is using SAM. Be sure to select a time that takes this into account.
4. Click **Back** to return to the previous screen, or click **Next** to proceed.
5. Click **OK** on the confirmation screen to verify what time your backup will take place. Once the backup is complete, you will receive a notification in the Message Center on the SAM Home Page.

NOTES/TIP

Backing up the database may take several hours to complete, based on the capacity of your school's server and the amount of data contained in it.
We recommend that you schedule system backups for after-school hours.

Restoring a Database

If for some reason your current database of student records is lost or has become corrupted, the most recent backup can be used to restore the data. Details on the SAM restore procedure can be found in the *SRI Installation Guide.*

Restoring a database will **write over the current database**. This function should only be performed by the School or District Technical Coordinator and **only** if the current database is lost or corrupted. If your school's database is lost or corrupted, regardless of your SAM permissions, you will see a notifcation on the SAM Home Page.

Contact Technical Support (1-800-927-0189) before restoring a database containing important student data.

Importing and Exporting Student Data

Students will often transfer into or out of your school. In these cases you may need to import or export their information into or out of your school's database. You may have student information stored in existing databases (either from previous Scholastic programs or from school databases) that you would like to use in SAM. If the information is in Comma Seperated Values (CSV) format, you can import these databases into SAM to create students' Profiles for Scholastic programs more quickly.

Importing Data Into SAM

To import student data:

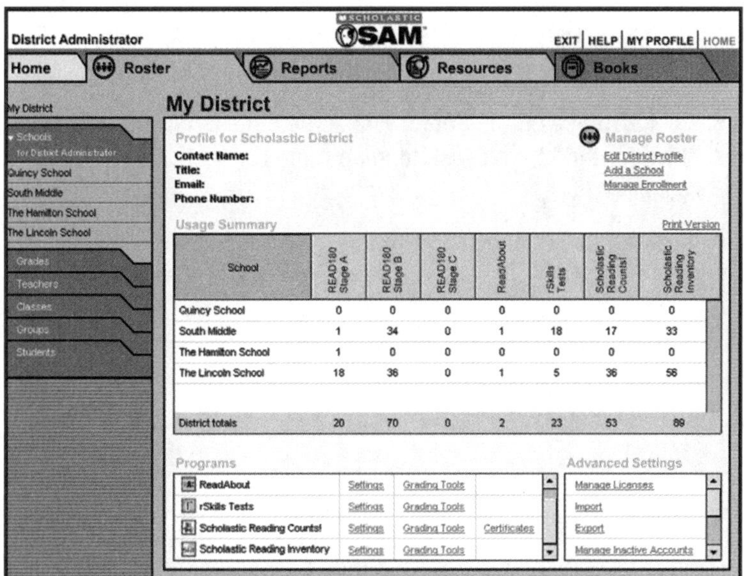

1. Back up your **SAM** database before importing any files.
2. Double-click **My District** at the top of the **SmartBar** to show your District Profile (if you are a District Administrator) or **My School** to show your School Profile (if you are a School Administrator).

3. Select **Import** from the **Advanced Settings** menu in the lower right of the screen. The Import Wizard will open in a separate screen.
4. Select the purpose of your import from the opening screen, then click **Next**. Choose from the following types of imports:
   - **Aggregate data:** Copy roster and student performance data to include it in school- or district-wide, aggregated reports.
   - **Transfer student data into SAM:** Move students' roster and performance data from another SAM server onto your current SAM database.
   - **Import roster data:** Import student roster information from a different software application into your current SAM Server (*.csv, *.xml files).
   - **Import SRI data:** Copy selected students' SRI Lexile scores from another SAM database into your current SAM database.
5. Click **Browse** on the **Select File** screen to search your computer's hard drive for the file you wish to import into SAM. Click **Next** once you have selected a file.
6. Click **Import** to import the file.

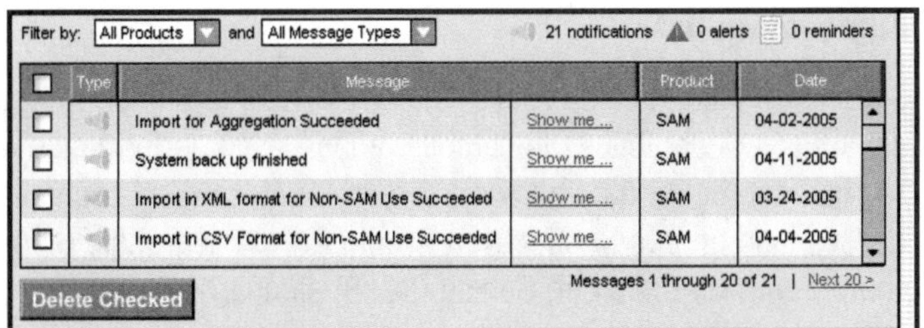

You will receive a notification in the Message Center on your SAM Home Page once the import is complete.

NOTES/TIP

Always back up your files on SAM before Importing or Exporting any files.

NOTES/TIP

We recommend that you install a server specifically for aggregating data, rather than using a server devoted to running SAM in your district or school.

Aggregating Data

Data aggregation is the process of combining information from several different SAM databases to compile broad-based performance reports. You can aggregate data across a district, but also within schools, grades, classes, and groups to effectively create AYP demographic reports to comply with No Child Left Behind (NCLB) standards.

Once you have aggregated data, you can run reports based on that information, such as demographically specific reports for your district or school.

For more detailed information about how to aggregate data, see the *SRI Installation Guide.*

Exporting Student Data

If you wish to use the data stored in SAM's database for purposes other than what is included amongst SAM's capabilities, you can export various data in order to repurpose it for your specific needs.

To export data from SAM's database:

1. Double-click **My District** or **My School** on the top of the **SmartBar** to access District or School Profile screen.
2. Click the **Export** link in the **Advanced Settings** menu on the lower right of the screen to open the Export Wizard.
3. Select the purpose of your export from the opening screen, then click **Next**. Choose from the following file export types:
   - **Aggregate data:** Copy and export roster and student performance data to include it in school- or district-wide, aggregated reports.
   - **Export roster data:** Export student roster information from your current SAM database for use in another application.
   - **Export SRI data:** export students' *SRI* Lexile scores from your current SAM database for use in another application.

Depending on which purpose you select for your export, the Export Wizard will show you the following screens:

- **For aggregation:** you will see a confirmation screen. Click **Export** to export aggregated data.
- **For roster and performance data:** you will see a time period selection screen. Select a date range over which you wish to export data and information, then click **Next**. Click **Export** on the following screen to export roster and performance data.
- **For *SRI* Lexile scores:** select a school, class, or students for which you would like to export scores, then click **Next**. Click **Export** on the following screen to export Lexile scores.

NOTES/TIP

Exporting files and data may take several hours to complete, based on the amount of data you export. We recommend that you schedule exports for after-school hours.

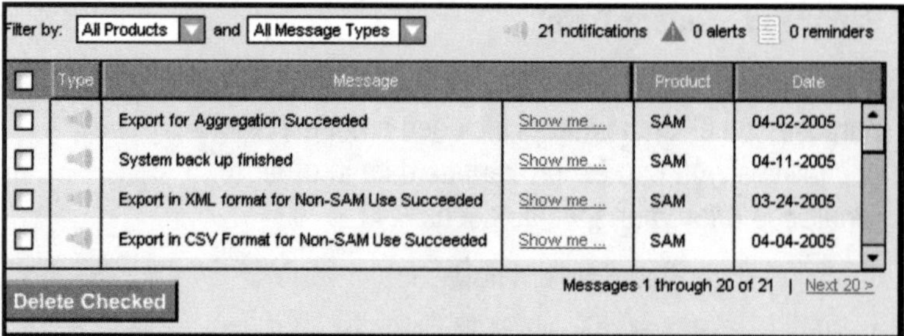

Once the export is complete, you will receive a notification in the Message Center on the SAM Home Page. You can either store the exported data files in SAM's database or save them to a different location on your computer.

Saving Your Exported Data

If you perform multiple exports over time, or would like to use the exported data for purposes other than what are included in SAM's capabilities, you can save them to a location on your computer's hard drive. To save your files to a location other than SAM's database:

1. Click the **Show me. . .** link next to the file you wish to save in the Message Center on the SAM Home Page.
2. Click the link under the **Export File** column on the following screen for the file you wish to save.
3. Select a file location in the directory window, then click **Save**.

Using Tab Key Navigation

SAM is designed so that you can navigate through all of the on-screen elements without the use of a mouse. You can use the **Tab** key on your keyboard to move to and choose executable functions on-screen.

Tab selections move from left to right, then down on the screen. For example, on a **Roster** page, first pressing **Tab** will place a red border around **Logout** on the Quick Menu. Pressing **Tab** again moves the red border to the selection on the right, then down to the on-screen tabs, then to the main display. After reaching the most bottom right on-screen element, pressing **Tab** returns you to the topmost right element on the screen.

To use **Tab** key navigation:

1. Press the **Tab** key on any screen in SAM. A red border will highlight the element that is on the topmost left corner of the screen, which is **Logout** in the Quick Menu.
2. Press the **space bar** to execute the function. For example, if the red border is on the **Roster** tab, pressing the **space bar** will bring you to a **Roster** page. You can also use the **space bar** to access any on-screen links, such as in the **Advanced Settings** menu.
3. To access pull-down menus using the **Tab** key, once you have placed the red border on a pull-down menu, use the **up** and **down** arrows to move between selections. After you have made a choice, press **Tab** to continue, and your choice will remain in the field.
4. To select (or deselect) check boxes and buttons, use the **Tab** key to navigate to them, then press the **space bar** to select (or deselect) options.
5. To enter information, press **Tab** until the red border highlights the field. Type in the information, then press **Tab** to continue and the information will remain in the field.

Setting Up Your Classroom

SAM is the central management component that maintains the information for all of the classes, students, and groups in the Scholastic programs. Once you've set up your classes, students, and groups, you can use the appropriate Profile screen to organize your classroom, access and maintain student information, track performance, and generate reports to differentiate instruction.

Creating the structure for your classes, groups, and students in SAM is the easiest way to begin monitoring both your students' use of Scholastic programs and their reading progress.

For more information on how to use the SmartBar to navigate SAM, refer to page 37.

Here are the steps to get started in setting up your classes, groups, and students.

NOTES/TIP

Your technical administrator will have created classes and groups for you. It's a good idea to review the Class and Group Profile screens to be sure the information is correct.

Adding a Class

Students working on Scholastic programs will need to be associated with a class. Creating a class also allows you to run reports for classes from the **SmartBar**.

To add a class:

1. Click the **Add a Class** link under **Manage Roster** in your **My Classes** Profile screen.
2. The **Add a Class** window automatically opens to the **Profile** tab. Use the pull-down menus and check boxes to enter the correct Teacher and Grade information and enable Scholastic programs. Items with an asterisk (*) are required.

NOTES/TIP

Set up your Class and Group Profiles first, then create Student Profiles and associate them with Classes and Groups.

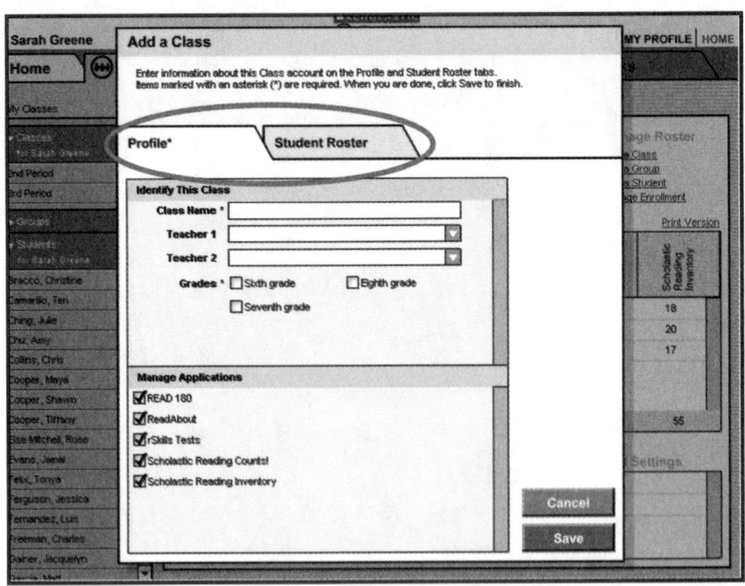

3. Click the **Student Roster** tab.
   - Use the check boxes to select the students to be included in the class, or click the check box in the menu heading to add all of the students listed to the class.

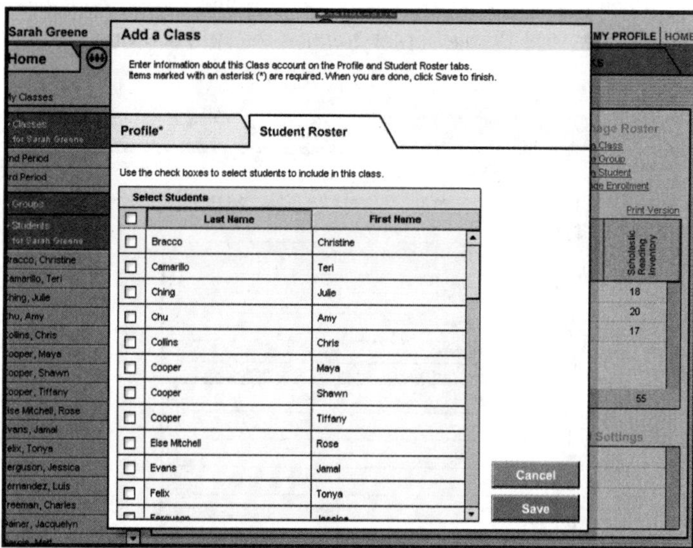

NOTES/TIP

Students will only appear on the **Student Roster** tab if you have already added Profiles for them. Add *classes* before adding students so you can enroll each student in a class as you set up their Profiles.

4. Click **Save** when you are done to return to your **My Profile** screen.

Adding a Group

Creating groups within a class of students allows you to run reports by group. However, you are not required to set up groups for your students.

To create a group:

1. Click the **Add a Group** link under **Manage Roster** on your **My Classes** Profile screen to open the **Add a Group** window.

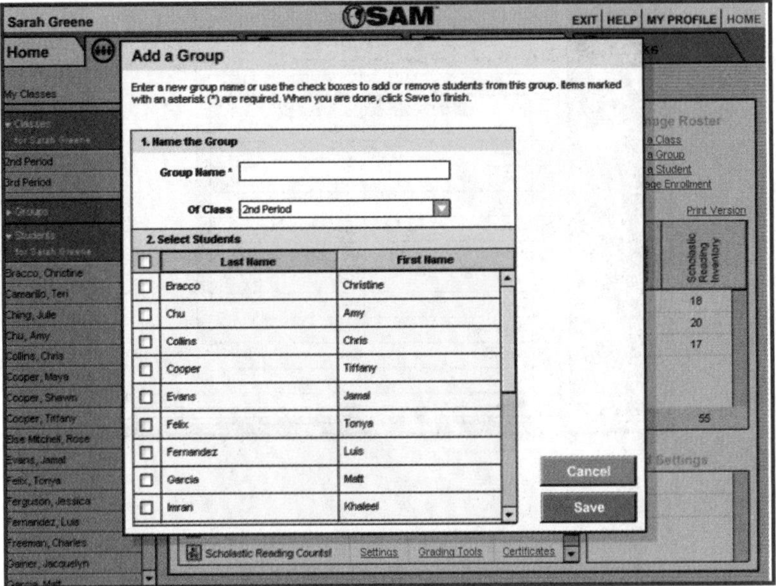

2. Type in the **Group Name**, then use the **Of Class** pull-down menu to select the students from the class you want to associate with the group (groups can only be created with students who are in the same class). The table below will list the students in the selected class.

3. Use the check boxes in the **Select Students** table to select students for the group. Use the check box in the **Select Students** heading to select all of your students.
4. Click **Save** to save your selections when you are done.

Adding and Editing a Student

You will need to enter information for any student who will be using any Scholastic program. If your district has imported this information, you can use the **Edit Student Profile** link under **Manage Roster** on the student's Profile screen to review and edit that student's Profile.

To add a student:

1. Click the **Add a Student** link under **Manage Roster** on the **My Classes** Profile screen to open the **Add a Student** window.
2. The **Add a Student** window has three tabs:
    - **Profile**
    - **Demographics**
    - **Guardian**

Only the **Profile** screen is required information.

NOTES/TIP

To enroll a student in a Scholastic program, there must be available licenses. You can check on licenses on your Profile screen in the **Usage Summary** table.

3. Click **Save** when you have entered all the student information to save the data and close the **Add a Student** window.

   - Enter information in each field to create the student's Profile. Information with an asterisk (*) is required.
   - Use the check boxes to enroll the student in Scholastic programs.
   - Use the check boxes to select or deselect the class or group(s) that the student is a member of.

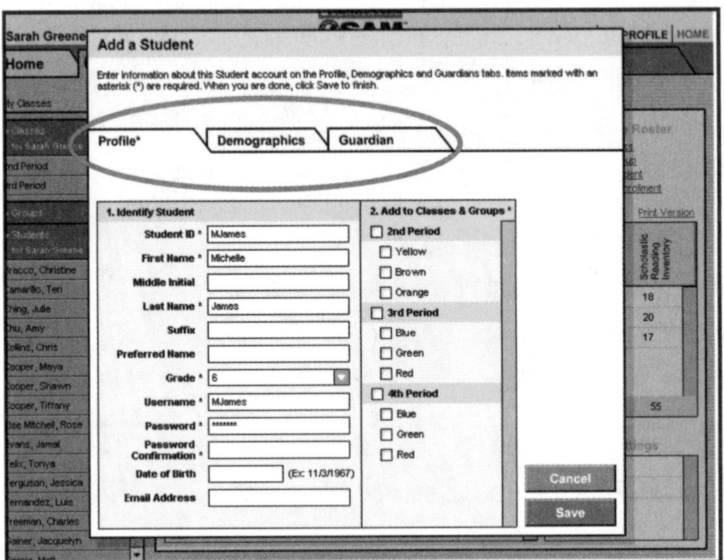

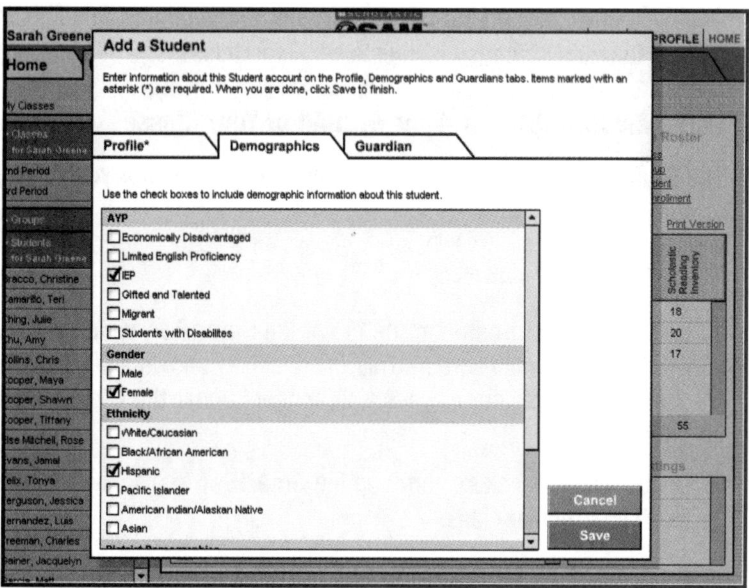

4. Click the **Demographics** tab to provide information about individual students. Use the check boxes to provide more specific information that will make it easier to track student performance, determine which students qualify for special programs, and establish AYP Criteria.

5. The **Guardian** tab has contact information to make it easy for you to access home contact details. This way you can keep a student's family or guardian informed of his or her progress in Scholastic programs.

   Students must be enrolled in at least one Scholastic class before you can add guardian information to their Profiles.

NOTES/TIP

A good way to keep a student's family or guardian informed of their progress is to run periodic Parent Reports from SAM. For more information on how to run reports, see page 97.

Working With All of Your Classes

Once you have set up your classes, groups, and students, you can begin using the **My Classes** screen, which lists all of your classes.

Using the SmartBar to Work With All of Your Classes

The **SmartBar** quickly takes you to any Profile screen for your classes, groups, or students.

To view all of your classes:

1. Double-click your name at the top of the **SmartBar**, which will open your **My Classes** Profile screen. This main display shows a list of all your classes. A list of your classes also appears under the **Classes** tab on the **SmartBar**.
2. Double-click any class name on the **SmartBar** to display the Profile screen for that particular class.

See page 84 for details about working with individual classes.

3. Click on the **Reports** tab to run reports for all your classes or just one class.

About the My Classes Profile Screen

The **My Classes** Profile screen provides an overview of the classes assigned to you in SAM. On this page, you can:

- Access links that can help you monitor and manage students, including grading tools and program settings.
- Get a snapshot of all of your classes using Scholastic programs.
- Manage and edit your Profile.

NOTES/TIP

You can get to the **My Classes** Profile screen from anywhere in SAM by clicking **My Profile** in the Quick Links.

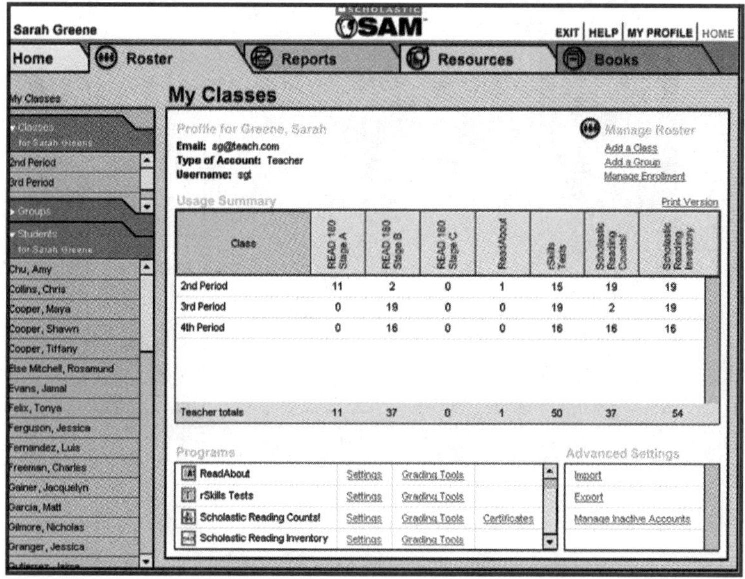

NOTES/TIP

Teacher Profiles in SAM can only be removed by those with administrative permissions.

Editing Your Profile

Basic information from your Profile is listed by your name at the top left of the **My Classes** Profile screen. You can view your full Profile and make any necessary changes by clicking **My Profile** in the Quick Links at the top right of any SAM screen.

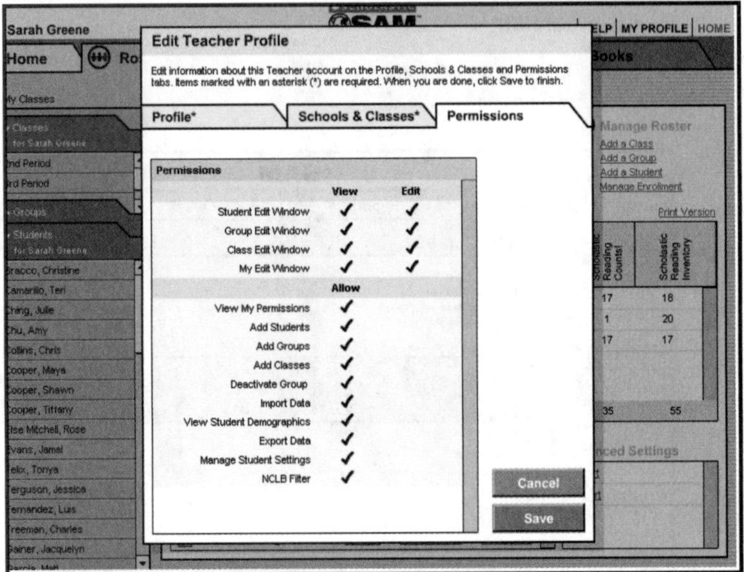

There are three tabs on the **Edit Profile** window:

- **Profile**
- **Schools & Classes**
- **Permissions**

To change any information on your Profile, delete the existing text and enter any new information. Click **Save** to keep your changes or **Cancel** to exit the **Edit Profile** window without saving any of your changes.

Viewing Program Usage for All of Your Classes

The **My Profile** screen has a **Usage Summary** table that shows information about each class that is using Scholastic programs, such as the number of students enrolled in each class, and their performance totals in each program.

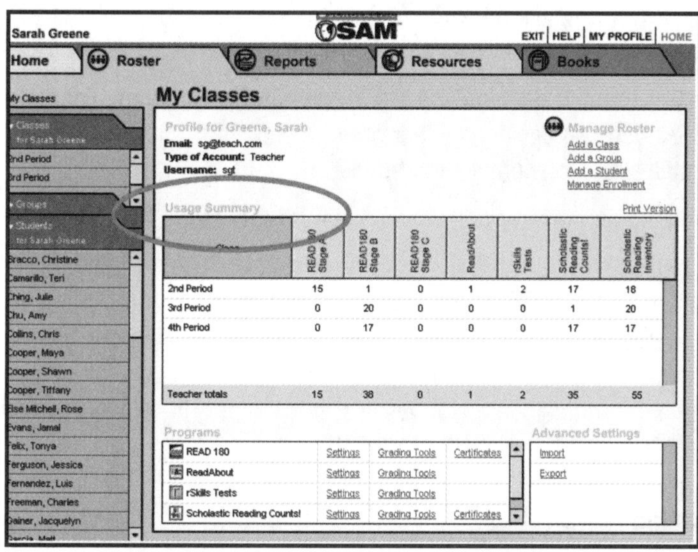

- The information in the **Usage Summary** table is sorted alphabetically by class name. However, you can click on the column headings to re-sort the information in the table.
- The bottom border of the **Usage Summary** table shows the total number of students enrolled in each Scholastic program and indicates how many licenses are still available to your school.

NOTES/TIP

Click the **Print Version** link above the **Usage Summary** table to display an Adobe Acrobat file (PDF) that you can print.

Changing Program Settings

Program settings affect how the students interact with Scholastic programs. You can set these adjustments for individual students, groups, or classes.

To access program settings from your Profile window:

1. On the **Programs** menu located at the bottom right of the screen, click the **Settings** link next to the program for which you would like to change settings.
2. Use check boxes to adjust the options for that program. For instance, for *SRI,* you can decide whether or not a student is shown his or her Lexile measure upon completing the test.
3. Click **Save** to save adjustments and return to your **My Profile** screen.

Changes that you make to program settings from your Profile screen will apply to all of the students assigned to you. If you have students with special needs, you can change program settings for those students individually from their Profile screens. For example, if you have set ELL support for all your classes, then select one student and deselect this option. This student now no longer has this support, but all other students will.

Grading Tools

Each Scholastic program has grading tools which you can use to enter information on how students are performing in the programs and in related activities. You can access grading tools from the **Programs** menu on a student's Profile screen.

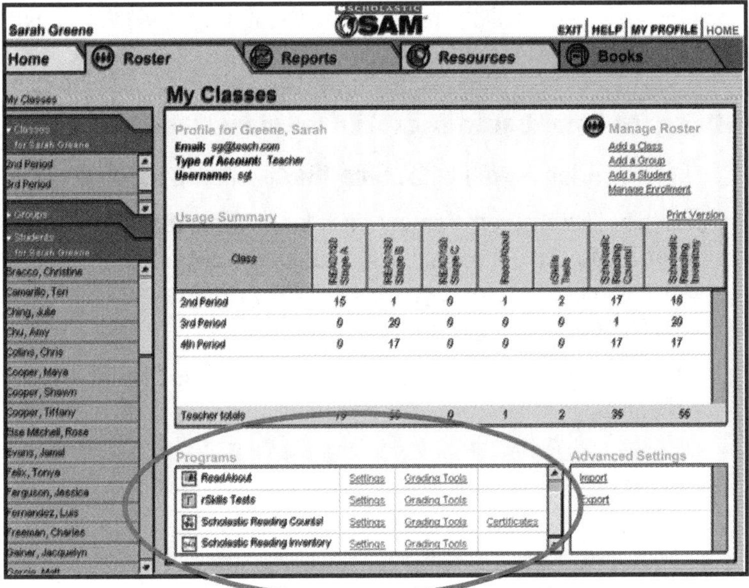

Grading tools are only applicable to individual students; they cannot be used for classes or groups. To access grading tools:

1. Click the **Grading Tools** link next to a program in the **Programs** menu at the bottom of the Student Profile screen to open the grading tool window.
2. Use check boxes to adjust how students will be graded in Scholastic programs.
3. Click **Save** to keep your changes and return to the Student Profile screen.

Working With Individual Classes

Each class has a Profile screen that makes it easy to view, edit, and add information specific to that class.

Using the SmartBar to Work With Individual Classes

1. Click the **Classes** tab in the **SmartBar** to show a list of all of your classes.
2. Double-click the name of any class in the **SmartBar**. The **SmartBar** expands to show the groups and students assigned to that class. On the right side of the screen, you will see the **Profile** screen for the class that is highlighted.
3. Double-click on a different class name to see the **Profile** screen for that class.

About the Class Profile Screen

The Class Profile screen gives you a snapshot of the students in one class and of the Scholastic programs they are using.

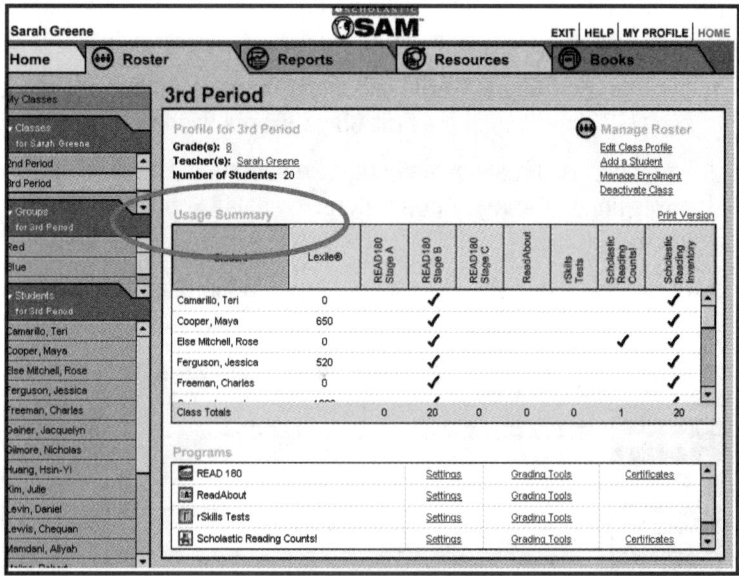

The Class Profile window has a **Usage Summary** table that shows information about how each student in that class is performing in Scholastic programs, such as their current Lexile scores, and their level of progress in each program.

Editing a Class Profile

You may at one point need to change a class's Profile. For example, you may install a new program or need to enroll new students in the class. At the top of the Class Profile screen in the main display is basic information about the class, like the number of students and how many grades are enrolled within it. You can view the full Profile and make any necessary changes. To do so:

1. Click the **Edit Class Profile** link under **Manage Roster** on the Class Profile screen. This will open the **Edit Class Profile** window.
2. Edit the Class Profile by entering new information or clicking the check boxes under **Manage Applications** to enable Scholastic programs for your class.
3. Click **Save** when you are done to return to the Class Profile window.

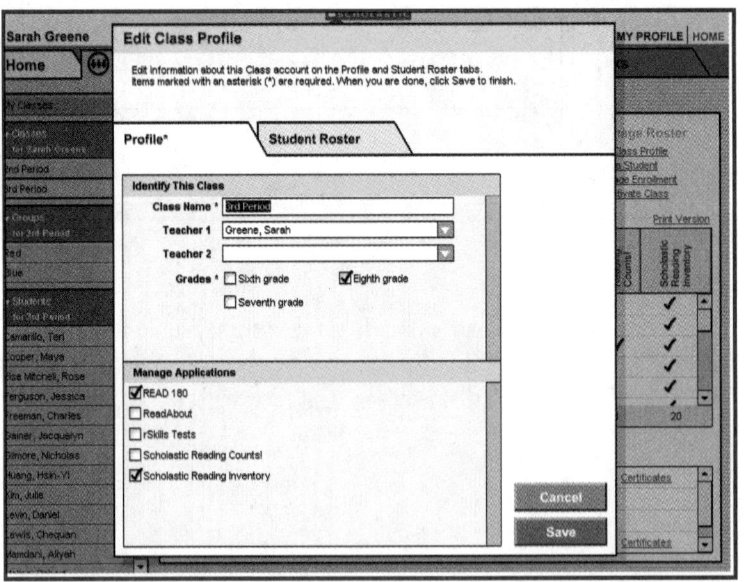

Deleting a Class Profile

You can delete classes that no longer use Scholastic programs. While this will remove the class from the **SmartBar** and automatically delete any groups associated with the class, it does not delete any of the students enrolled in the class. Deleting a class removes students from the **SmartBar** and changes their status to inactive, but they remain in the SAM database.

To delete a class:

1. Click the **Deactivate Class** link under **Manage Roster** in the upper right hand corner of the Class Profile screen. A confirmation window will appear, to ask if you really want to deactivate the class.
2. Click **Yes** to proceed and deactivate the class, or **No** to return to the **My Classes** Profile screen.

Changing Program Settings for a Class

Program settings affect how the students interact with Scholastic programs. You can set these adjustments for individual students, groups, or whole classes.

To access program settings for a class from your Profile screen:

1. Click the **Settings** link next to the program for which you would like to change settings in the **Programs** menu at the bottom of the screen.
2. Use check boxes to adjust the options for that program. For instance, for *SRI,* you can require students to always take a practice test.
3. Click **Save** to save your adjustments and return to the Class Profile screen.

You can change program settings for individual students from their Profile screens. For example, if you have set ELL support for all your classes, then select one student and deselect this option in that student's settings screen. This student now no longer has this support, but all other students will.

Working With Groups

Many teachers organize their classes into groups. These might be used for reading groups, groups with different institutional needs, or your instructional rotations. Students may be placed in more than one group at a time. Assigning students to multiple groups may be useful for reporting purposes.

SAM makes it easy to organize students into groups within a class so you can track and monitor their progress and work in Scholastic programs.

Using the SmartBar to Work With Groups

If you have set up Group Profiles, these group names will appear under Groups in the **SmartBar**.

To display a group:

1. Single-click the class name on the **SmartBar**, the **Groups** tab will expand to display a list of groups associated with the highlighted class.
2. Double-click a group name on the **SmartBar**. It expands to display a list of the students belonging to that group. On the right side of the screen, you will see the group's **Roster** screen, which also shows a list of students in the group. Double-click another group name in the **SmartBar** to see the Profile screen for that group.
3. If you wish to work with a group from a different class, you have to first select the class name by clicking the name of the class the group is associated with.

Editing a Group Profile

At the top of the Group Profile screen is the basic information for that group. You can view the full Profile and make any necessary changes by clicking the **Edit Group Profile** link in the top right-hand side of the window to open a screen where you can edit or delete the Profile information.

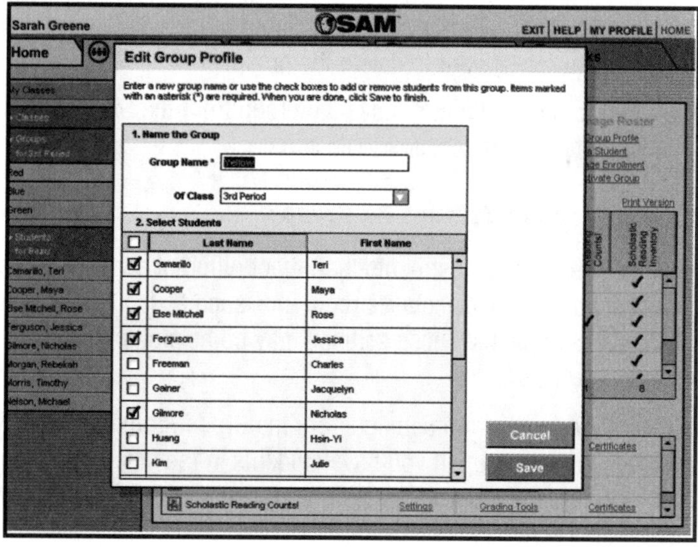

NOTES/TIP

As group needs change frequently depending on students' needs, use the **Edit Group Profile** link to avoid deleting or changing the name of the group.

Deleting a Group Profile

You may wish to remove a group from your classes. This is done by deleting that group, which does not delete any of the Student Profiles in the group from the SAM database or from their classes. It only removes the group from the database.

To delete a group:

1. Click the **Deactivate Group** link under **Manage Roster** in the upper right corner of the Group Profile screen. A confirmation window will appear, asking if you really want to delete the group.
2. Click **Yes** to proceed and remove the group from the SAM database, or **No** to return to the Group Profile screen.

Changing Program Settings for Groups

Program Settings are adjustments that affect different aspects of the student experience when using Scholastic programs, such as language support and different display options. These settings may be helpful to accommodate a group's special needs.

Changes made to program settings from the Group Profile screen will apply to all students in that group. If you have students in the group with special needs, you may change the program settings for those students individually from their Student Profile screens.

See page 95 for instructions on changing an individual student's program settings.

Working With Individual Students

Just as you can work with all of your classes, an individual class, or groups on SAM, you can get information and adjust program settings for individual students. Furthermore, grading tools are accessible from the Student Profile screen, too.

Using the SmartBar to Work With Students

1. Double-click on any student's name in the **SmartBar** to bring up the student's Profile screen.
2. To open up the Profile for a student from a different class or group, first select the appropriate class name, then the group name from the **SmartBar**, then double-click a student's name to access their Student Profile screen.

See pages 92–94 for details on the Student Profile screen.

About the Student Profile

The Student Profile screen displays the information that was created when the student was added to the database.

See page 75 for details on adding a student.

From the Student Profile screen, you can view, edit, and delete student information. All students in SAM have a Profile screen, even if they are not enrolled in a Scholastic program.

NOTES/TIP

The Usage Summary provides a great snapshot you can look at before a student, small-group, or personal conference.

Viewing a Student's Program Usage

The **Usage Summary** table on the Student Profile screen shows detailed status for each of the programs in which a student is enrolled. Click on any program name in the **Usage Summary** table to see high-level, recent data points of the student's progress and performance in that program.

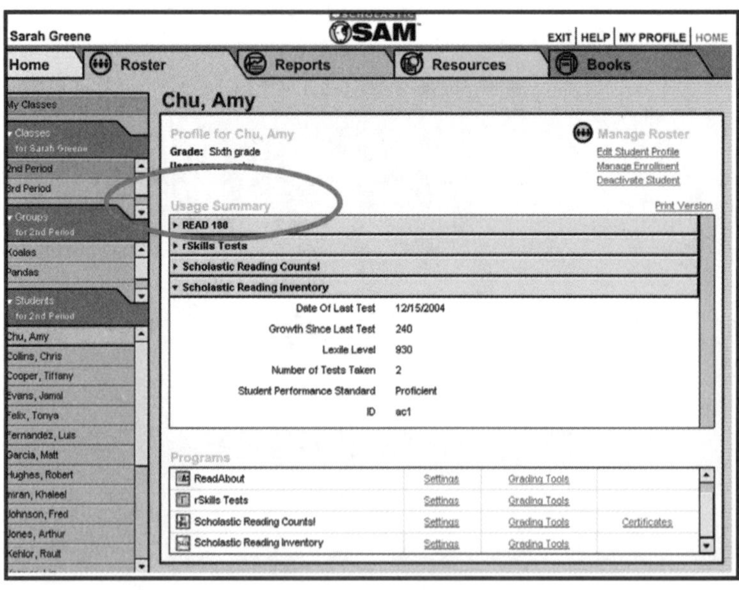

Editing a Student Profile

To edit a student's Profile:

1. Click the **Edit Student Profile** link under **Manage Roster** on the upper right-hand corner of the Student Profile screen. This will open the **Edit Student Profile** window that shows the student's Profile information.

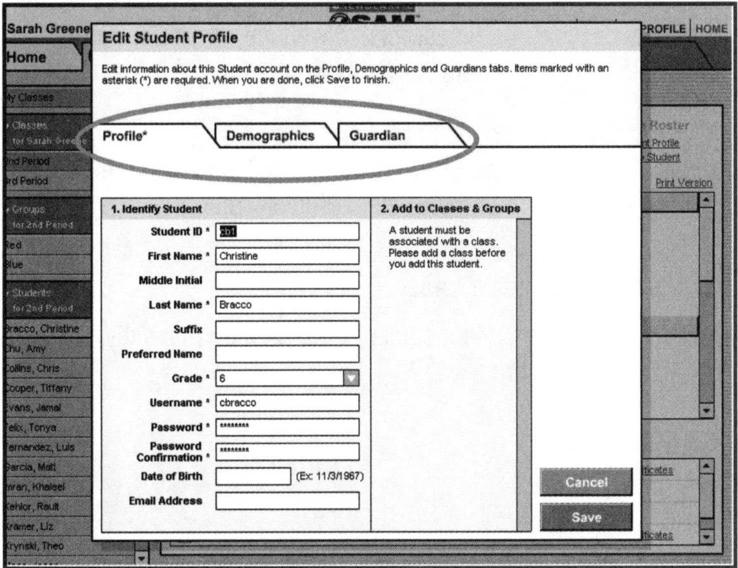

For more information on the different tabs for creating a Student Profile, see page 75.

2. Click anywhere inside the fields to change, enter, or delete information. Click the **Demographics** or **Guardian** tab headings to change the student's information.

3. Click **Save** when you are done to close the window and return to the Student Profile screen. If you switch from one tab to another without clicking **Save**, any information you entered or changed will be automatically saved.

Deactivating a Student Profile

If a student leaves your class or school, or is no longer enrolled with a Scholastic program, then you should remove his or her Profile from program enrollment. This way their data will not be included when you generate reports.

Deactivating a student removes that student's connection with any class or group he or she is assigned to. This does not delete the student from the database. The student, however, will still be visible to users with administrative privileges, but will not be associated with any teachers, classes, or groups in the school and will not appear in the **SmartBar**.

To deactivate a student from SAM:

1. Click the **Deactivate Student** link under **Manage Roster** on the upper right-hand corner of the Student Profile screen.
2. Click **Yes** to proceed and remove the student from SAM, or **No** to return to that student's Profile screen.

If you wish to deactivate a student from SAM permanently, contact your School or District Administrator.

Changing Program Settings for Individual Students

At the bottom of every Student Profile screen for an individual student is the **Programs** menu. Once a student is enrolled in Scholastic programs, this menu provides you with quick access to the settings that affect your students' experience when they use Scholastic programs. For example:

- for *READ 180*, you can turn on English-language support;
- for SRI, you can allow students to see their scores after testing;
- for *Reading Counts!*, you can set the number of quiz attempts allowed;
- for *ReadAbout*, you can choose audiovisual and support options for students with special needs.

Use the **Settings** links in the **Programs** menu to change settings for a program. A window will appear in which you may make your settings selections. Changing program settings from a Student Profile screen will affect only that student's settings.

For information on changing settings for an entire class, see page 87 and for a group, see page 90.

Evaluating Student Performance With Grading Tools

The student grading tools offer a selection of tools that can assist you in evaluating your students' performance.

To access student grading tools from any screen in SAM:

NOTES/TIP

Using grading tools is particularly useful for adding assessment scores, Lexiles, or other assignments that may be completed in class or not on any software programs.

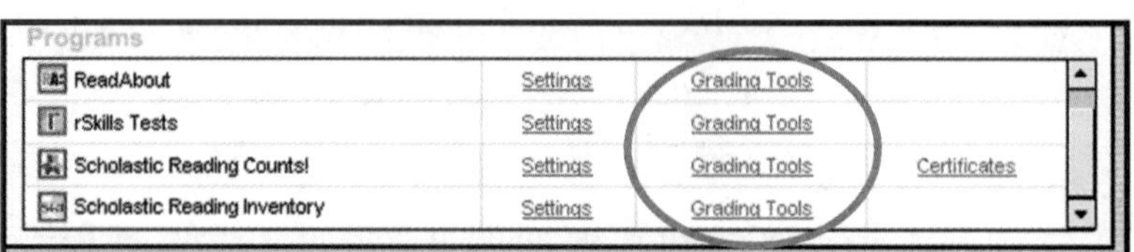

1. Double-click on a student's name in the **SmartBar**. The student's Profile will display on the right side of the screen.
2. Click the **Grading Tools** link next to a Scholastic program name in the **Programs** menu at the bottom of the screen to bring up the grading tools for that program.

Using SAM Reports

Reports provide detailed information about your students' time-on-task reading progress in a variety of different reading areas and skills. They also contain information on students' status in the programs or can be used for communicating with parents.

Reports help you:

- Monitor student progress
- Check software usage
- Plan instruction
- Diagnose student needs

When students work in Scholastic programs, SAM periodically saves the results of their work. This information is organized into a variety of different reports that can be generated from each of the Scholastic programs.

You can run reports for the Scholastic programs your district or school is using. This section explains how to generate reports in SAM, the various reports displays, as well as several of the reporting options that will help you assess your students' performance.

For details on reports and suggestions on how to use them, see pages 142–183.

NOTES/TIP

You have different reporting options based on your Profile's permissions. For example, as a teacher you are able to run reports for individual students, groups, classes, but not for grades, schools, and districts.

Finding the Right Reports

Types of Reports

NOTES/TIP

You can easily identify the type of report by looking at the icon in the upper left-hand corner of any reports screen.

For all Scholastic programs, there are six different types of reports you can run in SAM:

- **Progress Monitoring:** These provide information on skills progress and time spent on various activities, and keep teachers up-to-date on how individual students, classes, or groups are doing over time.

- **Diagnostic Reports:** These provide information on students' strengths and weaknesses in specific areas in order to help teachers differentiate instruction to meet individual needs.

- **Instructional Planning:** These help teachers plan targeted, data-driven instruction. In these reports, teachers may group students according to their skill needs or according to the activities or topics students are working on.

- **Alerts & Acknowledgments:** These reports provide automatic updates via messages to teachers about milestones in their students' performance or achievements.

- **School-to-Home:** These are letters to parents or guardians that are available in English and Spanish. They include student-specific progress information as well as home-involvement suggestions.

- **Management:** These reports provide lists of enrolled students and all teachers using Scholastic programs, or other basic program management.

About the Reports Index

The Reports Index lists a selection of recommended reports based on your **SmartBar** selection. The Reports Index is organized by the Scholastic programs, report types, and the dates reports were last run. Clicking the blue **Reports** tab from any screen in SAM will open the Reports Index. (If you are on the Home Page, click the blue **Reports** button.)

For more information on how your SmartBar selection affects the Reports Index, see page 101.

To return to the Reports Index, click **My District** (if you are an administrator) **My Classes** (if you are a teacher) at the top of **SmartBar**, which shows all available reports for your permissions level in the main display.

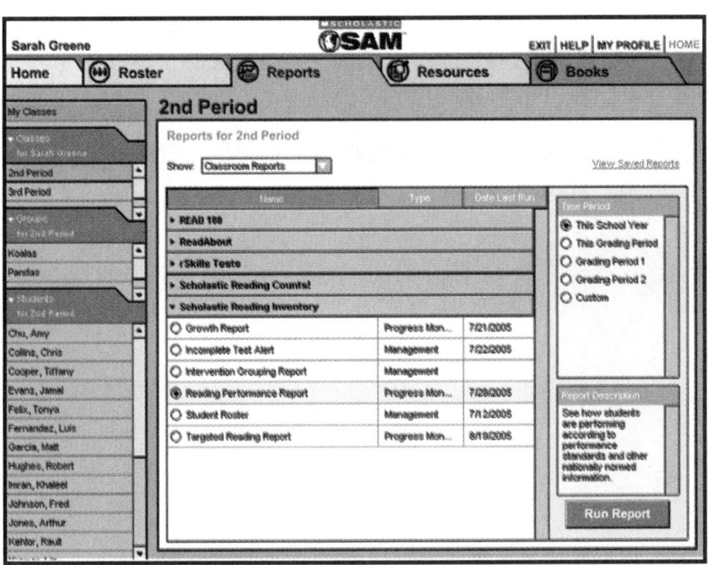

Filtering the Reports List

There are several ways you can use the Reports Index to filter through the reports you wish to run.

At the top of the Reports Index are four different options you can use to filter reports. Use the pull-down menu next to **Show** at the top of the Reports Index to choose from a report grouping. Select from the following:

- Multi-Classroom reports include data aggregated across several different classrooms or schools.
- Classroom reports show reports for students in one or more classes.
- Student reports show reports for individual students.
- All Reports show the complete list of reports available for use.

Once you choose a grouping, click on the column headings in the Reports Index to sort by report Program, Type, or Date last run. Once you have made your selections, the Reports Index display will change based on the filters.

For detailed information about types of reports, see pages 142–143 in this guide.

Browsing for Reports

Double-click a **Student**, **Group**, **Class**, **Grade**, **School**, or **District** (depending on your account) on the **SmartBar** from the Reports Index screen to change the reports we recommend for your selection.

Use the pull-down menu next to **Show** at the top of the Reports Index main display to chose a report grouping. We recommend the following report groupings for each **SmartBar** selection:

- **Multi-Classroom** reports are best used for districts, schools, and grades.
- **Classroom** reports are best used for classes, groups, and teachers.
- **Student** reports, which you can run by double-clicking a student's name in the **SmartBar**, are the best ways to evaluate individual performance.

NOTES/TIP

When you are viewing an on-screen report, you can make a different selection on the **SmartBar** without having to go back to the Reports Index.

Running Reports

You can generate reports easily and flexibly in SAM. Filter your reports by type, and run them over long or short time periods. To run a report:

1. Click the **Reports** tab from any screen in SAM to show the Reports Index.
2. Double-click a name in the **SmartBar** to select the **Student**, **Group**, **Class**, **Grade**, **School**, or **District** for which you would like to run a report.
3. Select the report you want to run by clicking the button to the left of the report name in the main display of the Reports Index. Time period selections will appear to the right of the main display.

NOTES/TIP

Click the **Using this Report** link on the top of any report for suggestions on how to apply each report to your class's or students' goals.

4. Depending on the report you select and your permissions level in SAM, run reports over the following time periods:
   - This School Year
   - This Grading Period
   - This Week
   - Last Week
   - Today
   - Custom

   When you select **Custom**, use the calendar tool in the pop-up window to tailor dates on which you would like to run a report.
5. Click **Run Report** once you have made your selections to display the interactive report on your screen.

Running the Same Report for Another Time Period

To change the time period for a report you just generated:

1. Click the **Time Period** link at the top of the report and use the calendar tool to select a different time period over which you would like to re-run the report.
2. Click **Run Report** to run the same report over the new time period.

Running the Same Report for Another Student, Group, or Class

To run a single report for a different **SmartBar** selection from the Report screen:

1. Double-click on the name of another **Student**, **Group**, or **Class** on the **SmartBar** and the report will rerun according to your selection.
2. Click the **Time Period** link at the top of the report to make any changes to the time period and click **Run Report** to run the same report with new dates.

Viewing Reports

Once you have selected and run your report for a chosen time period, it will appear on the screen.

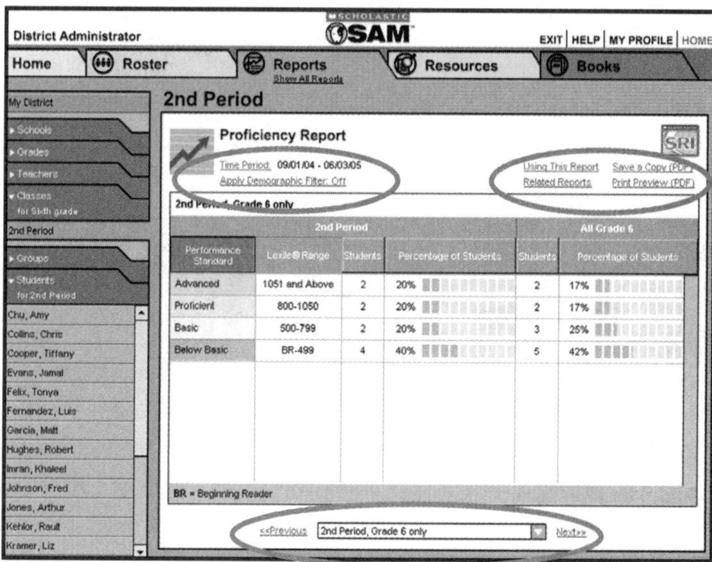

Depending on which report you run, you can use the **Reports** screen features to:

- Click on column headings to sort information in the report;
- Access resources related to your report;
- Click links to change the time period, use the demographic filter, view related reports, print a copy, or save the report in SAM;
- Use the pull-down menu at the bottom of the screen to run different reports from the same **SmartBar** selection.

Viewing Related Reports

Some report data or further information may be elaborated in greater detail on other reports. **Related Reports** selections are available for each report based on Scholastic recommendations for exploring your data further. Click the **View Related Reports** link in the upper right corner of a **Report** screen to open a window that has a list of reports that provide further or related data. Click the link for the related report you wish to see to run that report.

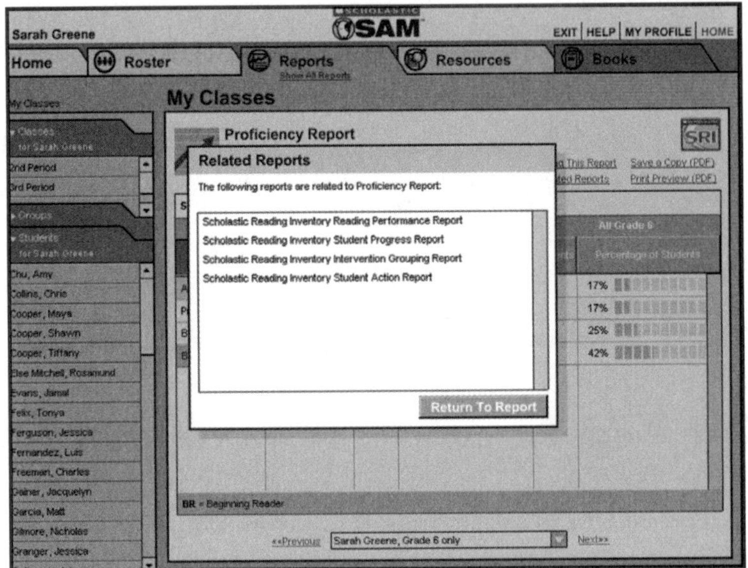

Using the Demographic Filter

Student Profiles contain demographic data that supports administrators to run reports based on No Child Left Behind (NCLB) reporting categories. This disaggregated data helps districts and schools to track, monitor, and demonstrate Adequate Yearly Progress (AYP). The **Demographic Filter** provides focused reporting based on various categories, including:

- **AYP criteria:** Make distinctions between students with economic disadvantages, gifted and talented students, students with limited English proficiency, students with disabilities and migrant students.
- **Ethnicity:** Identify students from various ethnic backgrounds, such as Asian/Pacific Islander, Hispanic or African-American.
- **Grade:** Filter reports by grade.
- **Gender**
- **Scholastic Program:** Make distinctions based on whether a student or class is enrolled in *SRI READ 180, ReadAbout, Scholastic Reading Counts!*, or any other Scholastic program powered by SAM.

You can use the **Demographic Filter** to run any Multi-Classroom or Classroom report (up to 30 students in a class) by one or more of the demographic categories. Choosing more than one category will generate more specific reports. (For example, selecting both "male" and "migrant" will display only students who are migrant *and* male.)

NOTES/TIP

District Administrators can use the Grade Filter to run district-wide reports for a single grade.

NOTES/TIP

To run a report using a different set of criteria, click **Demographic Filter** and check the appropriate categories. This will allow you to compare data among different groups or students in your school or district.

To apply AYP filters to a report from a **Reports** screen:

1. Click the **Demographic Filter** link on the top of the reports screen to open the **Demographic Filter** window.
2. Use the check boxes to select students based on the categories which you would like to run a report.
3. Click **Run Report** to rerun the report to include and display the students that match your selections.

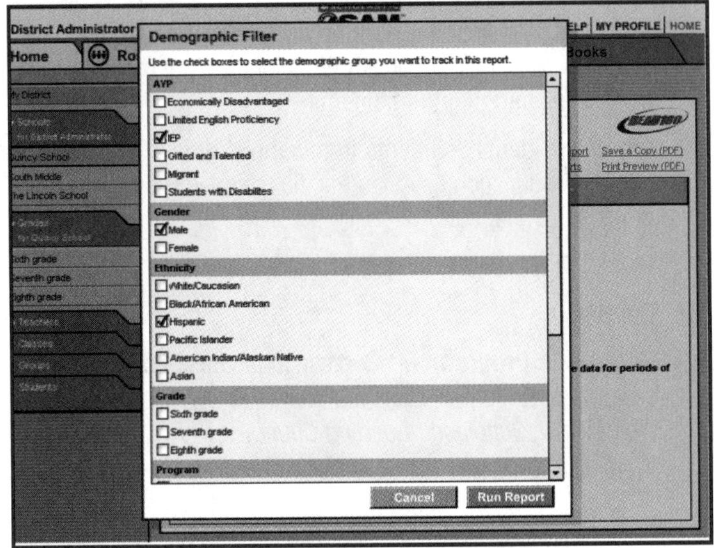

Returning to the Reports Index

From any reports screen, use the **View All Reports** link under the **Reports** tab to return to the Reports Index. The Reports Index will show you a list of all the reports available for the Profile selected on the **SmartBar**.

Printing, Saving, and Archiving Reports

You may want to keep the reports you generated, either for record-keeping purposes or to reuse them at another time. You can print, save, and archive any report you run in SAM for these purposes.

Printing a Report

To print a report from the reports screen:

1. Click the **Print Preview (PDF)** link to open the report in Adobe Acrobat Reader in a new window.
2. Click **File** from the Adobe Acrobat Reader menu at the top left of the screen. Choose **Print** in the menu to print the report.

NOTES/TIP

Adobe Acrobat Reader should have been included during installation. If it was not, contact your Technical Administrator.

Reading Performance Report

TEACHER: SARAH GREENE

PROGRESS MONITORING

School: The Lincoln School
Grade: 6, 7, 8

Time Period: 09/01/04 – 06/03/05

STUDENT	GRADE	LEXILE®	TEST DATE	PERFORMANCE STANDARD	NORMATIVE DATA: PERCENTILE RANK	NCE	STANINE
Chu, Amy	6	930	12/15/04	Proficient	58	54.0	5
Collins, Chris	6	820	12/15/04	Proficient	40	45.0	4
Cooper, Maya	8	650	12/01/04	Basic	11	24.0	2
Cooper, Shawn	7	1030	02/01/05	Proficient	63	57.0	6
Cooper, Tiffany	6	1080	12/15/04	Advanced	82	69.0	7
Evans, Jamal	6	410	12/15/04	Below Basic	3	10.0	1
Felix, Tonya	6	690	12/01/04	Basic	24	35.0	4
Ferguson, Jessica	8	520	12/01/04	Below Basic	3	10.0	1
Fernandez, Luis	6	320	12/15/04	Below Basic	1	1.0	1
Freeman, Charles	8	930	12/01/04	Proficient	39	44.0	4
Gainer, Jacquelyn	8	1030	12/01/04	Proficient	56	53.0	5
Garcia, Matt	6	BR (0)	12/15/04	Below Basic	1	1.0	1
Gilmore, Nicholas	8	680	12/01/04	Basic	12	25.0	3
Granger, Jessica	7	930	02/01/05	Proficient	46	48.0	5
Gutierrez, Jaime	7	760	02/01/05	Basic	22	34.0	3
Horowitz, Jason	7	820	02/01/05	Basic	30	39.0	4
Huang, Hsin-Yi	8	780	12/01/04	Basic	20	32.0	3
Hudson, Orlando	7	780	02/01/05	Basic	25	36.0	4
Imran, Khaleel	6	620	12/15/04	Basic	18	31.0	3
James, Michelle	7	1080	02/01/05	Proficient	72	62.0	6
Kehlor, Rault	6	BR (75)	05/18/05	Below Basic	1	1.0	1
Kim, Julie	8	740	12/01/04	Basic	16	29.0	3
Kramer, Liz	PK	650	12/15/04	Advanced	96	87.0	9

BR = Beginning Reader

YEAR-END PROFICIENCY LEXILE® RANGES

GRADE 1	GRADE 2	GRADE 3	GRADE 4	GRADE 5	GRADE 6	GRADE 7	GRADE 8	GRADE 9	GRADE 10	GRADE 11	GRADE 12
100-400	300-600	500-800	600-900	700-1000	800-1050	850-1100	900-1150	1000-1200	1025-1250	1050-1300	1050-1300

Using This Report

Purpose: This report shows students' performance standards based on the results of their latest SRI tests.

Follow-Up: Use the information on the report to set goals for students, and to identify students who are performing at low performance standards.

Printed by: Sarah Greene | Page 1 of 2 | Printed on: 08/19/05
 v 1.38

NOTES/TIP

In Mac OS X, reports may open in the Preview application.

Saving a Report to Your Computer

You can save any report on your local computer once you have run it. This will help you compare data and monitor progress for students, classes, grades, or districts. To save a report from the **Reports** screen:

1. Click the **Print Preview (PDF)** link to open the report as a PDF file in Adobe Acrobat.
2. Once in Adobe Acrobat, click **File** and choose **Save a Copy** to save the report, or select the **Save** icon in the toolbar.
3. Select a location where you want to save the report using the **Save a Copy** pull-down menu. A file name will automatically appear in the **Save** window, but you should rename your file with something that you can easily recognize when you want to open it again (e.g., a student's name and the date the report was run).
4. Click **Save** and close Adobe Acrobat when you are finished.
5. Go to the folder where you saved the report and double-click on the file name to open it.

NOTES/TIP

When you Save a Copy of a report, it is stored on your local computer's hard drive. When you save a report on SAM, it is stored on the SAM server and you can access it from the Reports Index.

Saving a Report in SAM

You can save a report for any class, group, or student within SAM so that you can access it from the Reports Index using the **View Saved Reports** link.

To save a report you have just generated, click the **Save a Copy (PDF)** link in the upper right-hand corner of the **Report** screen. This will save the report in PDF format with the appropriate Profile information included.

To access a saved report from any screen in SAM:

1. Double-click a name in the **SmartBar**.
2. Click the blue **Reports** tab to access the Reports Index.
3. Click the **View Saved Reports** link in the upper right of the main display. A window opens with a list of already-saved reports for that selection in the **SmartBar**.
4. Click on the report name to open the PDF file. This will launch Adobe Acrobat.

Using Resources in SAM

SAM provides access to a variety of instructional resources that you can print and use in your classroom to enhance the effectiveness of your Scholastic programs.

Resources provide additional support for Scholastic's software-based activities and your classroom-based instruction. You can print resources to use in classroom instruction, with individual students, for your professional development needs, or for help implementing Scholastic programs.

NOTES/TIP

You can only access resources from SAM if your workstation is connected to the World Wide Web.

Finding the Right Resources

The Resource Finder is your tool for locating resources that you can use with Scholastic programs and for professional development.

To use the Resource Finder, click the green **Resources** tab along the top of any screen in SAM.

The Resource Finder has the following features to help you narrow your searches:

- **Quick Search by SAM Keyword:** This allows you to search for resources using SAM Keywords, which are found on many Scholastic print materials.
- **Advanced Search:** This function enables you to further tailor your resource searches by resource type, strand, skill, and Scholastic program.
- **Browse:** You can use this function to browse for types of resources associated with Small- or Whole-Group Instruction, individual students, and by Scholastic program.
- **Standards Lookup tool:** this allows you to view state standards related to Scholastic skills.

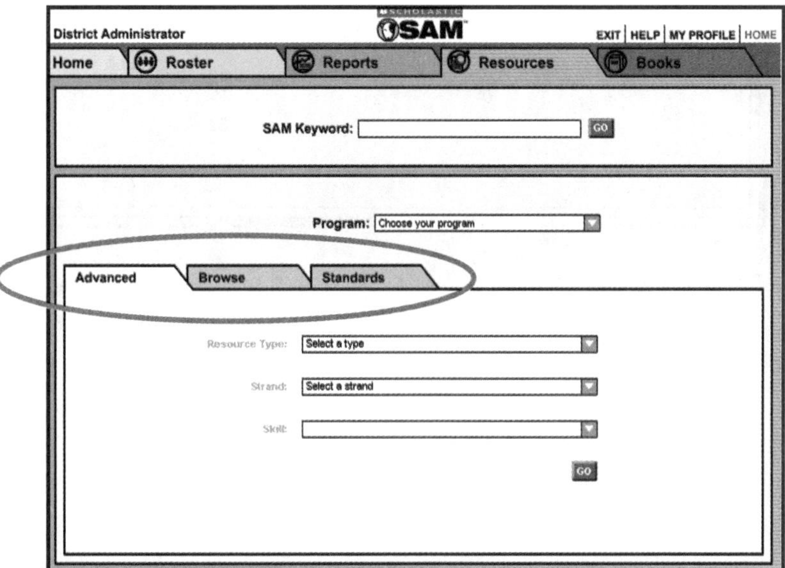

Using Quick Search

Scholastic's print-based teacher materials have SAM Keywords associated with them. You can use SAM Keywords in the Quick Search to access printable PDF files of these materials and activities to use in your classroom.

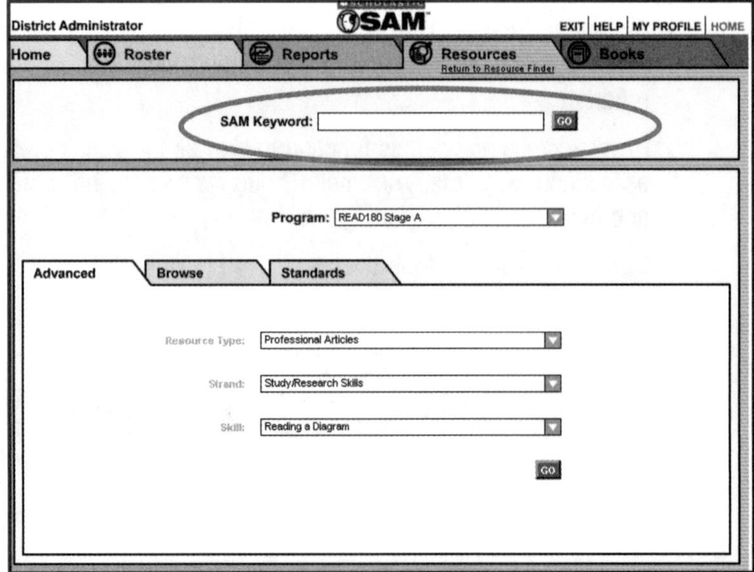

To use Quick Search, type a SAM Keyword in the **SAM Keyword** field at the top of the Resource Finder's main display and click **Go**. Your results will automatically display in the **Resource Search Results** screen.

Using Advanced Search

The Resource Finder also has an **Advanced Search** that allows you to search for materials by using more specific criteria. Click the **Advanced** tab to use the **Advanced Search** feature.

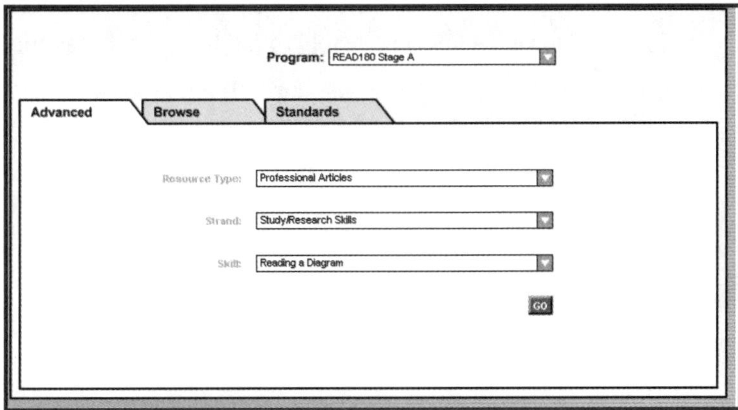

To use **Advanced Search**:

1. Use the pull-down menus to select any or all of the following:
   - Scholastic **Program**
   - **Resource Type**
   - **Strand**
   - **Skill**
2. Click **Go** to search using the selections you made. The **Resource Search Results** screen will display. Click on the **Resource Name** links to view PDF files of resources.

NOTES/TIP

Some searches may bring up many resources. Make sure to use as many fields as possible in **Advanced Search** to access resources specific to your needs.

Viewing, Printing, and Saving a Resource

The results of resource searches are displayed on the **Resource Search Results** screen. You can view these results as Adobe Acrobat PDF files.

Viewing a Resource

To view a resource in Adobe Acrobat from the **Search Results** screen:

1. Click the **Resource Name**, **Resource Type**, **Program**, **Resource**, or **Grade/Level** columns to re-sort the resources table.
2. Click any link in the **Resource Name** column of the **Resource Search Results** screen to view PDFs of Scholastic resources related to that skill.

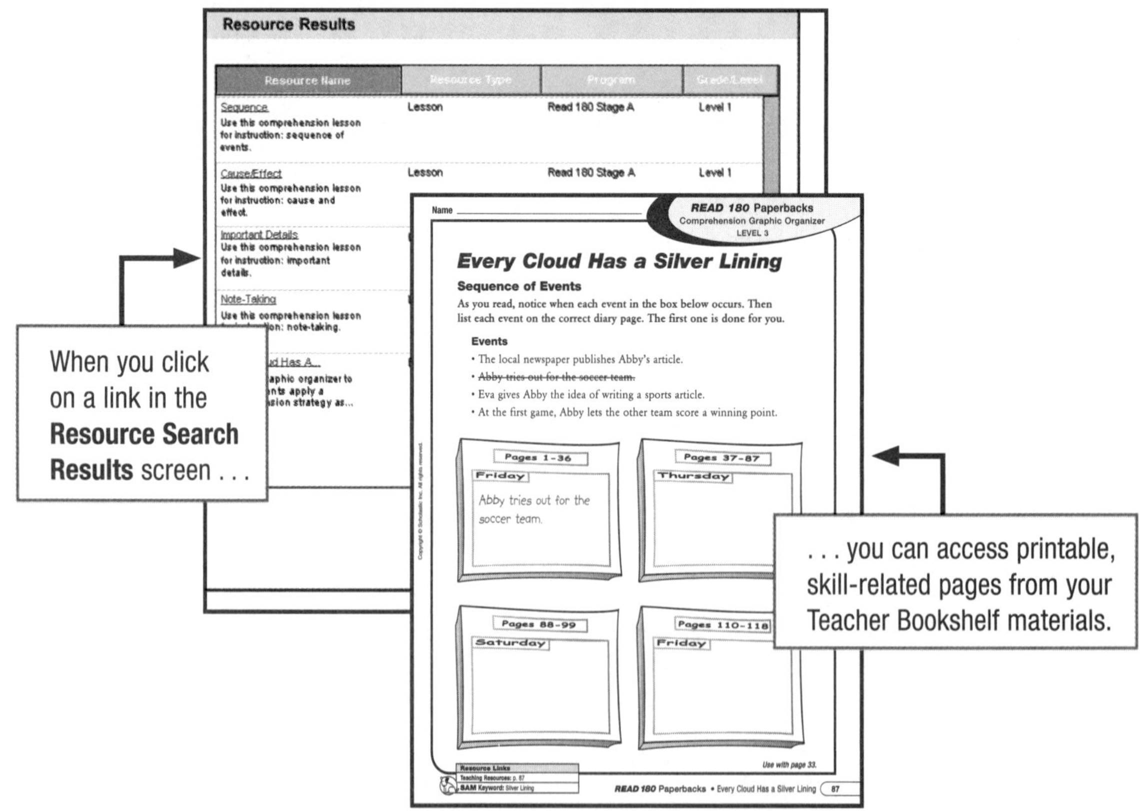

Printing or Saving a Resource

You can view Scholastic resources as Adobe Acrobat PDF files. Once you have viewed a resource, you can print and save it as you would any file on your computer.

To print a resource, click **File** from the Adobe Acrobat Reader menu at the top left of the screen. Choose **Print** in the menu to print the report.

You can also save any resource on your local computer once you viewed it. To save a report:

1. Click **File** in Adobe Acrobat and choose **Save a Copy** to save the report, or select the **Save** icon in the toolbar.
2. Select a location where you want to save the resource using the **Save a Copy** pull-down menu. A file name will automatically appear in the **Save** window, but you should rename your file with something that you can easily recognize when you want to open it again (e.g., the title of the resource).
3. Click **Save** and close Adobe Acrobat when you are finished.
4. Go to the folder where you saved the resource and double-click on the file name to open it.

Browsing for Resources

The Resource Finder has a **Browse** feature that allows you to search for resources associated with specific needs, either by Scholastic program or for more focused instructional purposes. The **Browse** tab organizes resources into several different categories as they relate to your classroom needs, including:

- **For Whole- and Small-Group Instruction:** Allows you to browse lessons, practice pages/BLMs, certificates, and Scholastic program-specific resources.
- **For individual students:** These types of resources are associated with student-intensive, specific instruction, such as Vocabulary Cards.

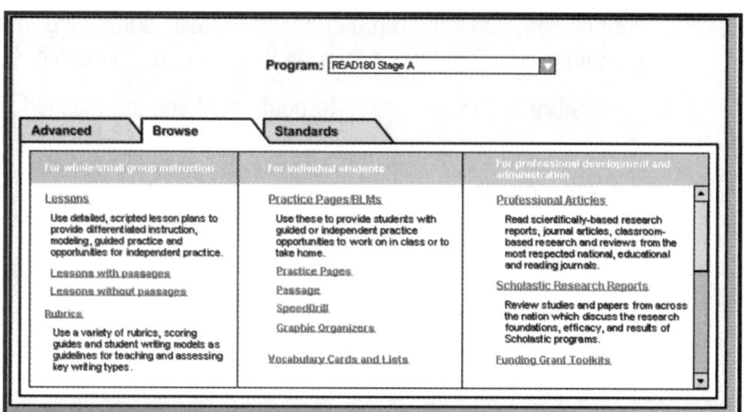

NOTES/TIP

Standards associated with resources can help you see how Scholastic programs align to meet your state's standards.

To browse for resources:

1. Click any resource type listed on the **Browse** tab. Your results will appear automatically in the **Resource Search Results** screen.
2. Click the column heads to sort the information in the table by **Resource Name**, **Resource Type**, **Program**, and **Grade/Level**.
3. Click any link under the **Resource Name** column to view a resource in Adobe Acrobat. Here you can view, save, or print the selected resource.

Searching for State Standards

If you would like to search directly for a specific standard as it relates to a Scholastic program, the Resources Finder **Search** tab includes a Standards Lookup Tool. This tool helps to access state standards correlation documents associated with some Scholastic programs.

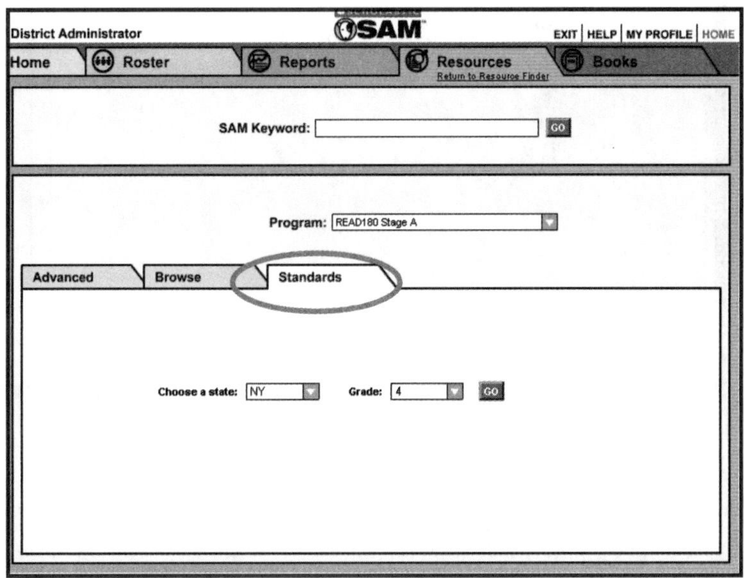

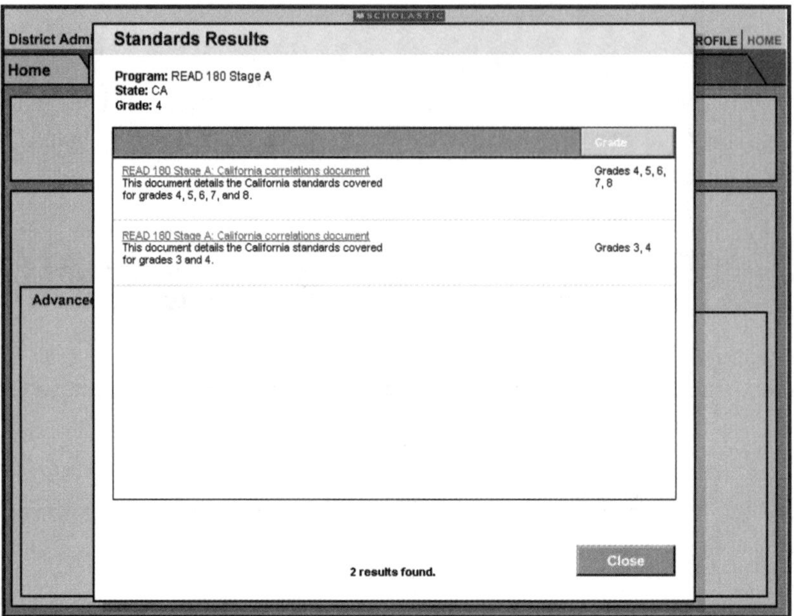

To search for state standards:

1. Click on **Standards** tab under **Resources**.
2. Use the pull-down menus to choose the state grade range for which you would like to view standards correlations.
3. Click **Go** to view a list of correlations documents in the **Standards Results** screen.
4. Click the links in the **Correlations Document** column to view PDF files of state standards.

Overview

The **Book Expert** is a powerful tool that searches the entire *Scholastic Reading Counts!* library to help you find books to match your curriculum needs. The **Book Expert** also lets you order and install quizzes to help you measure your students' reading progress if you have *Scholastic Reading Counts!* installed.

Finding the Right Books

To open the **Book Expert** search screen, click the **Books** button on the main display of the SAM Home Page, or click the **Books** tab along the top of any screen in SAM. The ***Scholastic Reading Counts!*** **Book Expert** automatically opens to its main display.

You can search the 35,000-plus books included in the **Book Expert** by title, author, Lexile, or ten other descriptive categories. From the **Book Expert**, you can:

- Use **Quick Search** to search by title or author's last name to find different book titles;
- Use **Advanced Search** to find books based on several different criteria.

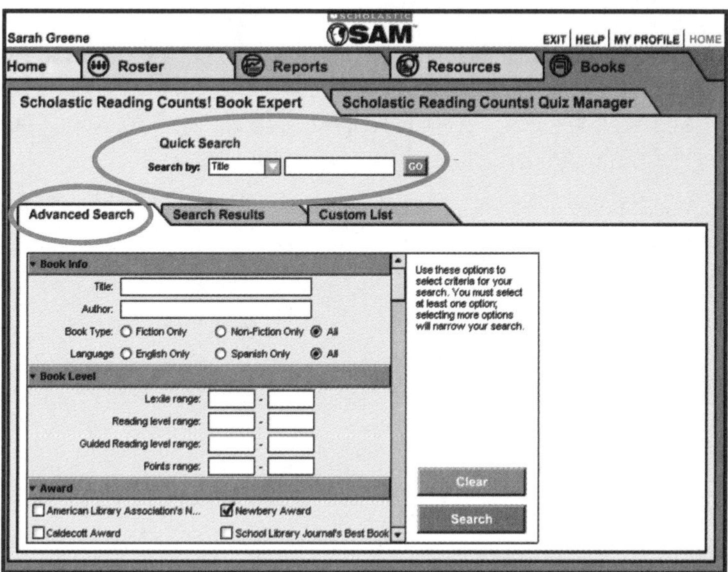

Using Quick Search to Find Books

You can use keywords, titles, or author names in **Quick Search** to search the *Scholastic Reading Counts!* library for books and suggestions to help you address your curriculum needs.

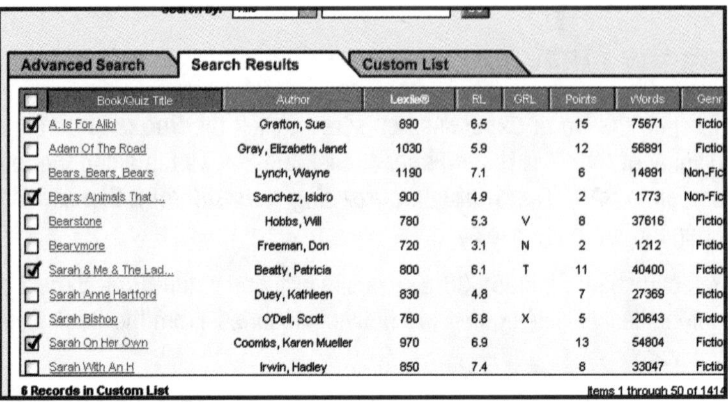

Advanced Search | Search Results | Custom List

☐	Book/Quiz Title	Author	Lexile®	RL	GRL	Points	Words	Genr
☑	A. Is For Alibi	Grafton, Sue	890	6.5		15	75671	Fictio
☐	Adam Of The Road	Gray, Elizabeth Janet	1030	5.9		12	56891	Fictio
☐	Bears, Bears, Bears	Lynch, Wayne	1190	7.1		6	14891	Non-Fic
☑	Bears: Animals That ...	Sanchez, Isidro	900	4.9		2	1773	Non-Fic
☐	Bearstone	Hobbs, Will	780	5.3	V	8	37616	Fictio
☐	Bearymore	Freeman, Don	720	3.1	N	2	1212	Fictio
☑	Sarah & Me & The Lad...	Beatty, Patricia	800	6.1	T	11	40400	Fictio
☐	Sarah Anne Hartford	Duey, Kathleen	830	4.8		7	27369	Fictio
☐	Sarah Bishop	O'Dell, Scott	760	6.8	X	5	20643	Fictio
☑	Sarah On Her Own	Coombs, Karen Mueller	970	6.9		13	54804	Fictio
☐	Sarah With An H	Irwin, Hadley	850	7.4		8	33047	Fictio

6 Records in Custom List — Items 1 through 50 of 1414

To use **Quick Search**:

1. Type a keyword in the **Quick Search** box, or choose a category from the **Search By** field to further narrow your search.
2. Click **Go**. Your results will automatically display on the **Search Results** screen. Click on the column headings to re-sort the results by book/quiz title, author, Lexile, reading level, Guided Reading Level (GRL), point value, words, genre, or number of copies in your library.
3. Use the check boxes to select (or deselect) book titles to include on your Custom Book List.

Using Advanced Search to Find Books

Advanced Search lets you use a number of specialized criteria to search the *Scholastic Reading Counts!* library for books to use in your classroom work. From the **Advanced Search** screen, you can either search by one criterion or use several to seek out books.

To use **Advanced Search**:

1. Click on the red bars in the Advanced Search main display to expand any of the following categories:
    - **Book Info:** Search for books by author, title, book type (fiction or nonfiction), or language (English and Spanish only).
    - **Book Level:** Find books appropriate to your students' or classes' Lexile, reading level, Guided Reading Level (GRL), and point ranges.
    - **Award:** Select books that have received notable awards, such as Newbury and State Book Awards.
    - **Comprehension Skill:** Find books that address specific comprehension skill issues your students may have.
    - **Culture:** Filters your search to find books that relate to the specific cultural backgrounds of your students.
    - **Genre:** Search for books from various genres, such as historical fiction, poetry, or myths and legends.
    - **Interest Level:** Search for books appropriate for various grade ranges, such as K–2, 3–5, Middle and High School.
    - **Program/Series:** Search for books that are part of popular childrens' series, such as Goosebumps, Harry Potter, and Dr. Seuss.
    - **Theme:** Specify themes that you would like to focus on in classroom use, such as art, music, and technology.
    - **Topic:** Specify topics that you would like to focus on in classroom use, such as African-American history, endangered species, and explorers.

Click the red bars again to compress the categories in the main display. Any changes you make to that category will be saved.

NOTES/TIP

The search criteria used the **Advanced Search** for Book Expert is the same for the ***Scholastic Reading Counts!*, Quiz Manager**.

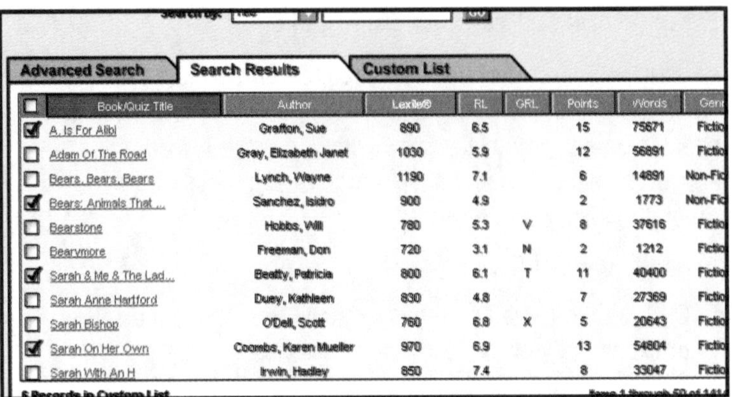

Advanced Search | Search Results | Custom List

Book/Quiz Title	Author	Lexile®	RL	GRL	Points	Words	Genr
A. Is For Alibi	Grafton, Sue	890	6.5		15	75671	Fictio
Adam Of The Road	Gray, Elizabeth Janet	1030	5.9		12	56891	Fictio
Bears, Bears, Bears	Lynch, Wayne	1190	7.1		6	14891	Non-Fic
Bears: Animals That ...	Sanchez, Isidro	900	4.9		2	1773	Non-Fic
Bearstone	Hobbs, Will	780	5.3	V	8	37616	Fictio
Bearymore	Freeman, Don	720	3.1	N	2	1212	Fictio
Sarah & Me & The Lad...	Beatty, Patricia	800	6.1	T	11	40400	Fictio
Sarah Anne Hartford	Duey, Kathleen	830	4.8		7	27369	Fictio
Sarah Bishop	O'Dell, Scott	760	6.8	X	5	20643	Fictio
Sarah On Her Own	Coombs, Karen Mueller	970	6.9		13	54804	Fictio
Sarah With An H	Irwin, Hadley	850	7.4		8	33047	Fictio

2. Click **Search** once you finish making all of your selections. Your results will automatically display on the **Search Results** screen. Click on the column headings to re-sort your results.
3. Click the **Advanced Search** tab to begin another search.

Using the Book Info Window

You can view and save details about any book on your list by clicking the book title link in the **Search Results** list to open the **Book Info** window.

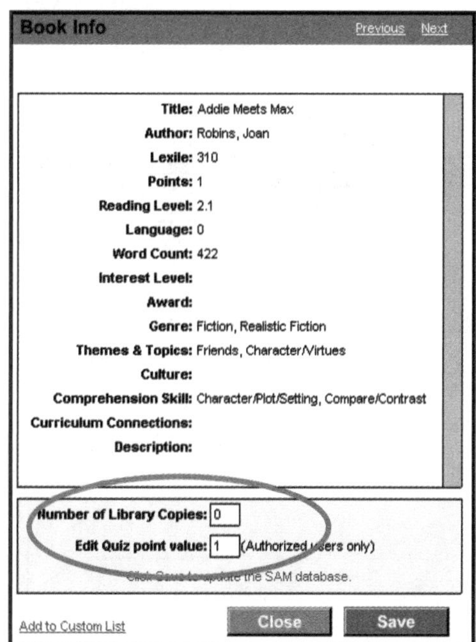

From the **Book Info** window, you can:

- View, record, and maintain the number of copies of a book in your school's library;
- Adjust *Reading Counts!* quiz point values (this option will be unavailable if you are not authorized to change point values);
- Add the book to a Custom Book List (this option will be unavailable if you opened the **Book Info** window from a Custom Book List).

Click the **Previous** and **Next** links to move to other books on the **Search Results** screen.

Once you have finished recording any information, click **Save** to keep the changes or **Close** to exit the **Book Info** window and return to the **Search Results** screen.

NOTES/TIP

Remember to click **Save** prior to closing the **Book Info** window to keep any changes you may have made.

Building, Editing, and Printing Custom Lists and Labels

Book Expert allows you to search and filter through the 35,000 titles in the *Scholastic Reading Counts!* library to seek out materials to match your curriculum needs. In the **Book Expert** you can:

- Create, edit and print custom book lists;
- Print quiz order forms;
- Print book labels for classroom use.

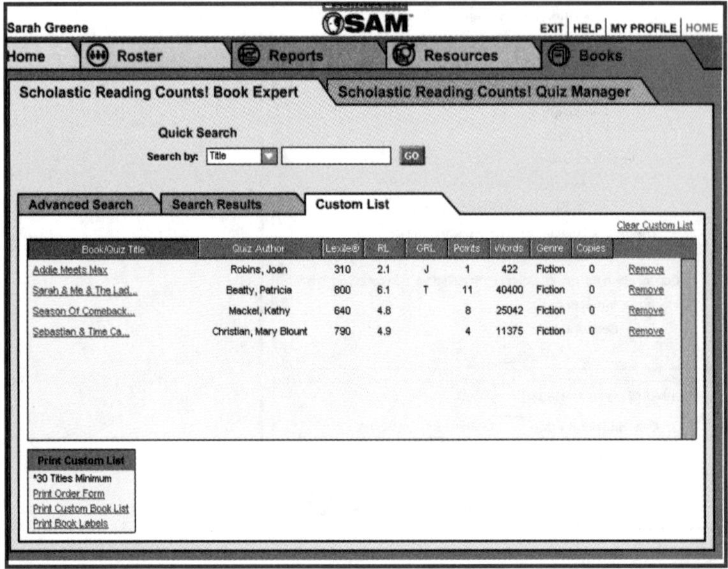

Building Custom Book Lists

After you search for books, you can narrow down your search results by creating a Custom Book List. To create a Custom Book List from the **Search Results** page:

1. Use the check boxes next to the search results to select (or deselect) titles to include on your Custom Book List. The counter on the lower left of the screen keeps track of how many titles you select.
2. Click the **View Custom List** button to view a list of titles you select. Click the column headings to re-sort the information for each title.

Printing Custom Book Lists

You can print hard copies of the lists you build in **Book Expert** for classroom planning or curriculum-related activities.

To print a Custom Book List from the **Custom List** screen:

1. Click the **Print Custom Book List** link in the **Print Custom List** menu on the lower left of the screen to open the **Print Custom Book List** window.
2. Use the check boxes to select (or deselect) the categories you would like to see displayed on your printed list.
3. Click the **Preview** button when you are finished making your selections to view a PDF file of the list. The PDF file will automatically open in Adobe Acrobat Reader, which is included in your Scholastic program installation package.
4. Click **File** then **Print** in the Adobe Acrobat toolbar to print your Custom Book List.

Printing Quiz Order Forms

You can use **Book Expert** to print customized Scholastic Quiz Order forms to add titles to your school's library or to use in classroom instruction.

To print Quiz order forms:

1. Click the **Print Order Form** link in the **Print Custom List** menu on the lower left of the screen to open the **Print Order Form** window. A PDF file will automatically open in Adobe Acrobat Reader, which is included in your Scholastic program installation package.
2. Click **File** then **Print** in the Adobe Acrobat toolbar to print your Scholastic Book Order Form.

Printing Book Labels

Book labels can be used to identify books for classroom use. You can use the labels to organize your school's library by any of the categories criteria provided in **Book Expert's Advanced Search**.

For a list of category criteria in Book Expert, see page 121.

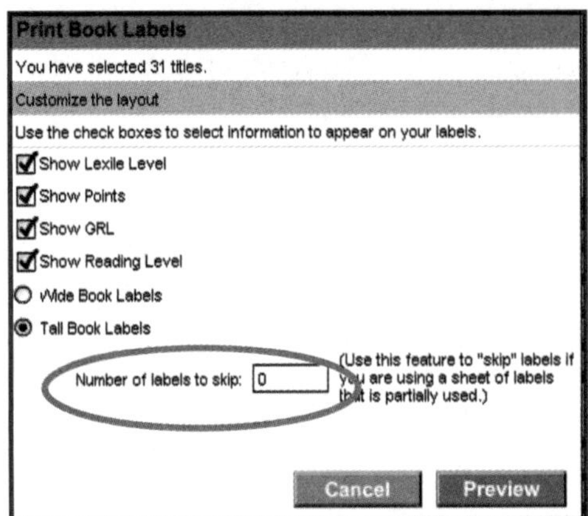

To print book labels:

1. Click the **Print Book Labels** link in the **Print Custom List** menu on the lower left of the screen to open the **Print Book Labels** window.
2. Use the check boxes to select (or deselect) whether or not you wish to display on the label the Lexile level of the book, its point value, reading level, or its Guided Reading Level (GRL). Use the buttons to choose wide book labels (to place on book covers) or tall book labels (to place on book spines).
3. Click the **Preview** button when you are finished making your selections to view a PDF file of the list. The PDF file will automatically open in Adobe Acrobat Reader, which is included in your Scholastic program installation package.
4. Click **File** then **Print** in the Adobe Acrobat toolbar to print your book labels.

NOTES/TIP

If you want to "skip" printing labels, enter the amount you would like to leave out in the **Number of Labels to Skip** field. You can skip up to 29 labels. Use this feature if you are using a sheet of labels that is partially used.

Teaching With *SRI:* Overview

SRI allows you to determine student reading levels, compare these levels to normative data, monitor student progress, and gauge the effectiveness of instruction and/or intervention. What's more, once you administer the test, you will be able to incorporate your understanding of student reading levels into your plans for instruction. With the *SRI* reports available through the Scholastic Achievement Manager, you can prescribe the appropriate instructional support material for your students to develop their reading skills and grow as readers.

SRI can also help you whenever you need to complete one of the following tasks:

- Set goals for reading growth.
- Identify students who may require intervention or additional testing or diagnosis.
- Create a plan for individual reading instruction.
- Find appropriately leveled books for your students to read.
- Create reading groups that are organized by reading level.

In order to get the most out of *SRI*, take this time now to review the following section. It contains helpful suggestions for administering the test easily and efficiently; pointers on understanding the *SRI* student test results; an overview of reports; instructions on how, when, and why you can use each report; a detailed explanation of the Lexile Framework; model schedules for use of the program during the Fall and Spring terms; and a number of other tips and strategies for how to use *SRI* and Lexile measures in the classroom.

SRI: Best Practices

Prepare Students for the Test Familiarize students with the format of the test. Copy a simple test item on the board or distribute copies of printed items and go through the items as a class. Then, prior to the test administration, make sure students understand how to use the computer interface to complete the test. Additionally, a guide to test-taking techniques is available in this guide on page 134. Finally, express to students the importance of taking the test seriously. The same expectations should be placed on students taking *SRI* as are placed during other testing experiences.

Make Judgments About Student Reading Levels As a default, students begin the test at a Lexile measure that is based on their grade level. *SRI* has been designed, then, to quickly "find" a student's reading ability range and adjust test items accordingly. However, the better a student is targeted when he or she first takes *SRI*, the more accurate his or her results will be. You have the ability through the *SRI* test settings to adjust students' starting points above or below grade level. In addition, if students have a prior history with *SRI* or another test that reports in Lexiles, use this information accordingly.

Time Test Administrations Judiciously *SRI* can be administered at different intervals, based on your classroom and educational needs. For example, the test can be administered once in the fall and once in the spring for a high-level snapshot of students' reading progress. Alternately, *SRI* can be administered monthly for a more regular tracking of students' reading progress. We recommend, however, that *SRI* not be administered too frequently as other factors, including test fatigue, may interfere with the accuracy of test results.

Capitalize on *SRI* Reports Make full use of the reports available through the Scholastic Achievement Manager. *SRI* reports provide you with student results, allow you to track student progress, help you plan instruction, assist you in managing the program, and help facilitate school-to-home communication.

Choose Reading Materials Based on Test Results Use student test results to help choose reading materials. With each test administration, students can create their own reading lists based on their own chosen interests and their test results. In addition, you can use the charts on pages 187–188 to help guide you in choosing appropriate texts for both independent and instructional reading at, above, and below students' current Lexile measures.

SRI for Administrators

SRI includes advanced features that allow district and school administrators to monitor and maximize product usage, assess and forecast reading performance through aggregated reports or filtered for Adequate Yearly Progress reporting groups, thus identifying schools, grades, and classes at risk of failing to meet proficiency goals. Moreover, *SRI* provides the data necessary to identify groups in need of additional resources or intervention.

A select group of *SRI* reports have been designed with the administrator in mind in order to accomplish these goals most effectively. See the chart on the next page for a summary of these reports, then refer to the more detailed presentation of the reports in the *SRI* reports section in Teaching With *SRI* (pp. 142–183).

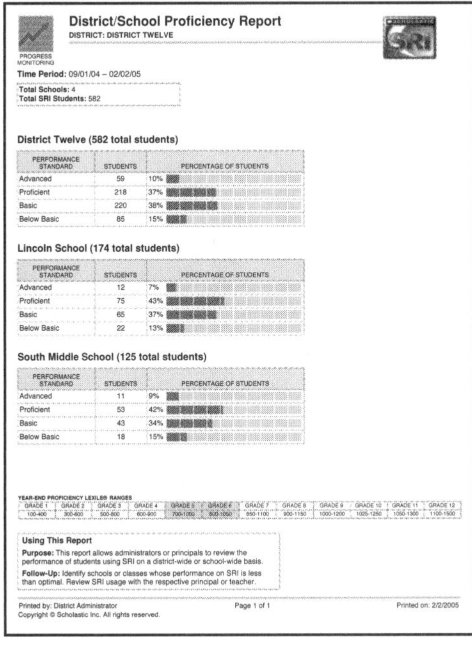

District/School Proficiency Report
DISTRICT: DISTRICT TWELVE

PROGRESS MONITORING

Time Period: 09/01/04 – 02/02/05

Total Schools: 4
Total SRI Students: 582

District Twelve (582 total students)

PERFORMANCE STANDARD	STUDENTS	PERCENTAGE OF STUDENTS
Advanced	59	10%
Proficient	218	37%
Basic	220	38%
Below Basic	85	15%

Lincoln School (174 total students)

PERFORMANCE STANDARD	STUDENTS	PERCENTAGE OF STUDENTS
Advanced	12	7%
Proficient	75	43%
Basic	65	37%
Below Basic	22	13%

South Middle School (125 total students)

PERFORMANCE STANDARD	STUDENTS	PERCENTAGE OF STUDENTS
Advanced	11	9%
Proficient	53	42%
Basic	43	34%
Below Basic	18	15%

YEAR-END PROFICIENCY LEXILE® RANGES

GRADE 1	GRADE 2	GRADE 3	GRADE 4	GRADE 5	GRADE 6	GRADE 7	GRADE 8	GRADE 9	GRADE 10	GRADE 11	GRADE 12
100-400	300-600	500-800	600-900	700-1000	800-1050	850-1100	900-1150	1000-1200	1025-1250	1050-1300	1100-1500

Using This Report

Purpose: This report allows administrators or principals to review the performance of students using SRI on a district-wide or school-wide basis.

Follow-Up: Identify schools or classes whose performance on SRI is less than optimal. Review SRI usage with the respective principal or teacher.

Printed by: District Administrator   Page 1 of 1   Printed on: 2/2/2005

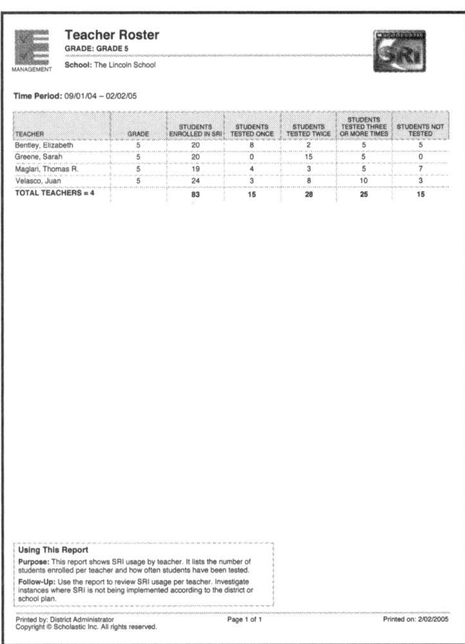

Teacher Roster
GRADE: GRADE 5
School: The Lincoln School

MANAGEMENT

Time Period: 09/01/04 – 02/02/05

TEACHER	GRADE	STUDENTS ENROLLED IN SRI	STUDENTS TESTED ONCE	STUDENTS TESTED TWICE	STUDENTS TESTED THREE OR MORE TIMES	STUDENTS NOT TESTED
Bentley, Elizabeth	5	20	8	2	5	5
Greene, Sarah	5	20	0	15	5	0
Maglari, Thomas R.	5	19	4	3	5	7
Velasco, Juan	5	24	3	8	10	3
TOTAL TEACHERS = 4		**83**	**15**	**28**	**25**	**15**

Using This Report

Purpose: This report shows SRI usage by teacher. It lists the number of students enrolled per teacher and how often students have been tested.

Follow-Up: Use the report to review SRI usage per teacher. Investigate instances where SRI is not being implemented according to the district or school plan.

Printed by: District Administrator   Page 1 of 1   Printed on: 2/02/2005

The District/School Proficiency Report and the Teacher Roster are just two SRI reports designed specifically for administrators.

SRI Reports: If You Want...

IF YOU WANT...	LOOK AT THE...
an overall summary of *SRI* performance	**Proficiency Summary Report** (page 150) for a pie chart that provides an easy-to-visualize summary of performance standard percentages on district- or school-wide levels.
a detailed summary of student performance standard data	**District/School Proficiency Report** (page 148) which shows, for a district and its schools, or a school and its grades, total number of students, number of students per performance standard, and percentages of students per performance standard, based on the latest *SRI* results.
a detailed summary of student performance standard data showing progress over time	**Proficiency Growth Report** (page 152), which shows performance standard data for districts, school, and grades from the first and last tests in a specified time period.
to see Lexile growth results for your district and schools	**Growth Summary Report** (page 154), which provides average test results in Lexiles for two tests in a specified time period, including the average growth in Lexile over the two testing sessions.
current *SRI* performance standard percentages for Adequate Yearly Progress groups	**Demographic Proficiency Report** (page 156), which lists eight AYP groups, the total numbers of students in each, and a bar graph showing performance standard breakdown.
to review performance standard results over time for Adequate Yearly Progress groups	**Demographic Growth Report** (page 158), which shows performance standard percentages over two testing sessions in a specified time period for the eight AYP groups.
to access data on how each school in a district, and the district overall, is utilizing *SRI*	**Test Activity Report** (page 160), which provides data on the number of teachers in a grade or school using *SRI*, the number of students enrolled, how many tests students have taken, and how many students have not been tested.
to access data on how individual teachers are utilizing *SRI*	**Teacher Roster** (page 161), which lists individual teachers in a school or grade, with the number of students each teacher has enrolled in *SRI*, how many tests students have taken, and how many students have not been tested.

Adjusting Performance Standard Proficiency Bands

A powerful feature of *SRI* that school or district administrators have at their disposal is the ability to customize the number, name, and Lexile range of the performance standards that are used for reporting *SRI* scores. The ability to adjust the performance standard proficiency bands allows you to customize the reporting of *SRI* scores to your own state or district's expectations. Administrators can adjust Lexile ranges for each performance standard at each grade, and also change the actual number of performance standards. (See pp. 19–20 in the Getting Started section of this guide for detailed instructions on how to adjust and rename the proficiency bands.)

As you make your judgment as to whether to change the performance standard proficiency bands for your district, or individual schools within your district, you may wish to keep in mind the default *SRI* performance standards, which are summarized below:

Advanced: Students scoring in this range exhibit superior performance when reading grade-level appropriate text and can be considered as reading "above Grade Level."

Proficient: Students scoring in this range exhibit competent performance when reading grade-level appropriate text and can be considered as reading "On Grade Level."

Basic: Students scoring in this range exhibit minimally competent performance when reading grade-level appropriate text and can be considered as reading "below Grade Level."

Below Basic: Students scoring in this range do not exhibit minimally competent performance when reading grade-level appropriate text and can be considered as reading significantly "below Grade Level."

For information on the development and standard-setting procedures used in *SRI*, see the *SRI Technical Guide.*

NOTE

If you choose to change the performance standard proficiency bands, the changes will be reflected in those *SRI* reports that include performance standard data and information.

Administering *SRI*

Create a Comfortable Testing Environment

- Emphasize that the purpose of *SRI* is to find out how well students are reading.
- Explain the test format to students and go over several sample items aloud with the class.
- Make sure students have the basic computer skills necessary to complete the test.
- Inform both students and parents ahead of time when the test will be administered.
- Explain that *SRI* is not a race and not meant to be competitive, so students should take their time to complete the test.

Administer the Test in Different Environments

- *SRI* can be administered wherever computer systems are available: in the classroom, in a computer lab, or in a library media center. Typically, students take between 20 and 30 minutes to complete the test.
- For single-computer environments, test students throughout the week. Assign time slots for students to take the test each day. Be sure to give students enough time, particularly younger students or students with special needs. When students are taking tests, organize quiet activities for the rest of the class so that test-takers are not disturbed.
- When there is a computer for every student, administer the test to all students at one time. Do not put a time limit on the test. Students will finish at different times. Allow students who finish before others to read silently upon completing the test, so that other students are not disturbed.

Moderate Test Taking

- Make sure that you or another adult is available to answer questions during testing, or to help if there are technical problems with the computer.
- Assist younger students as they get started, if necessary, by helping them log on and enter their passwords.
- Make sure that students pay attention to the directions as they read aloud before the test begins. Encourage students to read along with the spoken directions. Ask if everyone understands the directions.
- Emphasize that students will take a Practice Test the first time they take the test, if you have decided to use this feature.
- Encourage students to use earphones if they need help concentrating or avoiding distraction.
- On subsequent administrations, review the test procedures to ensure that each test is taken correctly, with the same degree of seriousness.

Administering *SRI*

Teach Test-Taking Strategies

SRI also helps students develop their test-taking skills. By creating a supportive testing environment, you can help students succeed on standardized tests in all subject areas.

Prior to administering the test, reinforce appropriate test-taking strategies. Review basic strategies of careful reading, answer selection, and pausing between selections. Practice reading passages of text as a class, and modeling the way in which you would arrive at an answer. You may wish to share the following specific strategies with your students:

- **Look for Important Ideas** When you read a comprehension passage, look for ideas you think might be important. Take mental notes as you read.
- **Complete the Sentence** When you think you've got the right answer, read the sentence, inserting the answer you choose. Does the meaning match the passage?
- **Eliminate Incorrect Answers** If an answer choice seems clearly incorrect, you can eliminate it. If you can eliminate two answers, you'll only have two left to choose from. Of course, only one of them is the right answer, so consider them both carefully and then make your choice.
- **Use Context Clues to Figure Out Unfamiliar Words** You might come across vocabulary words you don't know. Slow down and take some time to see if you can figure out what the words mean. Look at the context clues before and after the word, as well as surrounding sentences. Ask yourself questions about what the passage is saying to determine the meaning of the word or eliminate wrong answer choices. Sound out the words if you need to.
- **Apply Reading Strategies** As you read each passage, use reading strategies—such as identifying the main idea, making an inference, drawing a conclusion, reading for details, or summarizing what you've read—to help find your answer.

Understanding *SRI* Test Results

SRI test results are based on the Lexile Framework for Reading, a scientifically accurate system for matching readers to text. Targeting readers to text enables students to practice reading strategies on materials they can understand. Targeted reading practice is essential for reading growth. *SRI* test results are actionable because teachers can guide instruction as well as book selection based on each student's test score (Lexile score)—leading to reading success.

The Lexile Framework

The Lexile Framework is a system that matches readers to text. The framework determines the reading level (Lexile text measure) of any written material, as well as a student's reading comprehension level (Lexile reader measure). When the Lexile measures of the text and reader are matched (the Lexile reader measure and the text measure are the same number), the reader experiences confidence and control. Targeting reading enables students to comprehend what they read, build their vocabulary by reading words in context, respond to text, and improve their independent reading skills. When students find success in reading, they develop a love for books.

The Lexile Framework levels both fiction and nonfiction texts from high-quality literature to newspapers and magazines, for beginning readers (under 100 Lexiles) up to graduate-school readers (1700 Lexiles). More than 30,000 books (including Spanish titles) from Scholastic and other publishers have been leveled according to the Lexile Framework. Grade-level ranges and performance standards correlate to Lexile text measures, providing a common frame of reference with which teachers can view students' performance. See the Glossary (pp. 214, 217) for the definition of grade-level range and performance standard.

Lexile Measures

A Lexile text measure is the specific number assigned to any text, as computed by the Lexile Analyzer. The Analyzer evaluates the text to measure characteristics related to reading comprehension, such as syntactic complexity and word frequency. It then reports a Lexile measure for text.

When determining the Lexile measure of a text that is designed for emergent, early, and transitional readers (generally below 200 Lexiles), picture support is considered. Research on the impact of other access features on text for young readers is ongoing.

Once measured, a book takes an invariant position on the Lexile Leveled Reading Framework (Map) in relation to every other book. (See the Lexile Leveled Reading Framework (Map), p. 140). In this sense, a Lexile measure is absolute because it is independent of other books that might be measured, or reader performances that might be observed.

A Lexile reader measure is converted from the results of the Scholastic Reading Inventory, or standardized tests that are linked to the Lexile Framework. When a reader and text are matched (have the same Lexile measure), the reader is "targeted." A targeted reader can read a book at an engaging and appropriate level of challenge. When the text is too difficult for a reader, the reader can become frustrated. If the text is too easy, the reader is often bored. When the text is just right for the reader, the reader can understand what he or she is reading, and still be challenged enough to actively apply and build reading skills.

Comprehension is a function of the match between reader and text. Lexile measures enable teachers to motivate students to read by matching them with material that they can understand.

Of course, targeting the reader with the Lexile Framework or any other system is only a starting point. Individual reader's level of motivation, their subject-matter interests, and the age appropriateness of individual books must also be taken into account.

Criterion- and Norm-Referenced Results

SRI provides both criterion-referenced and norm-referenced test results. Criterion-referenced test results indicate a student's knowledge or skills as determined by a fixed measure. Norm-referenced results indicate how a student is performing by comparing that student to other students' performance (a changing measure).

The Lexile measure is criterion-referenced because it tells you at what level the student is reading. One metric, the Lexile measure, is used from first grade through graduate school to assess the student's reading ability, making it easy to chart the student's growth over the years. To draw an analogy, consider a ruler that uses inches and feet to measure how tall a child is and how much the child has grown from age eight to age eleven. The Lexile measure works in much the same way, giving an accurate picture of reading growth.

SRI gives teachers an invariant and fixed measure—the Lexile measure of a book—against which they can interpret a student's test results and reading growth. A book's Lexile measure is invariant because the text does not change, therefore the level of reading ability needed to read that book will not change. For example, Judy Blume's *Tales of a Fourth Grade Nothing* will always require the same level of reading ability to understand the book.

Not only are the books fixed measures against which to interpret a student's ability, but they are also familiar benchmarks. For example, if a fourth grade student's Lexile measure matches that of *Charlotte's Web*, then the teacher knows from experience with this classic book that the student is reading on the appropriate level. Because the Lexile measure is applied to well-known books, teachers can interpret students' test results in a concrete way—by looking at the books the student can read.

To provide another familiar context in which to interpret Lexile measures, *SRI* provides norm-referenced results, including grade-level ranges and performance standards. A student's Lexile measure corresponds to the grade-level range at which the student is demonstrating proficiency in reading. *SRI* reports tell you whether the student is reading on, above, or below grade level. The reports also indicate the student's performance standard (Below Basic, Basic, Proficient, Advanced)—the level of proficiency at which the student is reading at that grade.

Norm-referenced metrics that are represented in *SRI* reports include national percentile rank, stanines, and normal curve equivalents. Other nationally normed tests, e.g. Stanford 9 (SAT9), the Stanford Diagnostic Reading Test (SDRT), and the North Carolina End-of-Grade Test have been linked to the Lexile Framework as well. For certain accountability purposes, norm-referenced measures (e.g., stanines or national percentiles) are required.

Grade Level	Performance Standard
Above	Advanced
On	Proficient
Below	Basic Below Basic

The correlation between Grade Level and Performance Standard

The Lexile Leveled Reading Framework (Map)

The Lexile Leveled Reading Framework (Map) provides a context for understanding reading comprehension levels (Lexile measures). Lexile measures (from 200 to 1700 Lexiles) are displayed on the map, as well as benchmark literature, sample text passages, and grade-level ranges. In this way, the map provides a comprehensive picture of the reading spectrum. You can use the map to assess where students are on that spectrum. The student's Lexile measure will show where he or she is situated on the map, and his or her reading choices can be analyzed according to the grade-level range at which the selections fall on the map. The map is also a useful tool for charting a reader's growth in reading comprehension over time. See a reproduction of the Framework (Map) on the next page. Both teachers and students can plot independent reading progress using a modified version of the map (see Reproducible 18).

SRI and the Lexile Framework®

The Best Choice to Measure Reading Progress

GRADE LEVEL	LEXILE LEVEL	BENCHMARK LITERATURE	SAMPLE TEXT PASSAGES
	1700L–1200L	**First Inaugural Address** *by George Washington* 1700 **The Good Earth** *by Pearl S. Buck* 1530 **The Life and Times of Frederick Douglass** *by Frederick Douglass* 1400 **Silent Spring** *by Rachel Carson* 1340 **Great Expectations** *by Charles Dickens* 1200	**The Life and Times of Frederick Douglass** It was not long, however, before I began to learn the sad fact that this house of my childhood belonged not to my dear old grandmother, but to someone I had never seen, and who lived a great distance off. I learned, too, the sadder fact, that not only the home and lot, but that grandmother herself and all the little children around her, belonged to a mysterious personage, called by grandmother, with every mark of reverence, 'old master'. Thus early, did clouds and shadows begin to fall upon my path.
	1100L	**The War of the Worlds** *by H. G. Wells* 1170 **Animal Farm** *by George Orwell* 1170 **Ethan Frome** *by Edith Wharton* 1160 **Pride and Prejudice** *by Jane Austen* 1100	**Ethan Frome** Ethan's love of nature did not take the form of a taste for agriculture. He had always wanted to be an engineer, and to live in towns, where there were lectures and big libraries and "fellows doing things." A slight engineering job in Florida, put in his way during his period of study at Worcester, increased his faith in his ability as well as his eagerness to see the world; and he felt sure that, with a "smart" wife like Zeena, it would not be long before he had made himself a place in it.
12, 11, 10, 9	1000L	**Anne Frank: The Diary of a Young Girl** *by Anne Frank* 1080 **One More River to Cross: The Stories of Twelve Black Americans** *by Jim Haskins* 1070 **20,000 Leagues Under the Sea** *by Jules Verne* 1030 **Freak the Mighty** *by Rodman Philbrick* 1000	**20,000 Leagues Under the Sea** What a spectacle! How can I depict it? How describe the aspect of the woods and rocks in this liquid element, their lower parts sombre and wild, the upper colored with red tints in the light which the reverberating power of the water doubled? We were climbing rocks which fell in enormous fragments directly afterwards with the noise of an avalanche. Right and left were deep dark galleries where sight was lost. Here opened vast clearings that seemed made by the hand of man, and I asked myself sometimes if some inhabitant of these submarine regions was not about to appear suddenly.
8	900L	**Exploring the *Titanic*** *by Robert Ballard* 980 **The Abracadabra Kid: A Writer's Life** *by Sid Fleischman* 940 **Dogsong** *by Gary Paulsen* 930 **Roll of Thunder, Hear My Cry** *by Mildred Taylor* 920	**The Abracadabra Kid: A Writer's Life** The Panama Canal disgorged us out into the Pacific Ocean, where I felt right at home. We paused to take on fuel in the bleak Galápagos Islands. I was dimly aware that somewhere in these South American waters Alexander Selkirk had been marooned, inspiring the tale of Robinson Crusoe. I wondered if someday I might use these remote, moody islands as story background, and made a few mental notes. Rocky. Scraggly yellow weeds. Sharks in the bay.
7, 6	800L	**Anthony Burns: The Defeat and Triumph of a Fugitive Slave** *by Virginia Hamilton* 860 **Julie of the Wolves** *by Jean Craighead George* 860 **Johnny Tremain** *by Esther Forbes* 840 **The Dark Is Rising** *by Susan Cooper* 820	**Julie of the Wolves** Propped on her elbows with her chin in her fists, she stared at the black wolf, trying to catch his eye. She had chosen him because he was much larger than the others, and because he walked like her father, Kapugen, with his head high and his chest out. The black wolf also possessed wisdom, she had observed. The pack looked to him when the wind carried strange scents or the birds cried nervously. If he was alarmed, they were alarmed.
5	700L	**Red Scarf Girl: A Memoir of the Cultural Revolution** *by Ji-Li Jiang* 780 **Harriet the Spy** *by Louise Fitzhugh* 760 **Pacific Crossing** *by Gary Soto* 750 **From the Mixed Up Files of Mrs. Basil E. Frankweiler** *by E. L. Konigsburg* 700	**Pacific Crossing** Mr. Ono was in the garden, playing a round of backyard golf. The golf club was rusty, and his single golf ball was chipped and yellow as an old tooth. "I'm on vacation. I can't worry about money," he said, concentrating on his putt and the dent in the earth twenty feet away. He swung the club, and the ball raced like a mouse under a cabbage leaf. He looked at the boys and said, "I need practice. Give me a couple of hours, and you'll see."
4	600L	**Charlotte's Web** *by E. B. White* 680 **Sadako and the Thousand Paper Cranes** *by Eleanor Coerr* 630 **Flossie and the Fox** *by Patricia McKissack* 610 **. . . If You Sailed on the Mayflower in 1620** *by Ann McGovern* 600	**. . . If You Sailed on the Mayflower in 1620** Plants called herbs were the medicine of the Pilgrims. When spring came, the women planted herbs in their gardens. Suppose you cut yourself. Your mother would make a medicine from the wild daisy. She would mix it with animal fat and smear it on your cut. Suppose you had a headache. Your mother would mix ground-up sage with fat and cornmeal. You would have to eat it, even if you hated the taste. Rose leaves and the fruit of the rose, called rose hips, were said to be good for almost anything.
3	500L	**Buffalo Woman** *by Paul Goble* 590 **The True Story of the Three Little Pigs by A. Wolf** *by Jon Scieszka* 570 **Encyclopedia Brown, Boy Detective** *by Donald J. Sobol* 560 **The Magic School Bus Inside the Earth** *by Joanna Cole* 500	**Encyclopedia Brown, Boy Detective** In the morning he made up his mind. He would go into the detective business and help people. He wouldn't wait until he grew up. It was summer and school was out. He could begin at once. Encyclopedia got out of bed and searched through his closet. He dug out a toy printing press, a Christmas gift from his Uncle Ben two years ago. As soon as Encyclopedia finished breakfast, he printed fifty handbills. When the ink was dry, he put the handbills in all the mailboxes in the neighborhood.
	400L	**Dinosaur Bones** *by Aliki* 460 **How My Parents Learned to Eat** *by Ina R. Friedman* 450 **Henry and Mudge and the Forever Sea** *by Cynthia Rylant* 420 **Frog and Toad Are Friends** *by Arnold Lobel* 400	**How My Parents Learned to Eat** One day, the captain of my father's ship said, "John, in three weeks the ship is leaving Japan." My father was sad. He wanted to marry my mother. How can I ask her to marry me? he thought. I don't even know if we like the same food. And if we don't, we'll go hungry. It's hard to be happy if you're hungry. I'll have to find out what food she likes. And I'll have to learn to eat with chopsticks. So he went to a Japanese restaurant.
2	300L	**Babushka's Doll** *by Patricia Polacco* 360 **The Best Way to Play** *by Bill Cosby* 360 **Noisy Nora** *by Rosemary Wells* 320 **Pet Show!** *by Ezra Jack Keats* 300	**The Best Way to Play** "My dad said there are too many toys these days," said Kiku. "So, what's wrong with toys?" I said. We sat around and felt sad together. Just then, Andrew came running toward us. "I got the game," he said. "Let's go to my house and play it!" "Let's go!" we shouted.
1	200L	**Mr. Rabbit and the Lovely Present** *by Charlotte Zolotow* 280 **Play Ball, Amelia Bedelia** *by Peggy Parish* 220 **Clifford, the Big Red Dog** *by Norman Bridwell* 220 **Danny and the Dinosaur** *by Syd Hoff* 200	**Play Ball, Amelia Bedelia** "I know there is a uniform here," said Amelia Bedelia. And there was one. She took a nip here and a tuck there. Soon that uniform was just right.

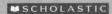

SCHOLASTIC

SRI SCHOLASTIC READING INVENTORY™ SCHOLASTIC READING COUNTS! LEXILE™

Monitoring Students' Lexile Measures

Monitoring students' Lexile measures is not only important, but it is easy to do. Administer *SRI* at least two to three times a year to accurately monitor students' Lexile measures, and check the *SRI* reports available through the Scholastic Achievement Manager to monitor progress, assess student growth, and set goals for reading achievement.

- Check reports such as the Student Progress Report or the Growth Report to gauge student achievement from test to test.
- Check the Intervention Grouping Report to monitor students who have scored below grade level (Basic or Below Basic Performance Standards).
- Readminister the test if a student's Lexile measure decreases over time or markedly increases, to make sure the results are consistent.
- Make sure that students read books that are on their Recommended Reading Reports, or other books that are within their independent reading range (fluent: 100–250 Lexiles below their level; challenging: 100 below to 50 Lexiles above their level) to maintain and ultimately increase their reading comprehension.
- Give every student a "reading physical," which not only utilizes *SRI* test results but other assessments as well, to gain a more comprehensive picture of students' reading ability. Multiple measures of assessment, such as reading records, fluency checks, projects and portfolios, self appraisals, and teacher observations are recommended. Consider the student's interests and experiences when evaluating the student's understanding of text and deciding which assessment to use.

SRI Reports: An Overview

One of the most powerful features of *SRI* is its ability to generate data that can be immediately used in the classroom to monitor and assess student progress. The Scholastic Achievement Manager organizes and analyzes the results gathered from student tests, and presents this information in a series of clear, understandable reports that will help you track reading growth over time, evaluate progress towards proficiency goals, and accomplish administrative tasks. *SRI* reports will help you effectively assess where your students are now and where they need to go.

SRI reports are organized according to purpose. There are five categories in all: Progress Monitoring, Instructional Planning, Alerts & Acknowledgments, School-to-Home, and Management. (See the chart on the next page.) Although each report is listed under only one category, reports can be used for many purposes.

With *SRI* reports, you can:

- detect trends in reading growth.
- review student Lexile measures, performance standards, and normative information.
- match student interests and reading skills to appropriate books.
- identify situations that might require intervention.
- facilitate administrative tasks.

SRI Reports Purposes Chart

SRI reports serve specific purposes to meet the needs of teachers, students, families, and administrators. The chart below explains these purposes and how the reports meet the distinct interests of each audience.

	PURPOSE	AUDIENCE	EXAMPLES
	Progress Monitoring	**Teachers** and **administrators** can use these reports for ongoing progress monitoring. **Teachers** may share these reports with **students**, **families**, and **administrators**.	• Growth Report, p. 164
	Instructional Planning	**Teachers** can use these reports to plan further instruction and intervention.	• Intervention Grouping Report, p. 174
	Alerts & Acknowledgments	**Teachers** will receive these reports automatically when logging on to the Scholastic Achievement Manager.	• Incomplete Test Alert, p. 181
	School-to-Home	**Families** will appreciate these reports, which may be sent home or shared during conferences.	• Parent Report I, p. 182
	Management	**Administrators** and teachers can use these reports to track participation and usage.	• Test Activity Report, p. 160

SRI Reports: If You Want to Know

IF YOU WANT TO KNOW...	LOOK AT THE...
. . . your students' current reading scores	Reading Performance Report (page 162), which provides a table showing students' scores and standings.
. . . how a student's reading and comprehension is changing from test to test	Student Progress Report (page 168), which provides an individual summary of *SRI* testing activity and scores for each student. Student Yearly Progress Report (page 170), which compares your student's Lexile scores to Lexile grade ranges for reading proficiency.
. . . which students did not complete *SRI* tests and should be retested	Incomplete Test Alert (page 181), which lists students who have attempted, but not completed, *SRI* tests.
. . . which students require additional intervention support and get ideas for grouping them	Intervention Grouping Report (page 174), which can help you identify groups of students who might need additional assistance.
how to fine-tune your reading instruction for an individual student	Student Action Report (page 176), which contains suggested targeted reading information and specific instructional recommendations.
. . . how to match your students to books	Targeted Reading Report (page 172), which indicates easy, on level, and challenging Lexile text ranges for individual students. Recommended Reading Report (page 178), which suggests books that pertain to students' expressed interests and match students Lexile scores.

SRI Reports in Detail

Reproductions of each *SRI* report, along with detailed annotations that explain the report information and how to use it, can be found on the following pages.

NOTE

Reports marked with an asterisk are for district and school administrators. See also p. 129–131 for further tips on how administrators can best help implement *SRI.*

SRI Reports: At a Glance

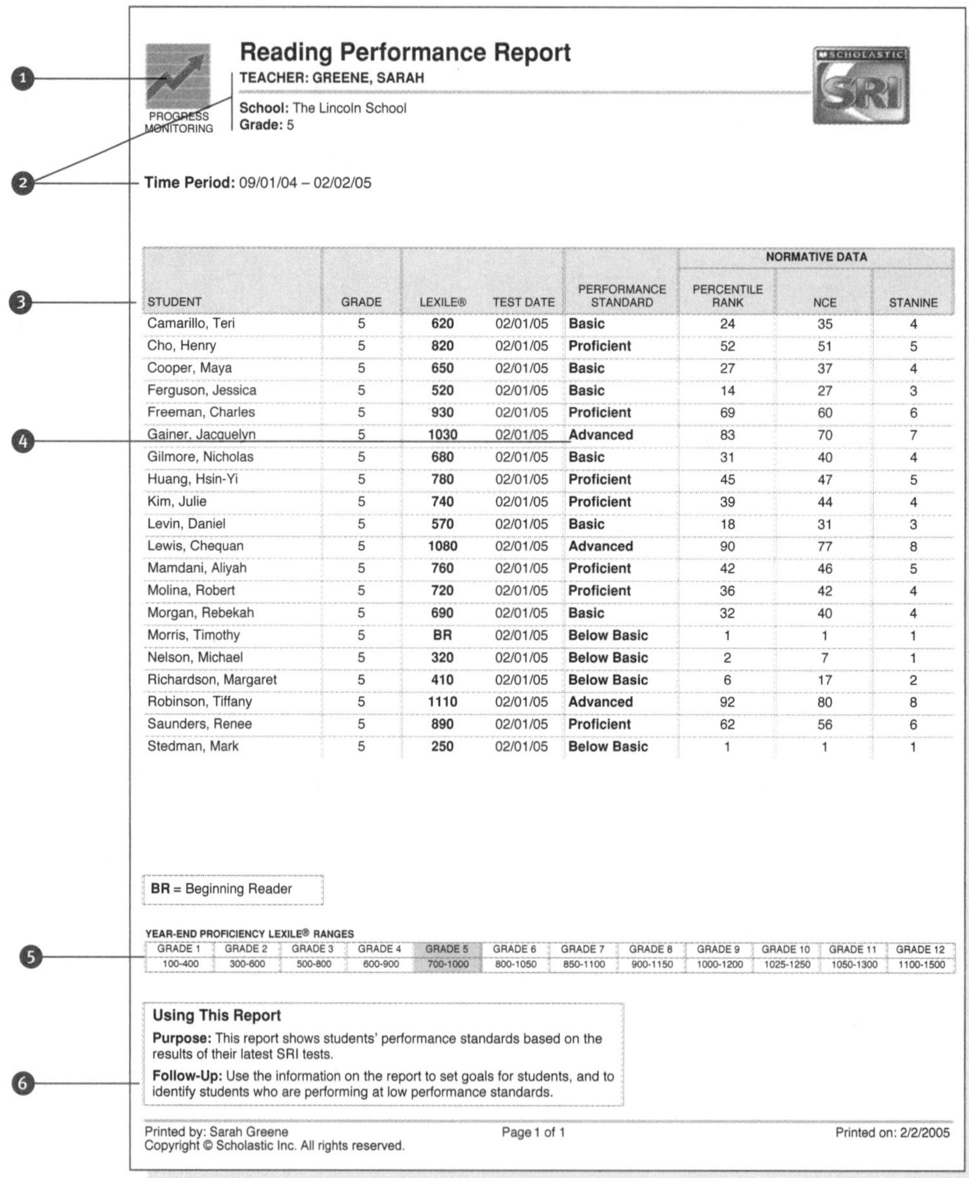

Reading Performance Report

PROGRESS MONITORING

TEACHER: GREENE, SARAH

SCHOLASTIC SRI

School: The Lincoln School
Grade: 5

Time Period: 09/01/04 – 02/02/05

					NORMATIVE DATA		
STUDENT	GRADE	LEXILE®	TEST DATE	PERFORMANCE STANDARD	PERCENTILE RANK	NCE	STANINE
Camarillo, Teri	5	**620**	02/01/05	**Basic**	24	35	4
Cho, Henry	5	**820**	02/01/05	**Proficient**	52	51	5
Cooper, Maya	5	**650**	02/01/05	**Basic**	27	37	4
Ferguson, Jessica	5	**520**	02/01/05	**Basic**	14	27	3
Freeman, Charles	5	**930**	02/01/05	**Proficient**	69	60	6
Gainer, Jacquelyn	5	**1030**	02/01/05	**Advanced**	83	70	7
Gilmore, Nicholas	5	**680**	02/01/05	**Basic**	31	40	4
Huang, Hsin-Yi	5	**780**	02/01/05	**Proficient**	45	47	5
Kim, Julie	5	**740**	02/01/05	**Proficient**	39	44	4
Levin, Daniel	5	**570**	02/01/05	**Basic**	18	31	3
Lewis, Chequan	5	**1080**	02/01/05	**Advanced**	90	77	8
Mamdani, Aliyah	5	**760**	02/01/05	**Proficient**	42	46	5
Molina, Robert	5	**720**	02/01/05	**Proficient**	36	42	4
Morgan, Rebekah	5	**690**	02/01/05	**Basic**	32	40	4
Morris, Timothy	5	**BR**	02/01/05	**Below Basic**	1	1	1
Nelson, Michael	5	**320**	02/01/05	**Below Basic**	2	7	1
Richardson, Margaret	5	**410**	02/01/05	**Below Basic**	6	17	2
Robinson, Tiffany	5	**1110**	02/01/05	**Advanced**	92	80	8
Saunders, Renee	5	**890**	02/01/05	**Proficient**	62	56	6
Stedman, Mark	5	**250**	02/01/05	**Below Basic**	1	1	1

BR = Beginning Reader

YEAR-END PROFICIENCY LEXILE® RANGES

GRADE 1	GRADE 2	GRADE 3	GRADE 4	GRADE 5	GRADE 6	GRADE 7	GRADE 8	GRADE 9	GRADE 10	GRADE 11	GRADE 12
100-400	300-600	500-800	600-900	700-1000	800-1050	850-1100	900-1150	1000-1200	1025-1250	1050-1300	1100-1500

Using This Report

Purpose: This report shows students' performance standards based on the results of their latest SRI tests.

Follow-Up: Use the information on the report to set goals for students, and to identify students who are performing at low performance standards.

Printed by: Sarah Greene
Page 1 of 1
Printed on: 2/2/2005

1. **Report Type:** This icon represents the report type, or category. There are five types in all: Progress Monitoring, Instructional Planning, Alerts & Acknowledgements, School-to-Home, and Management.

2. **Customized Information:** This area shows you the students (or teachers) you have selected. This area usually includes such information as school name, teacher name, and time period it covers.

3. **Common Reports Data:** While *SRI* reports come in a variety of formats (tables, graphs, text), most will include such basic information as student names, their grade, their most recent test date, and their current Lexile measure.

4. **Purposeful Data:** In addition to providing you with basic information about Lexile measures and test dates, each *SRI* report is designed to fulfill a specific purpose. For example, the Reading Performance Report helps you monitor class progress in their current performance standards and related normative data.

5. **Report Key:** Much like a map, each report also includes a key that will guide your understanding of the data. For example, the Reading Performance Report includes a listing of *SRI* Year-End Proficiency Lexile Ranges to help you determine if your students are reading at or are on target for reading at grade level.

6. **Report Purposes:** Look at the Using this Report box in each report to find suggestions for interpreting the data and to learn how to apply the data to your classroom instruction.

District/School Proficiency Report

Administrator Reports

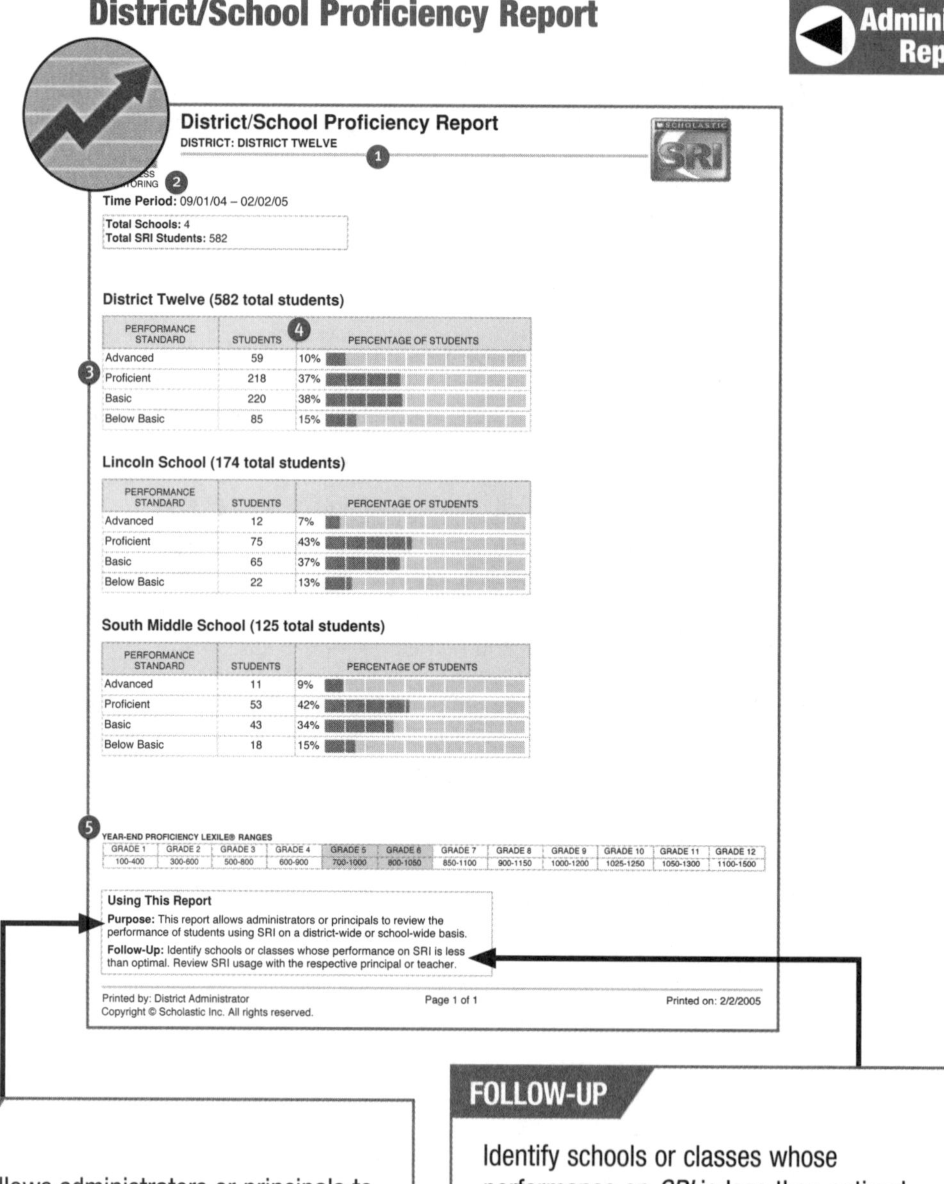

District/School Proficiency Report

DISTRICT: DISTRICT TWELVE 1

...SS ...ORING 2

Time Period: 09/01/04 – 02/02/05

Total Schools: 4
Total SRI Students: 582

District Twelve (582 total students)

PERFORMANCE STANDARD	STUDENTS	PERCENTAGE OF STUDENTS
Advanced	59	10%
Proficient	218	37%
Basic	220	38%
Below Basic	85	15%

Lincoln School (174 total students)

PERFORMANCE STANDARD	STUDENTS	PERCENTAGE OF STUDENTS
Advanced	12	7%
Proficient	75	43%
Basic	65	37%
Below Basic	22	13%

South Middle School (125 total students)

PERFORMANCE STANDARD	STUDENTS	PERCENTAGE OF STUDENTS
Advanced	11	9%
Proficient	53	42%
Basic	43	34%
Below Basic	18	15%

5 YEAR-END PROFICIENCY LEXILE® RANGES

GRADE 1	GRADE 2	GRADE 3	GRADE 4	GRADE 5	GRADE 6	GRADE 7	GRADE 8	GRADE 9	GRADE 10	GRADE 11	GRADE 12
100-400	300-600	500-800	600-900	700-1000	800-1050	850-1100	900-1150	1000-1200	1025-1250	1050-1300	1100-1500

Using This Report

Purpose: This report allows administrators or principals to review the performance of students using SRI on a district-wide or school-wide basis.

Follow-Up: Identify schools or classes whose performance on SRI is less than optimal. Review SRI usage with the respective principal or teacher.

Printed by: District Administrator Page 1 of 1 Printed on: 2/2/2005

PURPOSE

This report allows administrators or principals to review the performance of students using *SRI* on a district-wide or school-wide basis.

FOLLOW-UP

Identify schools or classes whose performance on *SRI* is less than optimal. Review *SRI* usage with the respective principal or teacher.

Using the Data

Who: This report is for district and school administrators.

What: This report provides performance standard data on a district- and school-wide basis. The district version of the report shows cumulative data for the entire district, which is then broken down by schools in the district. The school version of the report shows cumulative data for an individual school, which is then broken down by grade. For each entry on the report(s), the number of students per performance standard is given, along with percentages and a bar graph to help visualize the data.

When: This report is best generated monthly, or according to the management needs of the individual district or school administrator.

Related Reports

Run the following reports for more information on student proficiency levels:

- Proficiency Growth Report
- Proficiency Summary Report
- Growth Summary Report
- Demographic Proficiency Report
- Demographic Growth Report
- Proficiency Report

Understanding the Data

1. **District, etc.:** The district is listed at the top of the report, followed by the total number of students enrolled in *SRI*. When generated for an individual school, the school name appears with the total number of *SRI* students.
2. **Time Period:** The time period covered by the report.
3. **Performance Standard:** Each table is broken down by *SRI* performance standard: Advanced, Proficient, Basic, Below Basic.
4. **Students/Percentage of Students:** The total number of students per performance standard is given, followed by the corresponding percentage and a bar graph scaled to 100 percent.
5. **Year-End Proficiency Lexile Ranges:** Ranges within which students are considered to be reading proficiently at their grade level. Relevant grade or grades are shaded. This table is most useful for the school version of this report.

Time Period Settings

This report is based on student achievement up to the end of the selected time period. Make sure to adjust the time period to cover students' most recent *SRI* testing sessions.

Proficiency Summary Report

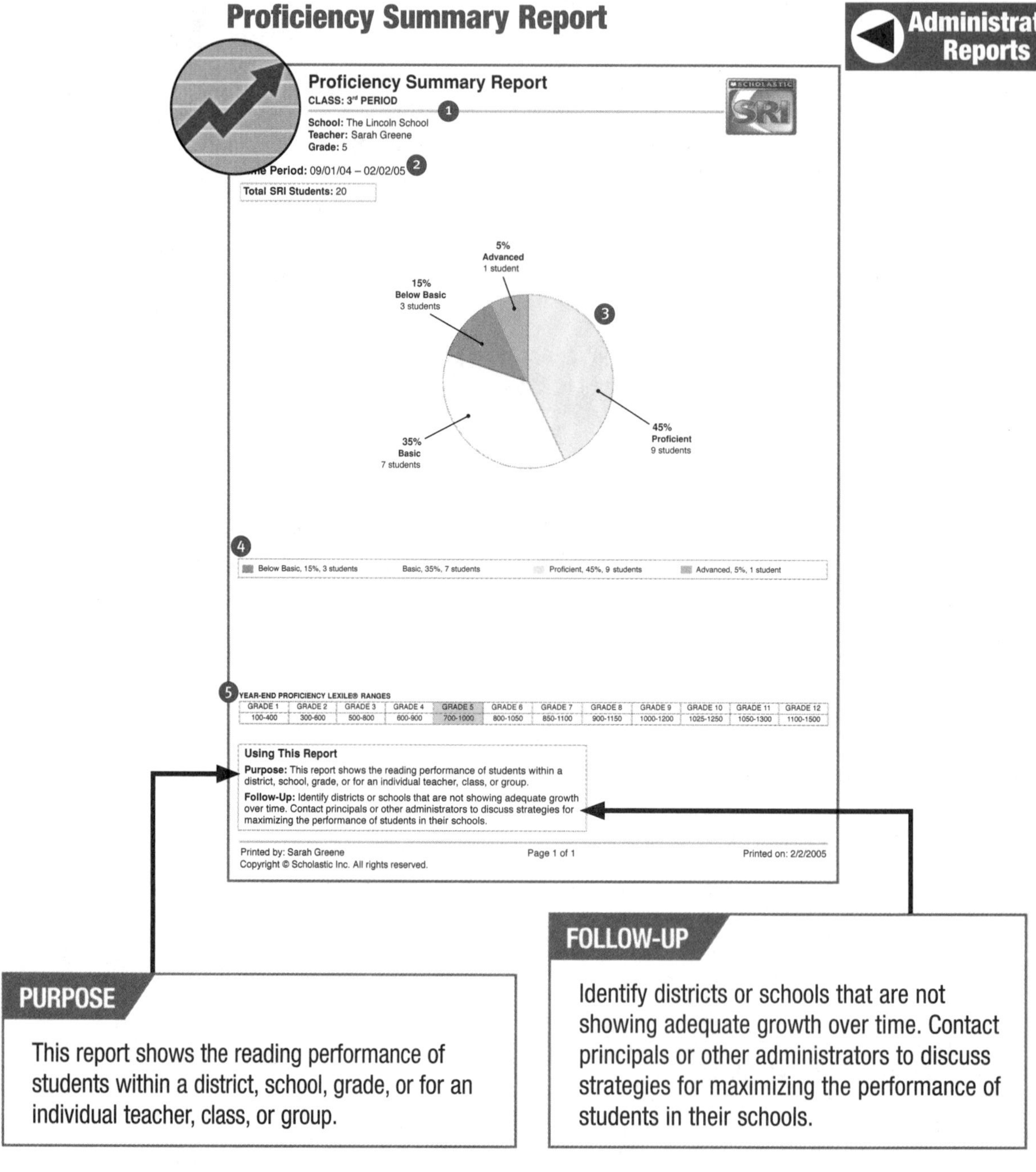

Proficiency Summary Report
CLASS: 3rd PERIOD

School: The Lincoln School
Teacher: Sarah Greene
Grade: 5

Time Period: 09/01/04 – 02/02/05

Total SRI Students: 20

Below Basic, 15%, 3 students | Basic, 35%, 7 students | Proficient, 45%, 9 students | Advanced, 5%, 1 student

YEAR-END PROFICIENCY LEXILE® RANGES

GRADE 1	GRADE 2	GRADE 3	GRADE 4	GRADE 5	GRADE 6	GRADE 7	GRADE 8	GRADE 9	GRADE 10	GRADE 11	GRADE 12
100-400	300-600	500-800	600-900	700-1000	800-1050	850-1100	900-1150	1000-1200	1025-1250	1050-1300	1100-1500

Using This Report

Purpose: This report shows the reading performance of students within a district, school, grade, or for an individual teacher, class, or group.

Follow-Up: Identify districts or schools that are not showing adequate growth over time. Contact principals or other administrators to discuss strategies for maximizing the performance of students in their schools.

Printed by: Sarah Greene

Page 1 of 1
Printed on: 2/2/2005

PURPOSE

This report shows the reading performance of students within a district, school, grade, or for an individual teacher, class, or group.

FOLLOW-UP

Identify districts or schools that are not showing adequate growth over time. Contact principals or other administrators to discuss strategies for maximizing the performance of students in their schools.

Using the Data

Who: This report is for district and school administrators.

What: District and school administrators can use this report to gain a high-level overview of *SRI* proficiency within a district, school, grade, or for an individual teacher, class, or group. The circle-graph format provides a quick visual reference of student performance. Percentages of performance standards and total numbers of students per standard are easily accessible.

When: Administrators will wish to view this high-level "snapshot" at least 3–4 times per school year.

Understanding the Data

❶ **District, etc.:** The district is listed at the top of the report, followed by the total number of schools, teachers, and students. When generated for an individual school, or for lower cohorts, the name of the cohort appears with the total number of students.

❷ **Time Period:** The time period covered by the report.

❸ **Performance Standard:** The circle graph is divided among the four *SRI* performance standards: Advanced, Proficient, Basic, Below Basic.

❹ **Key:** A key runs along the bottom reiterating for clarity the breakdowns in the circle graph.

❺ **Year-End Proficiency Ranges:** Ranges within which students are considered to be reading proficiently at their grade level. Relevant grade or grades are shaded. This table is most useful for the school, grade, teacher, etc., versions of this report.

Time Period Settings

This report is based on student achievement up to the end of the selected time period. Make sure to adjust the time period to cover two student *SRI* testing sessions, including the most recent session.

Related Reports

For other perspectives on student growth, run the following reports:

- District/School Proficiency Report
- Proficiency Summary Report
- Proficiency Growth Report
- Demographic Proficiency Report
- Demographic Growth Report
- Growth Report

Proficiency Growth Report

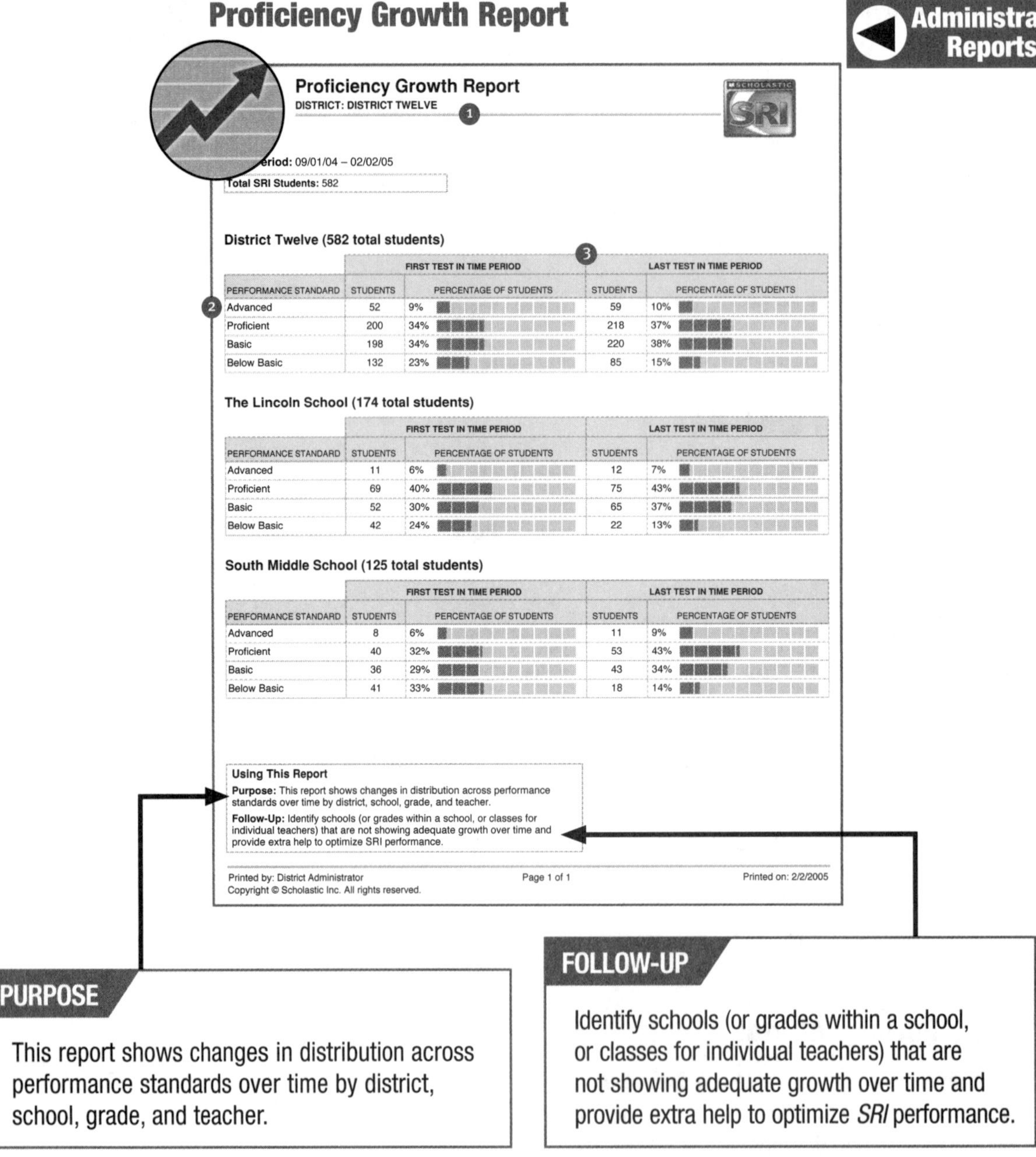

Proficiency Growth Report

DISTRICT: DISTRICT TWELVE

Time Period: 09/01/04 – 02/02/05

Total SRI Students: 582

District Twelve (582 total students)

	FIRST TEST IN TIME PERIOD		LAST TEST IN TIME PERIOD	
PERFORMANCE STANDARD	STUDENTS	PERCENTAGE OF STUDENTS	STUDENTS	PERCENTAGE OF STUDENTS
Advanced	52	9%	59	10%
Proficient	200	34%	218	37%
Basic	198	34%	220	38%
Below Basic	132	23%	85	15%

The Lincoln School (174 total students)

	FIRST TEST IN TIME PERIOD		LAST TEST IN TIME PERIOD	
PERFORMANCE STANDARD	STUDENTS	PERCENTAGE OF STUDENTS	STUDENTS	PERCENTAGE OF STUDENTS
Advanced	11	6%	12	7%
Proficient	69	40%	75	43%
Basic	52	30%	65	37%
Below Basic	42	24%	22	13%

South Middle School (125 total students)

	FIRST TEST IN TIME PERIOD		LAST TEST IN TIME PERIOD	
PERFORMANCE STANDARD	STUDENTS	PERCENTAGE OF STUDENTS	STUDENTS	PERCENTAGE OF STUDENTS
Advanced	8	6%	11	9%
Proficient	40	32%	53	43%
Basic	36	29%	43	34%
Below Basic	41	33%	18	14%

Using This Report

Purpose: This report shows changes in distribution across performance standards over time by district, school, grade, and teacher.

Follow-Up: Identify schools (or grades within a school, or classes for individual teachers) that are not showing adequate growth over time and provide extra help to optimize SRI performance.

Printed by: District Administrator   Page 1 of 1   Printed on: 2/2/2005

PURPOSE

This report shows changes in distribution across performance standards over time by district, school, grade, and teacher.

FOLLOW-UP

Identify schools (or grades within a school, or classes for individual teachers) that are not showing adequate growth over time and provide extra help to optimize *SRI* performance.

Using the Data

Who: This report is for district and school administrators.

What: This report provides performance standard data over time for a district and its schools, for a school and its grades, for a grade within a school and its individual classes, and for an individual teacher and his or her classes and/or groups. The performance standard data is supplied for the first and last *SRI* tests taken in the chosen time period. Numbers of students per performance standard are supplied, as are percentages per standard and a bar graph to help visualize the data.

When: This report is best generated every 6–9 weeks, or after students have taken at least two *SRI* test administrations, or according to the management needs of the individual district or school administrator.

Understanding the Data

1. District, etc.: The district is listed at the top of the report, followed by the total number of students enrolled in *SRI*, and the time period covered by the report. When generated for an individual school or smaller cohorts, the school name appears with the total number of *SRI* students.

2. Performance Standard: Each table is broken down by *SRI* performance standard: Advanced, Proficient, Basic, Below Basic.

3. Students/Percentage of Students: The total number of students per performance standard is given, for both the first and last tests in the time period, followed by the corresponding percentage and a bar graph scaled to 100 percent.

Time Period Settings

This report is based on student achievement up to the end of the selected time period. Make sure to adjust the time period to cover students' most recent *SRI* testing sessions

Related Reports

Run the following reports for more information on student proficiency levels:

- District/School Proficiency Report
- Proficiency Growth Report
- Growth Summary Report
- Demographic Proficiency Report
- Demographic Growth Report
- Proficiency Report

Growth Summary Report

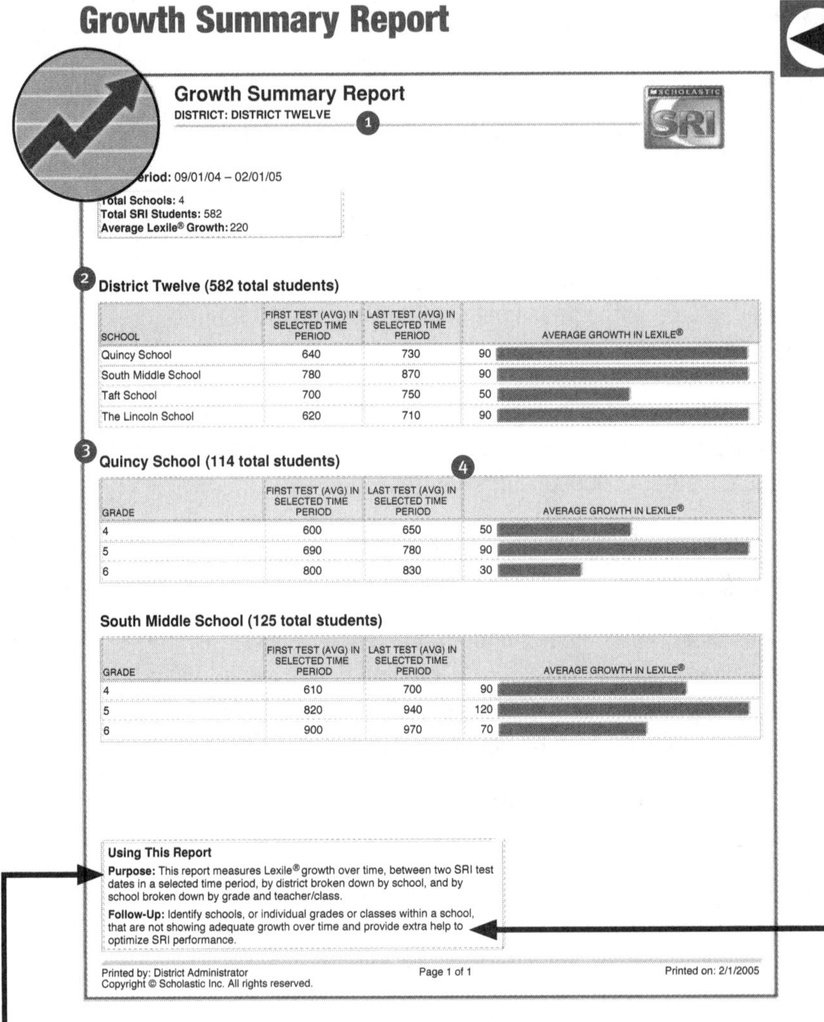

Growth Summary Report

DISTRICT: DISTRICT TWELVE

SCHOLASTIC SRI

riod: 09/01/04 – 02/01/05

Total Schools: 4
Total SRI Students: 582
Average Lexile® Growth: 220

District Twelve (582 total students)

SCHOOL	FIRST TEST (AVG) IN SELECTED TIME PERIOD	LAST TEST (AVG) IN SELECTED TIME PERIOD	AVERAGE GROWTH IN LEXILE®
Quincy School	640	730	90
South Middle School	780	870	90
Taft School	700	750	50
The Lincoln School	620	710	90

Quincy School (114 total students)

GRADE	FIRST TEST (AVG) IN SELECTED TIME PERIOD	LAST TEST (AVG) IN SELECTED TIME PERIOD	AVERAGE GROWTH IN LEXILE®
4	600	650	50
5	690	780	90
6	800	830	30

South Middle School (125 total students)

GRADE	FIRST TEST (AVG) IN SELECTED TIME PERIOD	LAST TEST (AVG) IN SELECTED TIME PERIOD	AVERAGE GROWTH IN LEXILE®
4	610	700	90
5	820	940	120
6	900	970	70

Using This Report

Purpose: This report measures Lexile® growth over time, between two SRI test dates in a selected time period, by district broken down by school, and by school broken down by grade and teacher/class.

Follow-Up: Identify schools, or individual grades or classes within a school, that are not showing adequate growth over time and provide extra help to optimize SRI performance.

Printed by: District Administrator

Page 1 of 1
Printed on: 2/1/2005

PURPOSE

This report measures Lexile growth over time, between two *SRI* test dates in a selected time period, by district broken down by school, and by school broken down by grade and teacher/class.

FOLLOW-UP

Identify schools, or individual grades or classes within a school, that are not showing adequate growth over time and provide extra help to optimize *SRI* performance.

Using the Data

Who: This report is for district and school administrators.

What: This report provides Lexile growth data over time for a district and its schools, for a school and its grades, for a grade within a school and its individual classes, and for an individual teacher and his or her classes and/or groups. The Lexile score (as an average) is supplied for the first and last *SRI* tests taken in the chosen time period. The total number of students per district, grade, etc. are supplied. The last column of each table supplies the average growth in Lexile both as a number and in bar-graph format.

When: This report is best generated every 6–9 weeks, or after students have taken at least two *SRI* test administrations, or according to the management needs of the individual district or school administrator.

Understanding the Data

1. **District, etc.:** The district (or school, grade, etc.) is listed at the top of the report, followed by the time period covered by the report. In the box below appears the total number of schools (or grades, or classes) profiled in the report, followed by the overall average Lexile growth of the main cohort.

2. **Top Table:** The top table breaks down the main subject of the report, in this case a district, into its component schools.

3. **Lower Tables:** The lower tables take the components of the top table, further breaking down the data into smaller cohorts, in this case individual grades per school.

4. **Table Data:** Each table lists the Lexile score of the first and last test in the selected time period, expressed as an average. The third column provides the average growth in Lexile, accompanied by a bar graph.

Time Period Settings

This report is based on student achievement up to the end of the selected time period. Make sure to adjust the time period to cover two student *SRI* testing sessions, including the most recent session.

Related Reports

For other perspectives on student growth, run the following reports:

- District/School Proficiency Report
- Proficiency Summary Report
- Proficiency Growth Report
- Demographic Proficiency Report
- Demographic Growth Report
- Growth Report

Demographic Proficiency Report

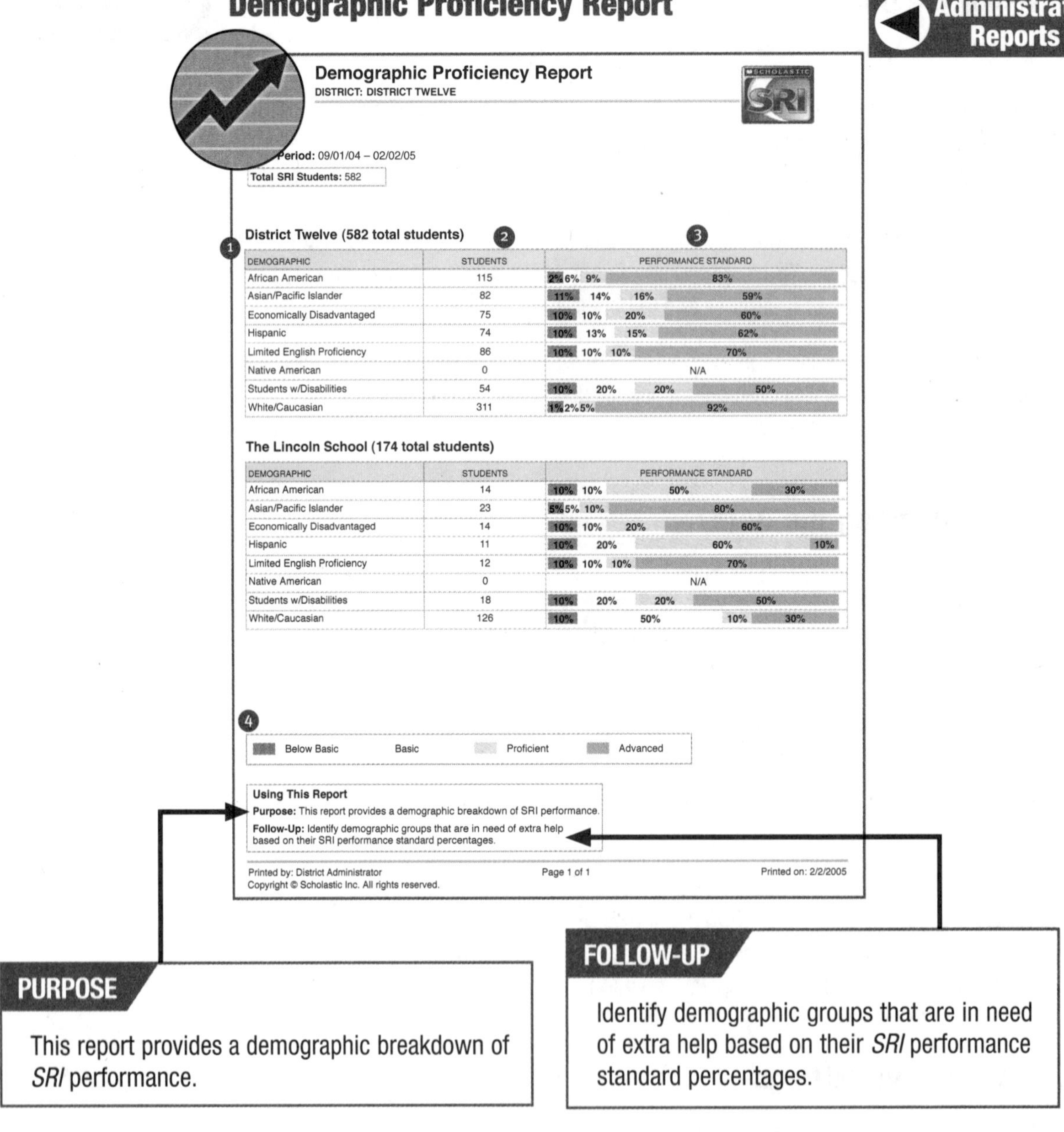

Demographic Proficiency Report

DISTRICT: DISTRICT TWELVE

SCHOLASTIC SRI

Period: 09/01/04 – 02/02/05

Total SRI Students: 582

District Twelve (582 total students)

DEMOGRAPHIC	STUDENTS	PERFORMANCE STANDARD
African American	115	2% 6% 9% 83%
Asian/Pacific Islander	82	11% 14% 16% 59%
Economically Disadvantaged	75	10% 10% 20% 60%
Hispanic	74	10% 13% 15% 62%
Limited English Proficiency	86	10% 10% 10% 70%
Native American	0	N/A
Students w/Disabilities	54	10% 20% 20% 50%
White/Caucasian	311	1% 2% 5% 92%

The Lincoln School (174 total students)

DEMOGRAPHIC	STUDENTS	PERFORMANCE STANDARD
African American	14	10% 10% 50% 30%
Asian/Pacific Islander	23	5% 5% 10% 80%
Economically Disadvantaged	14	10% 10% 20% 60%
Hispanic	11	10% 20% 60% 10%
Limited English Proficiency	12	10% 10% 10% 70%
Native American	0	N/A
Students w/Disabilities	18	10% 20% 20% 50%
White/Caucasian	126	10% 50% 10% 30%

Below Basic Basic Proficient Advanced

Using This Report

Purpose: This report provides a demographic breakdown of SRI performance.

Follow-Up: Identify demographic groups that are in need of extra help based on their SRI performance standard percentages.

Printed by: District Administrator Page 1 of 1 Printed on: 2/2/2005

PURPOSE

This report provides a demographic breakdown of *SRI* performance.

FOLLOW-UP

Identify demographic groups that are in need of extra help based on their *SRI* performance standard percentages.

Using the Data

Who: This report is for district and school administrators.

What: The Demographic Proficiency Report provides a breakdown of *SRI* performance standard data for a number of demographic groups. The report can be run to provide data for a district and its schools, for a school and its grades, for a grade within a school and its individual classes, and for an individual teacher and his or her classes and/or groups. Numbers of students per group are supplied, as are percentages per performance standard in a bar-graph format.

When: This report is best generated on a monthly basis, or according to the management needs of the individual district or school administrator.

Understanding the Data

1. **Demographic:** Demographic groups addressed in the report.
2. **Students:** Number of students in each group.
3. **Performance Standard:** Percentage of students in each performance standard.
4. **Table Key:** Key to performance standards shown in the table: Below Basic, Basic, Proficient, Advanced.

Time Period Settings

The information in this report is based on the last *SRI* test taken during the chosen time period.

Related Reports

Run the following reports for more information on student proficiency levels:

- District/School Proficiency Report
- Proficiency Summary Report
- Proficiency Growth Report
- Growth Summary Report
- Demographic Growth Report
- Proficiency Report

Demographic Growth Report

Administrator Reports

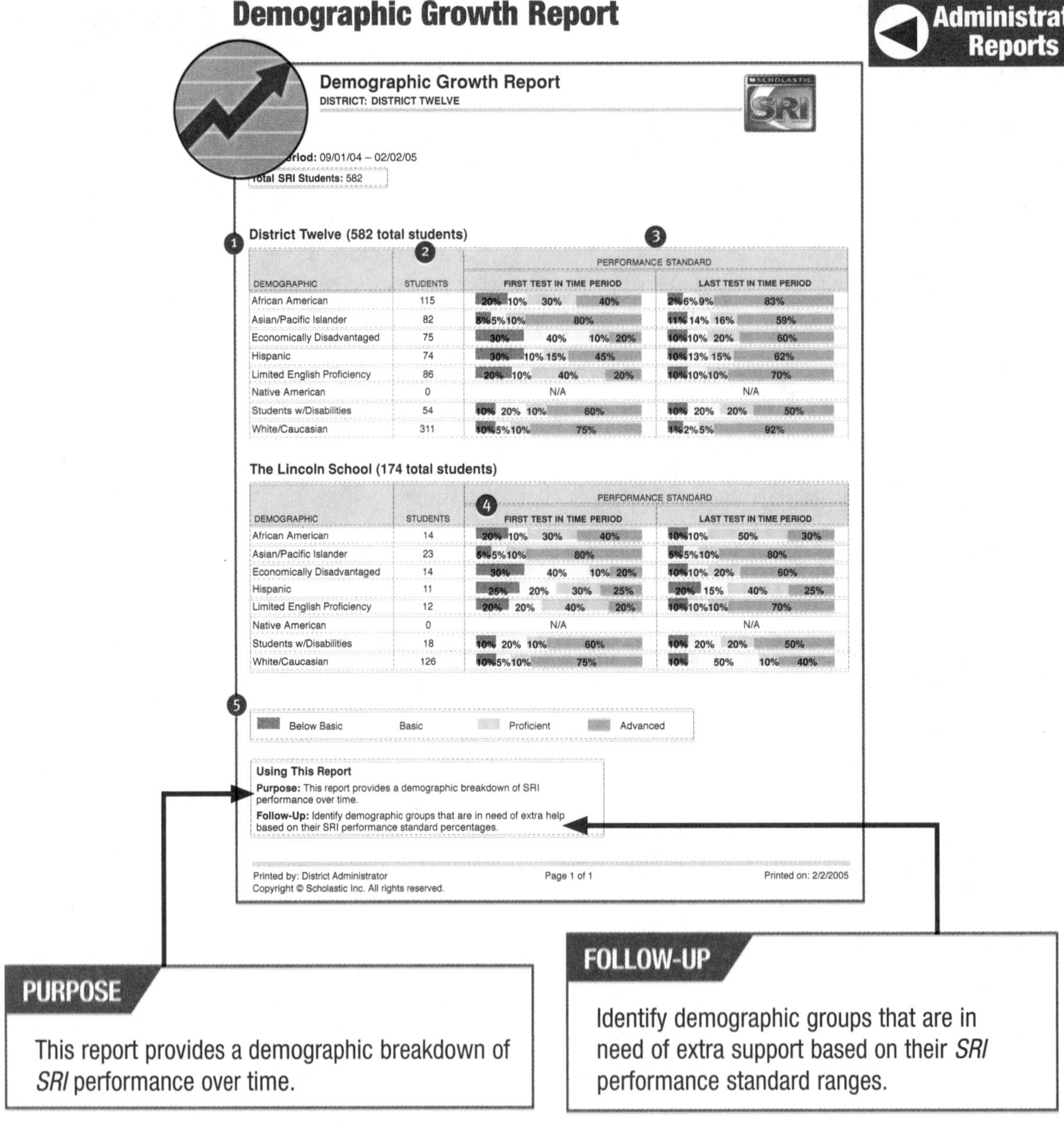

Demographic Growth Report

DISTRICT: DISTRICT TWELVE

SCHOLASTIC SRI

…riod: 09/01/04 – 02/02/05

…otal SRI Students: 582

District Twelve (582 total students)

DEMOGRAPHIC	STUDENTS	PERFORMANCE STANDARD	
		FIRST TEST IN TIME PERIOD	LAST TEST IN TIME PERIOD
African American	115	20% 10% 30% 40%	2% 6% 9% 83%
Asian/Pacific Islander	82	5% 5% 10% 80%	11% 14% 16% 59%
Economically Disadvantaged	75	30% 40% 10% 20%	10% 10% 20% 60%
Hispanic	74	30% 10% 15% 45%	10% 13% 15% 62%
Limited English Proficiency	86	20% 10% 40% 20%	10% 10% 10% 70%
Native American	0	N/A	N/A
Students w/Disabilities	54	10% 20% 10% 60%	10% 20% 20% 50%
White/Caucasian	311	10% 5% 10% 75%	1% 2% 5% 92%

The Lincoln School (174 total students)

DEMOGRAPHIC	STUDENTS	PERFORMANCE STANDARD	
		FIRST TEST IN TIME PERIOD	LAST TEST IN TIME PERIOD
African American	14	20% 10% 30% 40%	10% 10% 50% 30%
Asian/Pacific Islander	23	5% 5% 10% 80%	5% 5% 10% 80%
Economically Disadvantaged	14	30% 40% 10% 20%	10% 10% 20% 60%
Hispanic	11	25% 20% 30% 25%	20% 15% 40% 25%
Limited English Proficiency	12	20% 20% 40% 20%	10% 10% 10% 70%
Native American	0	N/A	N/A
Students w/Disabilities	18	10% 20% 10% 60%	10% 20% 20% 50%
White/Caucasian	126	10% 5% 10% 75%	10% 50% 10% 40%

Below Basic Basic Proficient Advanced

Using This Report

Purpose: This report provides a demographic breakdown of SRI performance over time.

Follow-Up: Identify demographic groups that are in need of extra help based on their SRI performance standard percentages.

Printed by: District Administrator Page 1 of 1 Printed on: 2/2/2005

PURPOSE

This report provides a demographic breakdown of *SRI* performance over time.

FOLLOW-UP

Identify demographic groups that are in need of extra support based on their *SRI* performance standard ranges.

Using the Data

Who: This report is for district and school administrators.

What: The Demographic Growth Report provides a breakdown of *SRI* performance standard data over time for a number of demographic groups. The report can be run to provide data for a district and its schools, for a school and its grades, for a grade within a school and its individual classes, and for an individual teacher and his or her classes and/or groups. Numbers of students per group are supplied, as are percentages per performance standard in a bar-graph format.

When: This report is best generated on a monthly basis, or according to the management needs of the individual district or school administrator.

Understanding the Data

1. **Demographic:** Demographic groups addressed in the report.
2. **Students:** Number of students in each group.
3. **Performance Standard:** Percentage of students in each performance standard.
4. **First/Last Test in Time Period:** The report is based on the first and last *SRI* tests taken during the chosen time period.
5. **Table Key:** Key to performance standards shown in the table: Below Basic, Basic, Proficient, Advanced.

Time Period Settings

The information in this report is based on the first and last *SRI* tests taken during the chosen time period. Make sure the time period setting you choose covers at least two *SRI* test administrations.

Related Reports

Run the following reports for more information on student proficiency levels:

- District/School Proficiency Report
- Proficiency Summary
- Proficiency Growth Report
- Growth Summary Report
- Demographic Proficiency Report
- Proficiency Report

Test Activity Report

Test Activity Report

DISTRICT: DISTRICT TWELVE

SCHOLASTIC SRI

iod: 09/01/04 – 02/02/05

AL SRI STUDENTS: 582

SCHOOL	TEACHERS	STUDENTS ENROLLED IN SRI	STUDENTS TESTED ONCE	STUDENTS TESTED TWICE	STUDENTS TESTED THREE OR MORE TIMES	STUDENTS NOT TESTED
The Lincoln School	7	174	20	100	30	24
Quincy School	10	116	5	75	22	14
South Middle School	5	125	10	75	15	25
Taft School	11	167	15	25	100	27

Using This Report

Purpose: This report provides data on how each school in a district is utilizing SRI.

Follow-Up: Contact principals or other administrators in schools where student SRI use is not meeting district plans or expectations.

Printed by: District Administrator

Page 1 of 1
Printed on: 2/2/2005

PURPOSE

This report provides data on how each school in a district is utilizing *SRI*.

FOLLOW-UP

Contact principals or other administrators in schools where student *SRI* use is not meeting district plans or expectations.

Teacher Roster

Teacher Roster

GRADE: GRADE 5

School: The Lincoln School

Period: 09/01/04 – 02/02/05

TEACHER	GRADE	STUDENTS ENROLLED IN SRI	STUDENTS TESTED ONCE	STUDENTS TESTED TWICE	STUDENTS TESTED THREE OR MORE TIMES	STUDENTS NOT TESTED
Bentley, Elizabeth	5	20	8	2	5	5
Greene, Sarah	5	20	0	15	5	0
Maglari, Thomas R.	5	19	4	3	5	7
Velasco, Juan	5	24	3	8	10	3
TOTAL TEACHERS = 4		**83**	**15**	**28**	**25**	**15**

Using This Report

Purpose: This report shows SRI usage by teacher. It lists the number of students enrolled per teacher and how often students have been tested.

Follow-Up: Use the report to review SRI usage per teacher. Investigate instances where SRI is not being implemented according to the district or school plan.

Printed by: District Administrator

Page 1 of 1

Printed on: 2/02/2005

PURPOSE

This report shows *SRI* usage by teacher. It lists the number of students enrolled per teacher and how often students have been tested.

FOLLOW-UP

Use the report to review *SRI* usage per teacher. Investigate instances where *SRI* is not being implemented according to the district or school plan.

Reading Performance Report

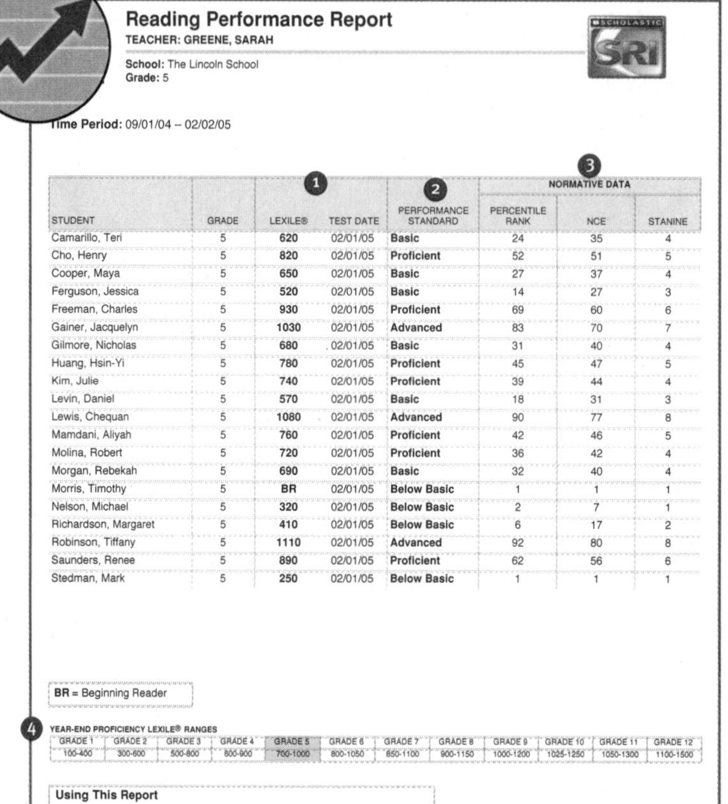

Reading Performance Report

TEACHER: GREENE, SARAH

School: The Lincoln School
Grade: 5

Time Period: 09/01/04 – 02/02/05

STUDENT	GRADE	LEXILE® (1)	TEST DATE	PERFORMANCE STANDARD (2)	NORMATIVE DATA (3) PERCENTILE RANK	NCE	STANINE
Camarillo, Teri	5	**620**	02/01/05	**Basic**	24	35	4
Cho, Henry	5	**820**	02/01/05	**Proficient**	52	51	5
Cooper, Maya	5	**650**	02/01/05	**Basic**	27	37	4
Ferguson, Jessica	5	**520**	02/01/05	**Basic**	14	27	3
Freeman, Charles	5	**930**	02/01/05	**Proficient**	69	60	6
Gainer, Jacquelyn	5	**1030**	02/01/05	**Advanced**	83	70	7
Gilmore, Nicholas	5	**680**	02/01/05	**Basic**	31	40	4
Huang, Hsin-Yi	5	**780**	02/01/05	**Proficient**	45	47	5
Kim, Julie	5	**740**	02/01/05	**Proficient**	39	44	4
Levin, Daniel	5	**570**	02/01/05	**Basic**	18	31	3
Lewis, Chequan	5	**1080**	02/01/05	**Advanced**	90	77	8
Mamdani, Aliyah	5	**760**	02/01/05	**Proficient**	42	46	5
Molina, Robert	5	**720**	02/01/05	**Proficient**	36	42	4
Morgan, Rebekah	5	**690**	02/01/05	**Basic**	32	40	4
Morris, Timothy	5	**BR**	02/01/05	**Below Basic**	1	1	1
Nelson, Michael	5	**320**	02/01/05	**Below Basic**	2	7	1
Richardson, Margaret	5	**410**	02/01/05	**Below Basic**	6	17	2
Robinson, Tiffany	5	**1110**	02/01/05	**Advanced**	92	80	8
Saunders, Renee	5	**890**	02/01/05	**Proficient**	62	56	6
Stedman, Mark	5	**250**	02/01/05	**Below Basic**	1	1	1

BR = Beginning Reader

(4) **YEAR-END PROFICIENCY LEXILE® RANGES**

GRADE 1	GRADE 2	GRADE 3	GRADE 4	GRADE 5	GRADE 6	GRADE 7	GRADE 8	GRADE 9	GRADE 10	GRADE 11	GRADE 12
100-400	300-600	500-800	600-900	700-1000	800-1050	850-1100	900-1150	1000-1200	1025-1250	1050-1300	1100-1500

Using This Report

Purpose: This report shows students' performance standards based on the results of their latest SRI tests.

Follow-Up: Use the information on the report to set goals for students, and to identify students who are performing at low performance standards.

Printed by: Sarah Greene

Page 1 of 1
Printed on: 2/2/2005

PURPOSE

This report shows students' performance standards based on the results of their latest *SRI* tests.

FOLLOW-UP

Use the information on the report to set goals for students, and to identify students who are performing at low performance standards.

Using the Data

Who: This report is for teachers.

What: This report summarizes students' reading performance by providing their latest *SRI* measure, along with the relevant test date, as well as performance-standard rankings and normative data.

When: This report is best generated on a monthly basis, or whenever a majority of students in a class or group have completed an *SRI* test.

Understanding the Data

1. **Lexile/Test Date:** Each student's current Lexile measure, and the date of their latest *SRI* test.
2. **Performance Standard:** *SRI* performance standards: Below Basic, Basic, Proficient, Advanced.
3. **Normative Data:** Data that shows a student's relative standing within a normative group.
    - **Percentile Rank:** A score that tells what percent of students in a particular group received lower scores than this student. Percentiles range from 1 to 99.
    - **Normal Curve Equivalent (NCE):** A normalized score with a mean of 50 and a standard deviation of 21.06. NCEs range from 1 to 99.
    - **Stanine:** A standardized score with a mean of 5 and a standard deviation of 2. Stanines range from 1 to 9.
4. **Year-End Proficiency Lexile Ranges:** Ranges within which students are considered to be reading proficiently at their grade level. Relevant grade or grades are shaded.

Time Period Settings

The information in this report is based on the last *SRI* test taken during the chosen time period. Make sure to adjust the time period to cover students' most recent testing sessions.

Related Reports

Consult the following reports for additional perspectives on student performance:

- Proficiency Report
- Student Progress Report
- Intervention Grouping Report
- Student Action Report

Growth Report

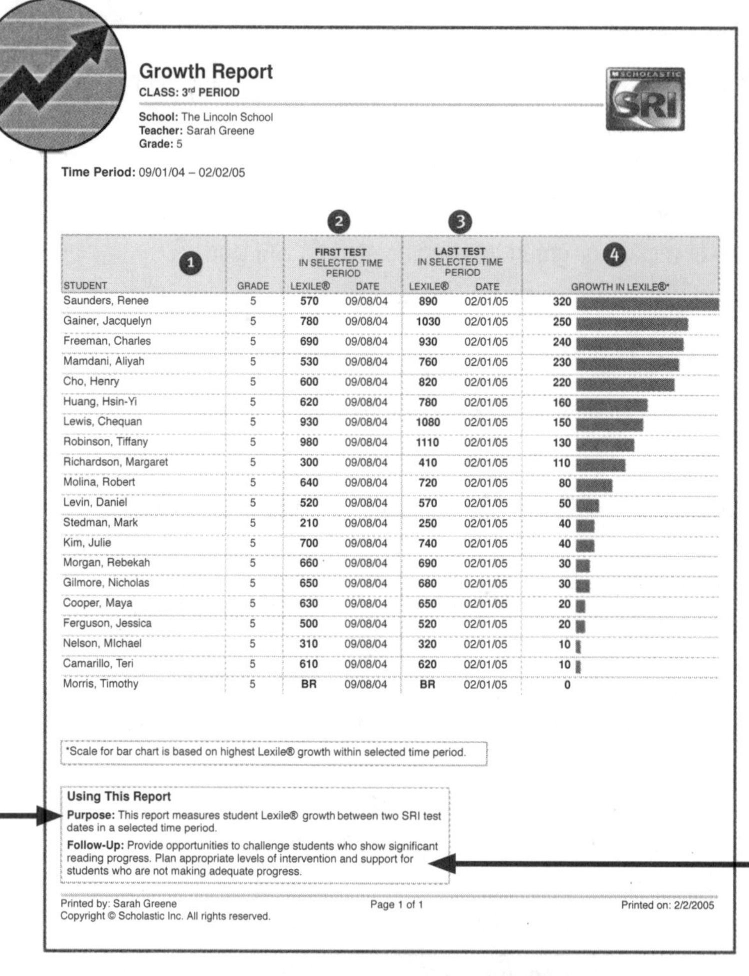

Growth Report

CLASS: 3rd PERIOD

School: The Lincoln School
Teacher: Sarah Greene
Grade: 5

Time Period: 09/01/04 – 02/02/05

STUDENT (1)	GRADE	FIRST TEST IN SELECTED TIME PERIOD (2) LEXILE®	DATE	LAST TEST IN SELECTED TIME PERIOD (3) LEXILE®	DATE	GROWTH IN LEXILE®* (4)
Saunders, Renee	5	570	09/08/04	890	02/01/05	320
Gainer, Jacquelyn	5	780	09/08/04	1030	02/01/05	250
Freeman, Charles	5	690	09/08/04	930	02/01/05	240
Mamdani, Aliyah	5	530	09/08/04	760	02/01/05	230
Cho, Henry	5	600	09/08/04	820	02/01/05	220
Huang, Hsin-Yi	5	620	09/08/04	780	02/01/05	160
Lewis, Chequan	5	930	09/08/04	1080	02/01/05	150
Robinson, Tiffany	5	980	09/08/04	1110	02/01/05	130
Richardson, Margaret	5	300	09/08/04	410	02/01/05	110
Molina, Robert	5	640	09/08/04	720	02/01/05	80
Levin, Daniel	5	520	09/08/04	570	02/01/05	50
Stedman, Mark	5	210	09/08/04	250	02/01/05	40
Kim, Julie	5	700	09/08/04	740	02/01/05	40
Morgan, Rebekah	5	660	09/08/04	690	02/01/05	30
Gilmore, Nicholas	5	650	09/08/04	680	02/01/05	30
Cooper, Maya	5	630	09/08/04	650	02/01/05	20
Ferguson, Jessica	5	500	09/08/04	520	02/01/05	20
Nelson, Michael	5	310	09/08/04	320	02/01/05	10
Camarillo, Teri	5	610	09/08/04	620	02/01/05	10
Morris, Timothy	5	BR	09/08/04	BR	02/01/05	0

*Scale for bar chart is based on highest Lexile® growth within selected time period.

Using This Report

Purpose: This report measures student Lexile® growth between two SRI test dates in a selected time period.

Follow-Up: Provide opportunities to challenge students who show significant reading progress. Plan appropriate levels of intervention and support for students who are not making adequate progress.

Printed by: Sarah Greene

Page 1 of 1
Printed on: 2/2/2005

PURPOSE

This report measures student Lexile growth between two *SRI* test dates in a selected time period.

FOLLOW-UP

Provide opportunities to challenge students who show significant reading progress. Plan appropriate levels of intervention and support for students who are not making adequate progress.

Using the Data

Who: This report is for teachers.

What: The Growth Report lists the results of two *SRI* test administrations and calculates the growth in Lexile that has occurred over time. Growth data is given both numerically and in bar-graph format.

When: This report is best generated on a monthly basis, or whenever a majority of students in a class or group have completed an *SRI* test administration.

Understanding the Data

1. **Student/Grade:** Names of students profiled in the report, with their grade levels.
2. **First Test in Selected Time Period:** Lexile measure and test date for the first *SRI* test in the selected time period.
3. **Last Test in Selected Time Period:** Lexile measure and test date for the last *SRI* test in the selected time period.
4. **Growth in Lexile:** Lexile increase between the first and last tests in the selected time period. The bar graph is scaled to the student with the largest increase.

Time Period Settings

The information in this report is based on the first and last *SRI* tests taken during the chosen time period. Make sure the time period setting you choose covers at least two *SRI* test administrations. If your students have taken more than two *SRI* tests, you may wish to run separate reports isolating the different dates; for example, testing sessions 1 and 3, sessions 1 and 2, and sessions 2 and 3.

Related Reports

Consult the following reports for additional perspectives on student growth:

- Student Progress Report
- Targeted Reading Report
- Student Yearly Progress Report

Proficiency Report

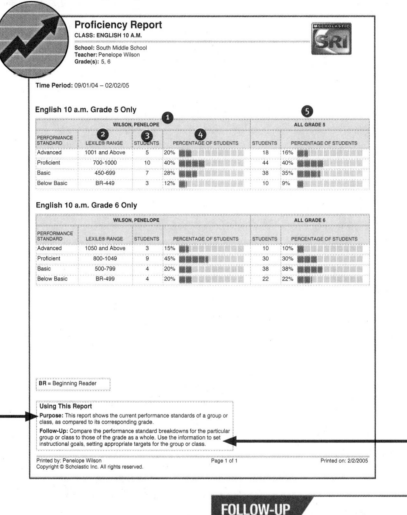

Proficiency Report

CLASS: ENGLISH 10 A.M.

School: South Middle School
Teacher: Penelope Wilson
Grade(s): 5, 6

Time Period: 09/01/04 – 02/02/05

English 10 a.m. Grade 5 Only

WILSON, PENELOPE ❶				ALL GRADE 5 ❺	
PERFORMANCE STANDARD	❷ LEXILE® RANGE	❸ STUDENTS	❹ PERCENTAGE OF STUDENTS	STUDENTS	PERCENTAGE OF STUDENTS
Advanced	1001 and Above	5	20%	18	16%
Proficient	700-1000	10	40%	44	40%
Basic	450-699	7	28%	38	35%
Below Basic	BR-449	3	12%	10	9%

English 10 a.m. Grade 6 Only

WILSON, PENELOPE				ALL GRADE 6	
PERFORMANCE STANDARD	LEXILE® RANGE	STUDENTS	PERCENTAGE OF STUDENTS	STUDENTS	PERCENTAGE OF STUDENTS
Advanced	1050 and Above	3	15%	10	10%
Proficient	800-1049	9	45%	30	30%
Basic	500-799	4	20%	38	38%
Below Basic	BR-499	4	20%	22	22%

BR = Beginning Reader

Using This Report

Purpose: This report shows the current performance standards of a group or class, as compared to its corresponding grade.

Follow-Up: Compare the performance standard breakdowns for the particular group or class to those of the grade as a whole. Use the information to set instructional goals, setting appropriate targets for the group or class.

Printed by: Penelope Wilson | Page 1 of 1 | Printed on: 2/2/2005

PURPOSE

This report shows the current performance standards of a group or class, as compared to its corresponding grade.

FOLLOW-UP

Compare the performance standard breakdowns for the particular group or class to those of the grade as a whole. Use the information to set instructional goals, setting appropriate targets for the group or class.

Using the Data

Who: This report is for teachers.

What: The Proficiency Report provides a performance-standard breakdown of a class or group, based on the students' most recent *SRI* scores. Also provided is a performance-standard breakdown of the corresponding grade as a whole. Teachers can use the report to compare group or class achievement in relation to their grade-level peers.

When: This report is best generated on a monthly basis, or whenever a majority of students in a class or group have completed an *SRI* test administration.

Understanding the Data

1. **Teacher Name:** The left part of the table provides data on the individual teacher's class or group. If the teacher has students from two different grades in his or her class or group, separate tables for each grade are provided.

2. **Performance Standard/Lexile Range:** *SRI* performance standards and corresponding grade-specific Lexile ranges.

3. **Students:** Number of students per performance standard.

4. **Percentage of Students:** Percentage of students per performance standard.

5. **All Grade:** Number and percentage of students per performance standard for grade as a whole.

Time Period Settings

The information in this report is based on the last *SRI* test taken during the chosen time period.

Related Reports

Consult the following related reports on student proficiency:

- Reading Performance Report
- Student Progress Report
- Intervention Grouping Report
- Student Action Report

Student Progress Report

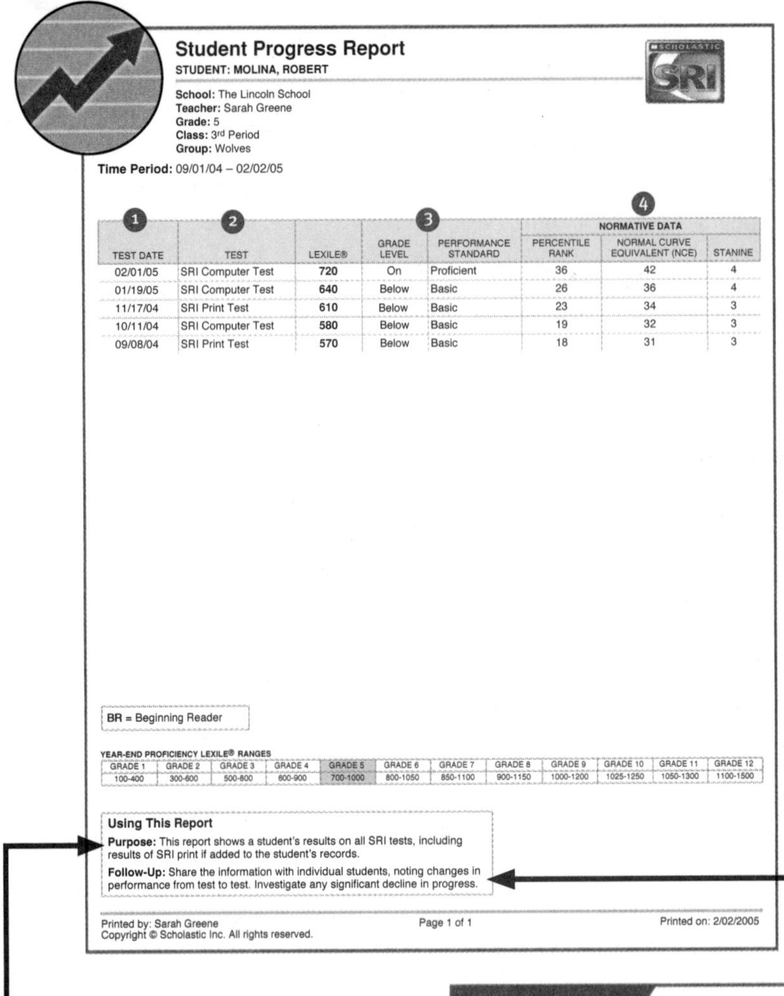

Student Progress Report

SCHOLASTIC SRI

STUDENT: MOLINA, ROBERT

School: The Lincoln School
Teacher: Sarah Greene
Grade: 5
Class: 3rd Period
Group: Wolves

Time Period: 09/01/04 – 02/02/05

1 TEST DATE	2 TEST	LEXILE®	GRADE LEVEL	3 PERFORMANCE STANDARD	4 NORMATIVE DATA: PERCENTILE RANK	NORMAL CURVE EQUIVALENT (NCE)	STANINE
02/01/05	SRI Computer Test	**720**	On	Proficient	36	42	4
01/19/05	SRI Computer Test	**640**	Below	Basic	26	36	4
11/17/04	SRI Print Test	**610**	Below	Basic	23	34	3
10/11/04	SRI Computer Test	**580**	Below	Basic	19	32	3
09/08/04	SRI Print Test	**570**	Below	Basic	18	31	3

BR = Beginning Reader

YEAR-END PROFICIENCY LEXILE® RANGES

GRADE 1	GRADE 2	GRADE 3	GRADE 4	GRADE 5	GRADE 6	GRADE 7	GRADE 8	GRADE 9	GRADE 10	GRADE 11	GRADE 12
100-400	300-600	500-800	600-900	700-1000	800-1050	850-1100	900-1150	1000-1200	1025-1250	1050-1300	1100-1500

Using This Report

Purpose: This report shows a student's results on all SRI tests, including results of SRI print if added to the student's records.

Follow-Up: Share the information with individual students, noting changes in performance from test to test. Investigate any significant decline in progress.

Printed by: Sarah Greene

Page 1 of 1
Printed on: 2/02/2005

PURPOSE

This report shows a student's results on all *SRI* tests, including results of *SRI* print if added to the student's records.

FOLLOW-UP

Share the information with individual students, noting changes in performance from test to test. Investigate any significant decline in progress.

Using the Data

Who: This report is for teachers.

What: The Student Progress Report shows an individual student's results on all *SRI* tests taken during the chosen time period. If a student has also taken an *SRI* print test, the results will be included if those results have been added to the student's records in the Scholastic Achievement Manager. Also provided for each test result is the corresponding grade-level and performance-standard ranking, as well as equivalent normative data.

When: This report is best generated after each *SRI* test administration.

Understanding the Data

1. **Test Date:** The date of each test included on the report.
2. **Test:** *SRI* Computer Test or *SRI* Print Test.
3. **Grade Level/Performance Standard:** Corresponding grade level and performance standard, based on year-end Lexile proficiency ranges.
4. **Normative Data:** Corresponding normative data: Percentile Rank, Normal Curve Equivalent (NCE), and Stanine.
    - **Percentile Rank:** A score that tells what percent of students in a particular group received lower scores than this student. Percentiles range from 1 to 99.
    - **Normal Curve Equivalent (NCE):** A normalized score with a mean of 50 and a standard deviation of 21.06. NCEs range from 1 to 99.
    - **Stanine:** A standardized score with a mean of 5 and a standard deviation of 2. Stanines range from 1 to 9.

Time Period Settings

This report includes the results of all *SRI* tests taken during the chosen time period. Make sure the time period setting you choose covers the student's latest *SRI* test administration.

Related Reports

Consult the following reports for additional perspectives on student progress:

- Growth Report
- Targeted Reading Report
- Student Action Report
- Student Yearly Progress Report

Student Yearly Progress Report

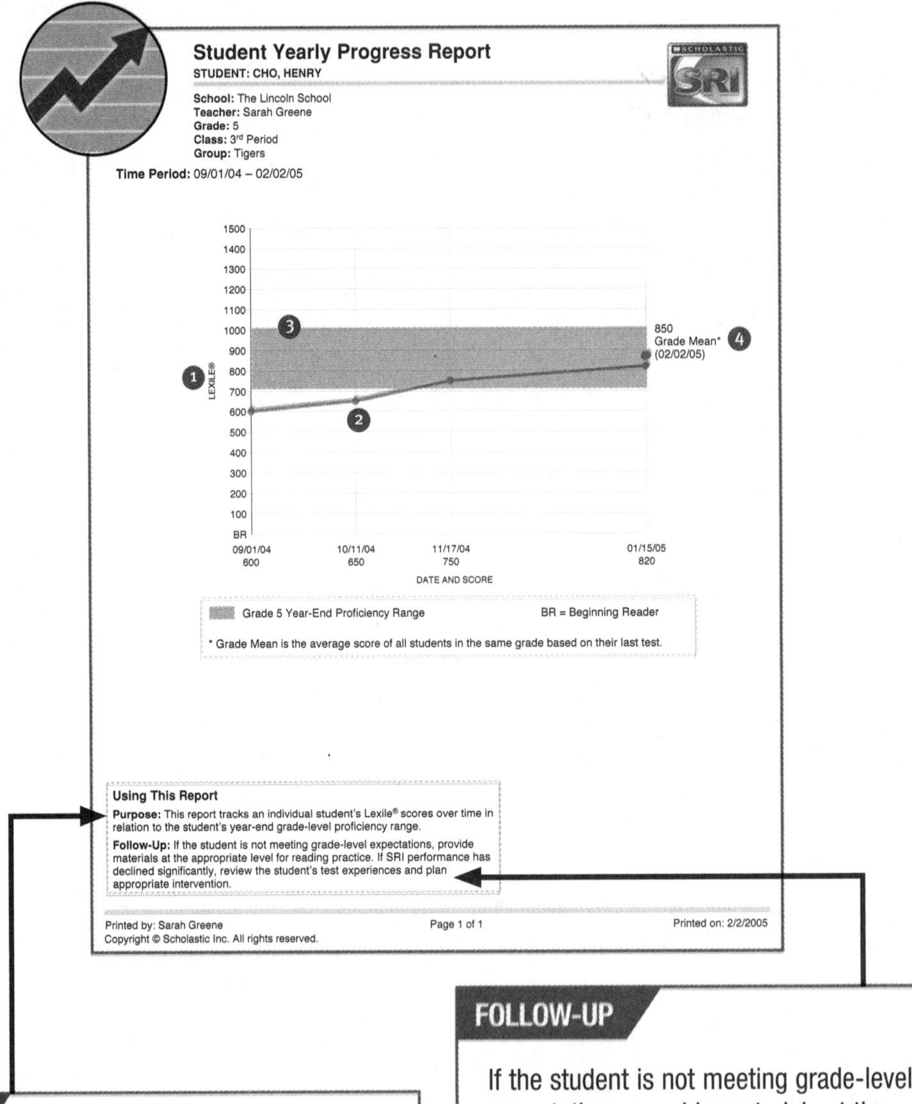

Student Yearly Progress Report
STUDENT: CHO, HENRY
SCHOLASTIC SRI
School: The Lincoln School
Teacher: Sarah Greene
Grade: 5
Class: 3rd Period
Group: Tigers
Time Period: 09/01/04 – 02/02/05
1500
1400
1300
1200
1100
1000
900
800
700
600
500
400
300
200
100
BR
LEXILE®
850
Grade Mean*
(02/02/05)
09/01/04
600
10/11/04
650
11/17/04
750
01/15/05
820
DATE AND SCORE
Grade 5 Year-End Proficiency Range
BR = Beginning Reader
* Grade Mean is the average score of all students in the same grade based on their last test.
Using This Report
Purpose: This report tracks an individual student's Lexile® scores over time in relation to the student's year-end grade-level proficiency range.
Follow-Up: If the student is not meeting grade-level expectations, provide materials at the appropriate level for reading practice. If SRI performance has declined significantly, review the student's test experiences and plan appropriate intervention.
Printed by: Sarah Greene
Page 1 of 1
Printed on: 2/2/2005
Copyright © Scholastic Inc. All rights reserved.

FOLLOW-UP

If the student is not meeting grade-level expectations, provide materials at the appropriate level for reading practice. If *SRI* performance has declined significantly, review the student's test experiences and plan appropriate intervention.

PURPOSE

This report tracks an individual student's Lexile scores over time in relation to the student's year-end grade-level proficiency range.

Using the Data

Who: This report is for teachers.

What: The Student Yearly Progress Report can be used to assess overall student performance over time. The report plots a student's test history on a chart that also displays the year-end proficiency range for the student's grade. Also included on the chart is the current average score for all students in the same grade.

When: This report is best generated after each *SRI* test administration.

Related Reports

Consult the following reports for additional perspectives on student progress:

- Growth Report
- Student Progress Report

Understanding the Data

1. **Line Graph:** The line graph is constructed to show Lexiles in 100-unit increments along the vertical axis and *SRI* test dates along the bottom axis.
2. **Graph Entries:** Each dot on the graph represents a student test result. The date of the test appears along the bottom of the graph.
3. **Year-End Proficiency Range:** The shaded area on the graph represents the year-end Lexile on-level proficiency range for the grade.
4. **Grade Mean:** The large dot represents the Grade Mean, the average score of all students in the grade based on their latest *SRI* tests.

Time Period Settings

This report includes the results of all *SRI* tests taken during the chosen time period. Make sure the time period setting you choose covers the student's latest *SRI* test administration.

Targeted Reading Report

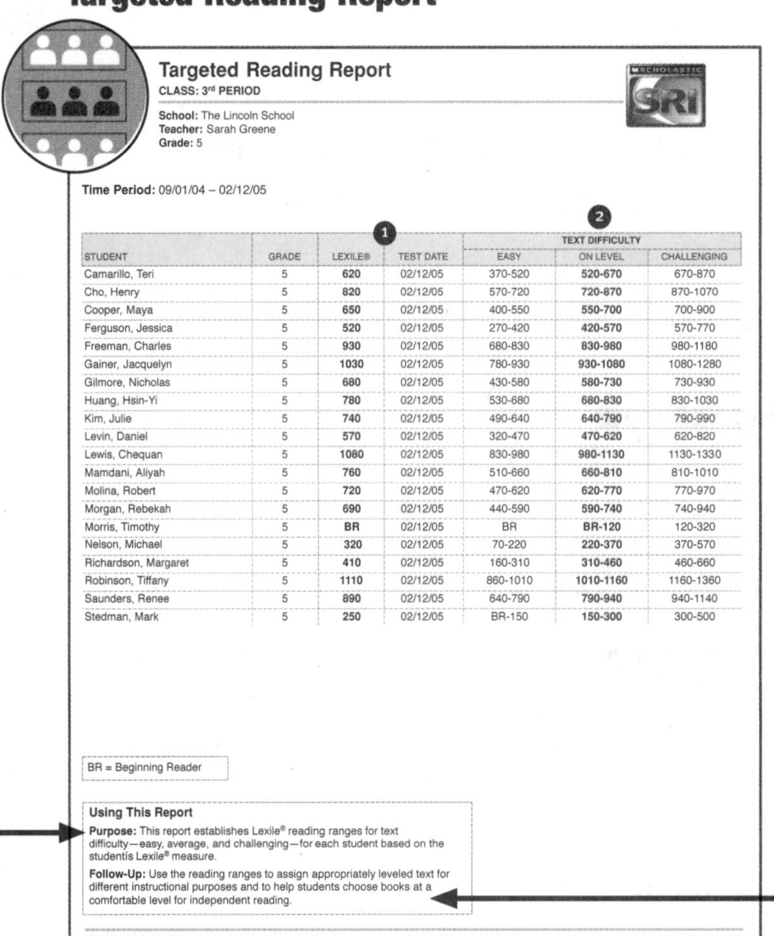

Targeted Reading Report

CLASS: 3rd PERIOD

School: The Lincoln School
Teacher: Sarah Greene
Grade: 5

Time Period: 09/01/04 – 02/12/05

STUDENT	GRADE	LEXILE®	TEST DATE	TEXT DIFFICULTY		
				EASY	ON LEVEL	CHALLENGING
Camarillo, Teri	5	**620**	02/12/05	370-520	**520-670**	670-870
Cho, Henry	5	**820**	02/12/05	570-720	**720-870**	870-1070
Cooper, Maya	5	**650**	02/12/05	400-550	**550-700**	700-900
Ferguson, Jessica	5	**520**	02/12/05	270-420	**420-570**	570-770
Freeman, Charles	5	**930**	02/12/05	680-830	**830-980**	980-1180
Gainer, Jacquelyn	5	**1030**	02/12/05	780-930	**930-1080**	1080-1280
Gilmore, Nicholas	5	**680**	02/12/05	430-580	**580-730**	730-930
Huang, Hsin-Yi	5	**780**	02/12/05	530-680	**680-830**	830-1030
Kim, Julie	5	**740**	02/12/05	490-640	**640-790**	790-990
Levin, Daniel	5	**570**	02/12/05	320-470	**470-620**	620-820
Lewis, Chequan	5	**1080**	02/12/05	830-980	**980-1130**	1130-1330
Mamdani, Aliyah	5	**760**	02/12/05	510-660	**660-810**	810-1010
Molina, Robert	5	**720**	02/12/05	470-620	**620-770**	770-970
Morgan, Rebekah	5	**690**	02/12/05	440-590	**590-740**	740-940
Morris, Timothy	5	**BR**	02/12/05	BR	**BR-120**	120-320
Nelson, Michael	5	**320**	02/12/05	70-220	**220-370**	370-570
Richardson, Margaret	5	**410**	02/12/05	160-310	**310-460**	460-660
Robinson, Tiffany	5	**1110**	02/12/05	860-1010	**1010-1160**	1160-1360
Saunders, Renee	5	**890**	02/12/05	640-790	**790-940**	940-1140
Stedman, Mark	5	**250**	02/12/05	BR-150	**150-300**	300-500

BR = Beginning Reader

Using This Report

Purpose: This report establishes Lexile® reading ranges for text difficulty—easy, average, and challenging—for each student based on the studentís Lexile® measure.

Follow-Up: Use the reading ranges to assign appropriately leveled text for different instructional purposes and to help students choose books at a comfortable level for independent reading.

Printed by: Sarah Greene | Page 1 of 1 | Printed on: 2/2/2005

PURPOSE

This report establishes Lexile reading ranges for text difficulty—easy, on level, and challenging—for each student based on the student's Lexile measure.

FOLLOW-UP

Use the reading ranges to assign appropriately leveled text for different instructional purposes and to help students choose books at a comfortable level for independent reading.

Using the Data

Who: This report is for teachers.

What: This report establishes Lexile reading ranges for text difficulty that can be used to find books at the appropriate level for instructional planning. Easy books range from 100 to 250 Lexiles below the student's Lexile measure. On Level books range from 100 Lexiles below to 50 Lexiles above the student's Lexile measure. Challenging books range from 50 to 250 Lexiles above the student's Lexile measure. See the bullet points below and pages 186–188 for more tips on matching readers to text.

When: This report is best generated after each *SRI* test administration, or according to the instructional needs of the individual teacher.

Related Reports

Run the following reports for more information on matching students to books:

- Recommended Reading Report
- Student Action Report

Understanding the Data

❶ **Lexile/Test Date:** Student's current Lexile measure and date of last test.

❷ **Text Difficulty:** Reading ranges, in Lexiles, for Easy, On Level, and Challenging texts. Reading ranges are customized for each student based on the student's current Lexile measure.

- **Instructional Reading Purposes:** Easy books can be used for skill instruction with remedial or reluctant readers, or to help students master a challenging subject or skill. On Level books can be used when asking students to read independently for instructional purposes. Challenging books should be used for read-alouds, guided reading, or with other forms of small-group or one-on-one support.
- **Independent Reading Choices:** Encourage students reading below grade level to choose Easy books for independent reading to boost confidence. Match students to books in the On Level range for overall engagement with text. Direct students to Challenging books when they are highly motivated and interested in the topic.

Time Period Settings

To assess your students' current reading ability, make sure to adjust the time period to cover their most recent *SRI* test.

Intervention Grouping Report

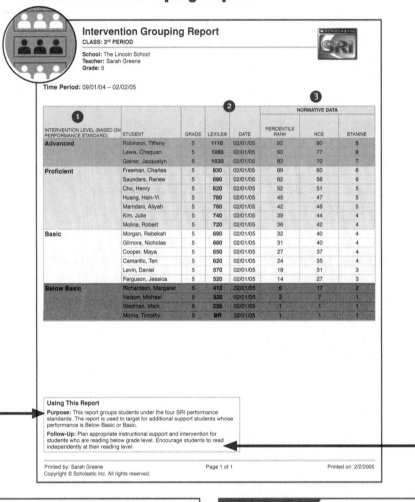

Intervention Grouping Report

CLASS: 3rd PERIOD

School: The Lincoln School
Teacher: Sarah Greene
Grade: 5

Time Period: 09/01/04 – 02/02/05

❶ INTERVENTION LEVEL (BASED ON PERFORMANCE STANDARD)	STUDENT	GRADE	❷ LEXILE®	DATE	❸ NORMATIVE DATA		
					PERCENTILE RANK	NCE	STANINE
Advanced	Robinson, Tiffany	5	**1110**	02/01/05	92	80	8
	Lewis, Chequan	5	**1080**	02/01/05	90	77	8
	Gainer, Jacquelyn	5	**1030**	02/01/05	83	70	7
Proficient	Freeman, Charles	5	**930**	02/01/05	69	60	6
	Saunders, Renee	5	**890**	02/01/05	62	56	6
	Cho, Henry	5	**820**	02/01/05	52	51	5
	Huang, Hsin-Yi	5	**780**	02/01/05	45	47	5
	Mamdani, Aliyah	5	**760**	02/01/05	42	46	5
	Kim, Julie	5	**740**	02/01/05	39	44	4
	Molina, Robert	5	**720**	02/01/05	36	42	4
Basic	Morgan, Rebekah	5	**690**	02/01/05	32	40	4
	Gilmore, Nicholas	5	**680**	02/01/05	31	40	4
	Cooper, Maya	5	**650**	02/01/05	27	37	4
	Camarillo, Teri	5	**620**	02/01/05	24	35	4
	Levin, Daniel	5	**570**	02/01/05	18	31	3
	Ferguson, Jessica	5	**520**	02/01/05	14	27	3
Below Basic	Richardson, Margaret	5	**410**	02/01/05	6	17	2
	Nelson, Michael	5	**320**	02/01/05	2	7	1
	Stedman, Mark	5	**250**	02/01/05	1	1	1
	Morris, Timothy	5	**BR**	02/01/05	1	1	1

Using This Report

Purpose: This report groups students under the four SRI performance standards. The report is used to target for additional support students whose performance is Below Basic or Basic.

Follow-Up: Plan appropriate instructional support and intervention for students who are reading below grade level. Encourage students to read independently at their reading level.

Printed by: Sarah Greene | Page 1 of 1 | Printed on: 2/2/2005

PURPOSE

This report groups students under the four *SRI* performance standards. The report is used to target for additional support students whose performance is Below Basic or Basic.

FOLLOW-UP

Plan appropriate instructional support and intervention for students who are reading below grade level. Encourage students to read independently at their reading level.

Using the Data

Who: This report is for teachers.

What: This report is organized specifically for teachers' grouping and intervention needs. Based on their latest *SRI* test results, students are grouped according to the *SRI* performance standard in which they currently fall: Advanced (above grade level), Proficient (on grade level), Basic (below grade level), and Below Basic (far below grade level). Use the report to target for additional support students whose performance is Below Basic or Basic, or students who are performing below or far below grade level. The report also includes normative data for each student.

When: This report is best generated after each *SRI* test administration, or according to the instructional needs of the individual teacher.

Understanding the Data

1. **Intervention Level:** Student reading level, based on the *SRI* performance standards: Below Basic, Basic, Advanced, and Proficient.

2. **Lexile/Date:** Student's current Lexile measure, and date of last test.

3. **Normative Data:** Corresponding normative data: Percentile Rank, Normal Curve Equivalent (NCE), and Stanine.
    - **Percentile Rank:** A score that tells what percent of students in a particular group received lower scores than this student. Percentiles range from 1 to 99.
    - **Normal Curve Equivalent (NCE):** A normalized score with a mean of 50 and a standard deviation of 21.06. NCEs range from 1 to 99.
    - **Stanine:** A standardized score with a mean of 5 and a standard deviation of 2. Stanines range from 1 to 9.

Time Period Settings

The information in this report is based on the last *SRI* tests taken during the selected time period.

Related Reports

Run the following reports for additional perspectives on student performance levels:

- Student Action Report
- Reading Performance Report
- Growth Report
- Student Progress Report
- Targeted Reading Report

Student Action Report

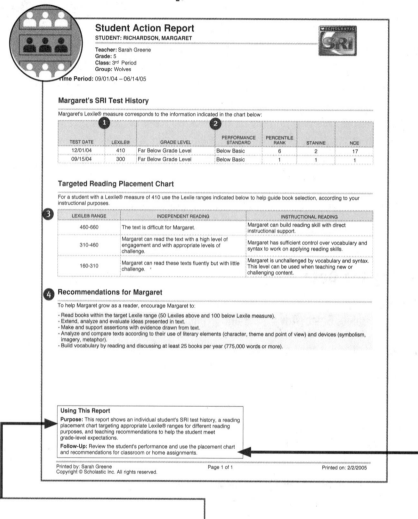

Student Action Report

STUDENT: RICHARDSON, MARGARET

Teacher: Sarah Greene
Grade: 5
Class: 3rd Period
Group: Wolves
Time Period: 09/01/04 – 06/14/05

Margaret's SRI Test History

Margaret's Lexile® measure corresponds to the information indicated in the chart below:

TEST DATE	❶ LEXILE®	GRADE LEVEL	❷ PERFORMANCE STANDARD	PERCENTILE RANK	STANINE	NCE
12/01/04	410	Far Below Grade Level	Below Basic	6	2	17
09/15/04	300	Far Below Grade Level	Below Basic	1	1	1

Targeted Reading Placement Chart

For a student with a Lexile® measure of 410 use the Lexile ranges indicated below to help guide book selection, according to your instructional purposes.

❸

LEXILE® RANGE	INDEPENDENT READING	INSTRUCTIONAL READING
460-660	The text is difficult for Margaret.	Margaret can build reading skill with direct instructional support.
310-460	Margaret can read the text with a high level of engagement and with appropriate levels of challenge.	Margaret has sufficient control over vocabulary and syntax to work on applying reading skills.
160-310	Margaret can read these texts fluently but with little challenge.	Margaret is unchallenged by vocabulary and syntax. This level can be used when teaching new or challenging content.

❹ Recommendations for Margaret

To help Margaret grow as a reader, encourage Margaret to:

- Read books within the target Lexile range (50 Lexiles above and 100 below Lexile measure).
- Extend, analyze and evaluate ideas presented in text.
- Make and support assertions with evidence drawn from text.
- Analyze and compare texts according to their use of literary elements (character, theme and point of view) and devices (symbolism, imagery, metaphor).
- Build vocabulary by reading and discussing at least 25 books per year (775,000 words or more).

Using This Report

Purpose: This report shows an individual student's SRI test history, a reading placement chart targeting appropriate Lexile® ranges for different reading purposes, and teaching recommendations to help the student meet grade-level expectations.

Follow-Up: Review the student's performance and use the placement chart and recommendations for classroom or home assignments.

Printed by: Sarah Greene

Page 1 of 1
Printed on: 2/2/2005

PURPOSE

This report shows an individual student's *SRI* test history, a reading placement chart targeting appropriate Lexile ranges for different reading purposes, and teaching recommendations to help the student meet grade-level expectations.

FOLLOW-UP

Review the student's performance and use the placement chart and recommendations for classroom or home assignments.

Using the Data

Who: This report is for teachers.

What: After providing a student's full *SRI* test history, this report goes on to present an action plan for helping the student grow as a reader. First, a reading placement chart targeted to the individual student is provided to help guide book selection. The chart is based on the student's Lexile measure and includes Lexile ranges at, on, and below the student's current reading level that correspond to different independent and instructional reading purposes. Second, the report includes recommendations for teaching strategies that have been customized to the student's grade level and reading ability as measured on *SRI*.

When: This report is best generated after each *SRI* test administration or according to the instructional needs of the individual teacher.

Understanding the Data

1. **Test Date/Lexile:** Date of test and corresponding student Lexile measure.
2. **Grade Level/Performance Standard:** For each test, grade-level determination is based on *SRI* performance standards.
3. **Placement Chart:** The Targeted Reading Placement Chart provides Lexile reading ranges, calculated from the student's current Lexile measure, that help guide book selection for independent reading and different instructional purposes.
4. **Recommendations:** The recommendations table offers a number of suggested teaching strategies you can use to help the individual student meet grade-level expectations. The recommendations are based on the student's current Lexile measure, taking into account the student's grade and his or her current *SRI* performance standard.

Time Period Settings

To assess the student's current reading ability, make sure to adjust the time period to cover their most recent *SRI* test.

Related Reports

Run the following reports for more information on matching students to books and strategies for helping students meet expectations:

- Targeted Reading Report
- Recommended Reading Report
- Student Test Printout
- Intervention Grouping Report

Recommended Reading Report

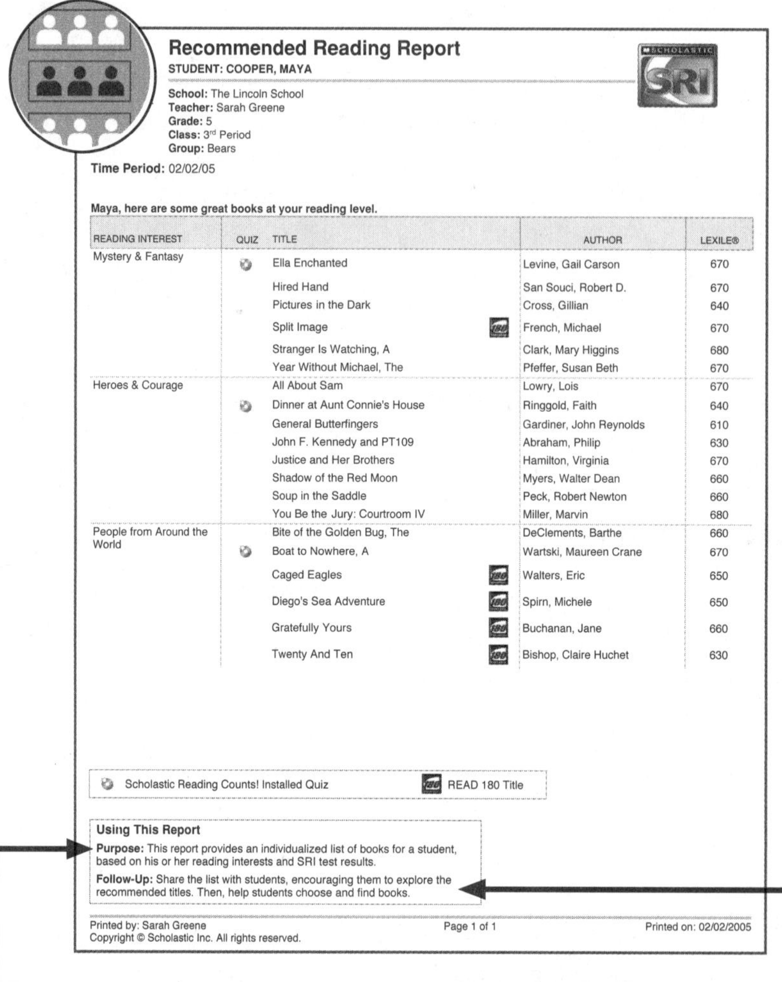

Recommended Reading Report

STUDENT: COOPER, MAYA

School: The Lincoln School
Teacher: Sarah Greene
Grade: 5
Class: 3rd Period
Group: Bears

Time Period: 02/02/05

Maya, here are some great books at your reading level.

READING INTEREST	QUIZ	TITLE		AUTHOR	LEXILE®
Mystery & Fantasy	●	Ella Enchanted		Levine, Gail Carson	670
		Hired Hand		San Souci, Robert D.	670
		Pictures in the Dark		Cross, Gillian	640
		Split Image	180	French, Michael	670
		Stranger Is Watching, A		Clark, Mary Higgins	680
		Year Without Michael, The		Pfeffer, Susan Beth	670
Heroes & Courage		All About Sam		Lowry, Lois	670
	●	Dinner at Aunt Connie's House		Ringgold, Faith	640
		General Butterfingers		Gardiner, John Reynolds	610
		John F. Kennedy and PT109		Abraham, Philip	630
		Justice and Her Brothers		Hamilton, Virginia	670
		Shadow of the Red Moon		Myers, Walter Dean	660
		Soup in the Saddle		Peck, Robert Newton	660
		You Be the Jury: Courtroom IV		Miller, Marvin	680
People from Around the World		Bite of the Golden Bug, The		DeClements, Barthe	660
	●	Boat to Nowhere, A		Wartski, Maureen Crane	670
		Caged Eagles	180	Walters, Eric	650
		Diego's Sea Adventure	180	Spirn, Michele	650
		Gratefully Yours	180	Buchanan, Jane	660
		Twenty And Ten	180	Bishop, Claire Huchet	630

● Scholastic Reading Counts! Installed Quiz 180 READ 180 Title

Using This Report
Purpose: This report provides an individualized list of books for a student, based on his or her reading interests and SRI test results.
Follow-Up: Share the list with students, encouraging them to explore the recommended titles. Then, help students choose and find books.

Printed by: Sarah Greene Page 1 of 1 Printed on: 02/02/2005
Copyright © Scholastic Inc. All rights reserved.

PURPOSE

This report provides an individualized list of books for a student, based on his or her reading interests and *SRI* test results.

FOLLOW-UP

Share the list with students, encouraging them to explore the recommended titles. Then, help students choose and find books.

Student Test Printout

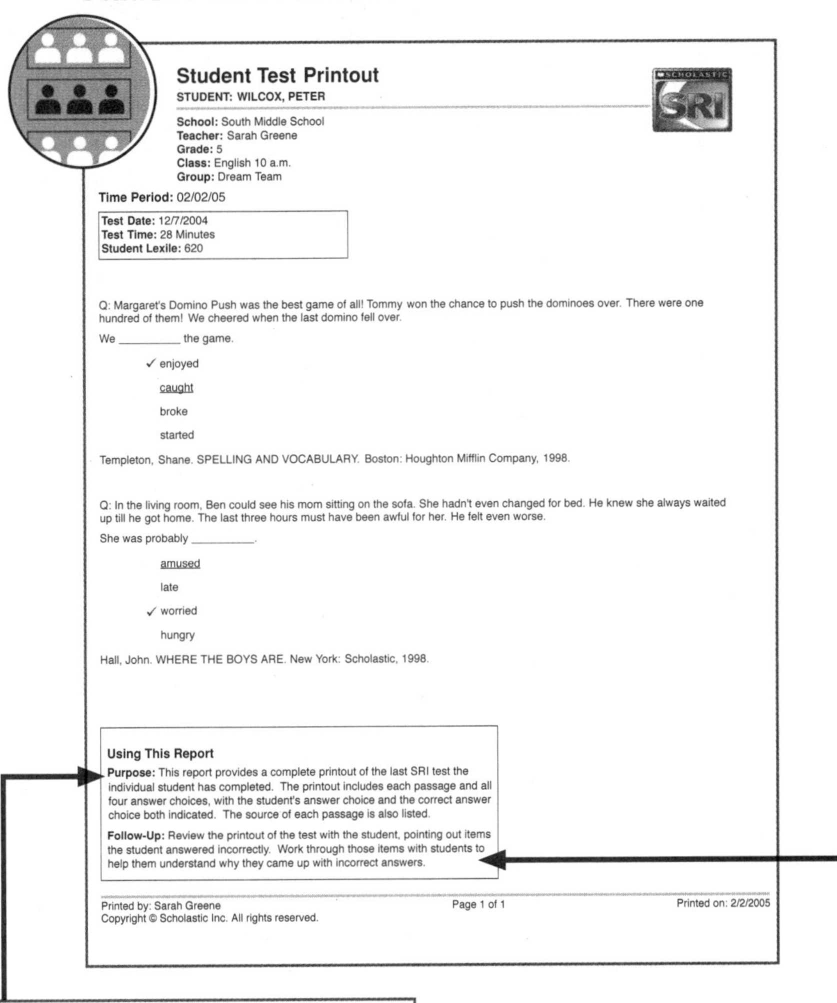
Student Test Printout
STUDENT: WILCOX, PETER

School: South Middle School
Teacher: Sarah Greene
Grade: 5
Class: English 10 a.m.
Group: Dream Team

Time Period: 02/02/05

Test Date: 12/7/2004
Test Time: 28 Minutes
Student Lexile: 620

Q: Margaret's Domino Push was the best game of all! Tommy won the chance to push the dominoes over. There were one hundred of them! We cheered when the last domino fell over.

We __________ the game.

✓ enjoyed

caught

broke

started

Templeton, Shane. SPELLING AND VOCABULARY. Boston: Houghton Mifflin Company, 1998.

Q: In the living room, Ben could see his mom sitting on the sofa. She hadn't even changed for bed. He knew she always waited up till he got home. The last three hours must have been awful for her. He felt even worse.

She was probably __________.

amused

late

✓ worried

hungry

Hall, John. WHERE THE BOYS ARE. New York: Scholastic, 1998.

Using This Report

Purpose: This report provides a complete printout of the last SRI test the individual student has completed. The printout includes each passage and all four answer choices, with the student's answer choice and the correct answer choice both indicated. The source of each passage is also listed.

Follow-Up: Review the printout of the test with the student, pointing out items the student answered incorrectly. Work through those items with students to help them understand why they came up with incorrect answers.

Printed by: Sarah Greene | Page 1 of 1 | Printed on: 2/2/2005

PURPOSE

This report provides a complete printout of the last *SRI* test the individual student has completed. The printout includes each passage and all four answer choices, with the student's answer choice and the correct answer choice both indicated. The source of each passage is also listed.

FOLLOW-UP

Review the printout of the test with the student, pointing out items the student answered incorrectly. Work through those items with students to help them understand why they came up with incorrect answers.

Student Roster

Student Roster

CLASS: 3rd PERIOD

School: The Lincoln School
Teacher: Sarah Greene
Grade: 5

Time Period: 09/01/04 – 02/02/05

STUDENT	GRADE	STUDENT ID	USERNAME	PASSWORD
Camarillo, Teri	5	99117	tcamarillo	sweater
Cho, Henry	5	69614	hcho	roast
Cooper, Maya	5	42237	mcooper	picnic
Ferguson, Jessica	5	20328	jferguson	leopard
Freeman, Charles	5	88947	cfreeman	wheel
Gainer, Jacquelyn	5	49997	jgainer	sponge
Gilmore, Nicholas	5	83775	ngilmore	lizard
Huang, Hsin-Yi	5	28697	hhuang	chair
Kim, Julie	5	90306	jkim	owl
Levin, Daniel	5	53512	dlevin	rhino
Lewis, Chequan	5	17312	clewis	dream
Mamdani, Aliyah	5	97972	amamdani	supercar
Molina, Robert	5	41743	rmolina	team
Morgan, Rebekah	5	93886	rmorgan	biblio
Morris, Timothy	5	33423	tmorris	gorp
Nelson, Michael	5	10036	mnelson	kittens
Richardson, Margaret	5	50339	mrichardson	prize
Robinson, Tiffany	5	54571	trobinson	elephant
Saunders, Renee	5	19486	rsaunders	pencil
Stedman, Mark	5	52010	mstedman	visit
TOTAL STUDENTS = 20				

Using This Report

Purpose: The Student Roster lists the students assigned to a selected group, class, or teacher. It includes each student's grade, ID, username, and password.

Follow-Up: Review the roster to track which students are enrolled in SRI.

Printed by: Sarah Greene

Page 1 of 1
Printed on: 2/2/2005

PURPOSE

The Student Roster lists the students assigned to a selected group, class, or teacher. It includes each student's grade, ID, username, and password.

FOLLOW-UP

Review the roster to track which students are enrolled in *SRI*.

Incomplete Test Alert

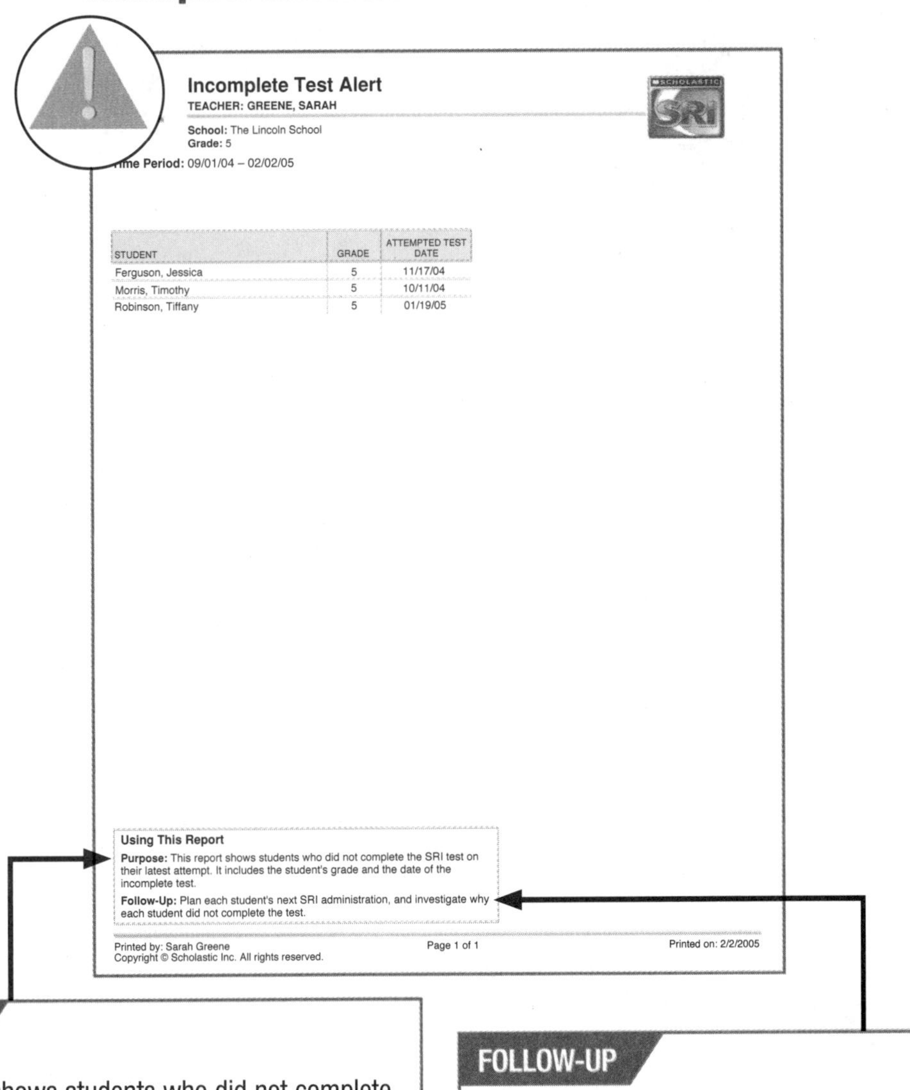

Incomplete Test Alert

TEACHER: GREENE, SARAH

School: The Lincoln School
Grade: 5
Time Period: 09/01/04 – 02/02/05

STUDENT	GRADE	ATTEMPTED TEST DATE
Ferguson, Jessica	5	11/17/04
Morris, Timothy	5	10/11/04
Robinson, Tiffany	5	01/19/05

Using This Report

Purpose: This report shows students who did not complete the SRI test on their latest attempt. It includes the student's grade and the date of the incomplete test.

Follow-Up: Plan each student's next SRI administration, and investigate why each student did not complete the test.

Printed by: Sarah Greene

Page 1 of 1
Printed on: 2/2/2005

PURPOSE

This report shows students who did not complete the *SRI* test on their latest attempt. It includes the Lexile measure of each student and the date of the incomplete test.

FOLLOW-UP

Plan each student's next *SRI* administration, and investigate why each student did not complete the test.

Parent Report I

STUDENT: COOPER, MAYA

School: The Lincoln School
Teacher: Sarah Greene
Grade: 5
Class: 3rd Period
Group: Bears

November 15, 2004

Dear Parent or Caregiver,

This year Maya will be completing the *Scholastic Reading Inventory* (SRI), a classroom-based assessment designed to evaluate students' reading ability, monitor student reading progress, and match students to books at their reading levels.

The SRI test involves reading a series of short passages taken from fiction and nonfiction books and articles. After each passage, the student is asked to complete a fill-in-the-blank sentence. The test is taken on a computer, and lasts about 20 minutes. Test results are reported using a readability measurement called the Lexile®. The Lexile score can be used to assess Maya's reading ability as well as to find books at an appropriate reading level.

Maya's SRI Results

Test Date	*Lexile® Test Results*
September 8, 2004	630

Grade 5 End-of-Year Target Range: 700–1000 Lexiles

There are a number of things that you can do at home to help support Maya's reading progress. Here are some suggestions:

- Set a goal with Maya of at least 20 minutes of daily reading.
- Help Maya find books that are at an appropriate reading level. Please contact me about how we can use the Lexile Framework to identify books at the appropriate reading ranges.
- Make connections between Maya's interests and books to read. For example, if Maya likes animals, try to locate books on animals, both fiction and nonfiction.
- Try to spend time every day with Maya looking through "nonbook" kinds of materials, such as pieces of mail, advertisements, and food labels, to demonstrate how important a part reading plays in daily life.
- Consider sharing with Maya the kinds of things you are reading. Tell Maya about interesting things you read in the newspaper, or about a magazine article that taught you something new.

Thank you for taking the time to help improve Maya's reading skills. If I can be of any assistance, or if you have any questions, please feel free to contact me.

Sincerely,

PURPOSE

Parent Report I, also available in Spanish, introduces *SRI* to parents or caregivers, summarizes the results of the student's first testing session, and offers several useful suggestions for how parents can help and encourage their child to build fundamental reading skills at home.

FOLLOW-UP

Send the report to the parent or caregiver. You may wish to contact parents personally to review the contents of the report.

Parent Report II

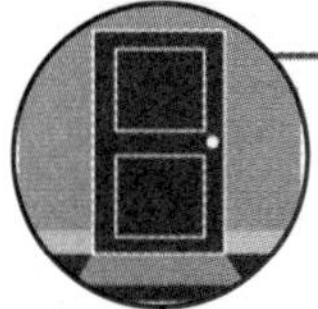

STUDENT: COOPER, MAYA

School: The Lincoln School
Teacher: Sarah Greene
Grade: 5
Class: 3rd Period
Group: Bears

February 2, 2005

Dear Parent or Caregiver,

Maya has just completed another Scholastic Reading Inventory (SRI) test, a classroom-based assessment designed to evaluate students' reading ability, monitor student reading progress, and match students to text. This letter is to inform you of Maya's latest results.

The results of Maya's SRI test are used in a number of ways. First, a student's score on the test is used to determine the student's reading ability compared to grade-level performance standards. These determinations can help tailor appropriate reading instructions based on the student's current abilities. The results of subsequent SRI tests are then used to monitor progress over time. Student results are also used to match students to texts at their reading level, which helps to make the student's reading experience rewarding, constructive, and enjoyable.

Maya's SRI Results

Test Date	*Lexile® Test Results*
February 1, 2005	650

Grade 5 End-of-Year Target Range: 700–1000 Lexiles®

Please continue to help support Maya's reading progress at home. Here are some further suggestions. Choose the ideas you think will work best for you and Maya:

- Set a goal with Maya of at least 20 minutes of daily reading. Try to set up a regular schedule, to provide some structure to Maya's reading efforts.
- Help Maya find books that are at an appropriate reading level. Please contact me about how we can use the Lexile Framework to identify books at the appropriate reading ranges.
- Continue to make connections between your child's interest and things Maya might like to read. For example, if Maya likes animals, try to locate books on animals, both fiction and nonfiction.
- Spend time every day with Maya looking through "nonbook" kinds of materials, such as pieces of mail, advertisements, and food labels, to demonstrate how important a part reading plays in daily life.
- Share with Maya the kinds of things you are reading. Tell Maya about interesting things you read in the newspaper, or about a magazine article that taught you something new.

Thank you for taking the time to help improve Maya's reading skills. If I can be of any assistance, or if you have any questions, please feel free to contact me.

Sincerely,

PURPOSE

Parent Report II, also available in Spanish, reintroduces *SRI* to parents or caregivers, provides them with an overview of their child's progress, and offers further useful suggestions for how parents can help and encourage their child to build fundamental reading skills at home.

FOLLOW-UP

Send the report to the parent or caregiver. You may wish to contact parents or caregivers personally to review the contents of the report.

Time Management Calendar

This Fall and Spring calendar provides tips for *SRI* test preparation and administration, as well as ideas for evaluation and teaching opportunities. These are optional tips and suggestions that you may adjust depending on your individual classroom needs.

FALL TERM	
Test Preparation and Administration	**Evaluation and Teaching Opportunities (posttest)**
• **Send parents a letter introducing them to *SRI*.** (See reproducibles 1–6.) • **Introduce students to *SRI*.** Emphasize that *SRI* will help them by providing an assessment of their reading abilities and by helping to match them with appropriate books that they will enjoy. • **Take a practice test with students.** Read several items aloud and model finding the correct answer. • **Practice test-taking strategies.** (See p. 134 for tips and instructional ideas.) • **Create a student-friendly test environment.** (See p. 132 for suggestions.) • **Administer the test.** If you do not have a computer available for every student, assign time slots for taking the test during the day and throughout the week.	• **Review *SRI* reports.** – Examine the **Reading Performance Report** to review individual test scores. You can evaluate student scores according to various measures: Lexile measure, Performance Standard, percentile rank, NCE, and Stanine. – Review the **Proficiency Report** to see how test scores are distributed within a class. – Use the **Intervention Grouping Report** to identify students who need extra help. Check for the **Incomplete Test Alert** for students who did not complete the test. • **Highlight student reading lists.** Encourage students to refer to their Recommended Reading Reports when making independent reading choices. • **Guide classroom instruction.** – Place students in reading groups according to their Lexile measures. With the Lexile measure in mind, select several books for students to read on the topics you are currently teaching. Ask each group to prepare a presentation on the book they read. – Adjust the Lexile measures of the books you choose according to whether you are reading aloud to the class or group, teaching specific skills, or scaffolding reading strategies. Review students' **Targeted Reading Report** and the Instructional Reading Chart on p. 188 when making your choices. • **Strengthen your library.** Share the **Recommending Reading Reports** with librarians, encouraging them to organize targeted collections for students and to help students select appropriately leveled books. • **Involve parents.** Print and send **Parent Report I** to share test results with parents or caregivers.

Time Management Calendar *continued*

Please note that *SRI* can be administered more than twice a year, and at any time during the year that you choose.

<table>
<tr><th colspan="2">SPRING TERM</th></tr>
<tr><th>Test Preparation and Administration</th><th>Evaluation and Teaching Opportunities (posttest)</th></tr>
<tr><td>

• **Inform students and parents about the test date.**
• **Adjust settings to accommodate student needs.** Review the *SRI* test settings and decide if a changed setting, such as continuing to take a practice test or not viewing the Lexile measure after the test, is appropriate for different students.
• **Administer the test.** Make sure that every student has a chance to take the test. Assign time slots for taking the test, if necessary.
</td><td>

• **Review *SRI* reports.**
– Examine the **Growth Report** to assess student progress from fall to spring.
– Print the **Reading Performance Report** to review individual test scores.
– Review the **Proficiency Report** to see how test scores are distributed within a class.
– Review the **Student Action Report** for individualized reading plans and teaching tips for students based on their test results.
• **Confer with students.**
– Print the **Student Test Printout** to evaluate students' incorrect answers and to gain an understanding of students' problem areas. As you review incorrect answers, model reading strategies and have students apply them as you work through individual items.
– Review students' **Recommended Reading Reports** and discuss the books they've read.
• **Guide classroom instruction.**
– Use the Book Expert to select books in your students' Lexile reading ranges that correspond to the cross-curricular units you are studying.
– For students with scores below grade level, focus on skill instruction using books that are up to 250 Lexiles below their level (a level at which they read with 90% comprehension).
• **Confer with administrators.**
Print the **Proficiency Report, Growth Report,** and **Reading Performance Report** to show administrators the range of Lexiles in your class and how students have progressed over time.
• **Involve parents.**
– Send **Parent Report II** home to share student test results.
– Send home a summer **Recommended Reading Report** to encourage reading when school is out.
</td></tr>
</table>

Using Lexile Measures in a Comprehensive Reading Program

A comprehensive reading program includes instructional and independent reading. Instructional reading provides students with an opportunity to build skills. Independent reading is necessary for students to grow as readers, practice reading skills, and develop a love of reading.

The charts on the following pages indicate how texts with different Lexile reading ranges can be used in a reading environment that consists of instructional and independent reading. While students are targeted at their Lexile measures, they can also read books within a Lexile reading range; that is, a number of Lexiles above and below their measures. The charts on the next pages indicate the ranges that can be used for different independent and instructional reading purposes. Think of a sliding scale as you consider what level of material is appropriate for students in different reading contexts. When students read down from their Lexile measure (as much as 250 Lexiles), they encounter text that is targeted to their independent level and becomes increasingly easy for them to read. When students read up from their Lexile measure (as much as 250 Lexiles), they encounter text that increases in challenge and should be targeted for instructional purposes. Within the instructional and independent reading zones, books may be used for a variety of purposes as illustrated in the charts.

INDEPENDENT READING

LEXILE READING RANGE	PURPOSE	RECOMMENDED CONTEXT	STUDENT EXPERIENCE
50 Lexiles above to 100 Lexiles below the student's Lexile measure	• Build comprehension skills and acquire new vocabulary while reading independently.	• This is optimal when the student has selected the book and is interested in the topic. • Use this range of text with confident readers.	**Challenging** • Student demonstrates a sufficient control of vocabulary and syntax to get over hurdles that he or she encounters, with relative ease. • An appropriate level of challenge—neither frustration nor boredom will occur.
100 to 250 Lexiles below the student's Lexile measure	• Read to build fluency and confidence.	• Motivate readers to engage in reading for pleasure, not skill building. • Text at this range is optimal for reluctant and remedial readers.	**Fluent** • Reader experiences automaticity with text. Both the vocabulary and syntax the reader encounters are easy.
50 Lexiles and above the student's Lexile measure	• Read for challenge.	• Only use text at this level if the student has prior knowledge or a deep interest or confidence in the subject of the book.	**Frustrating** • This is the student's frustration zone, except in cases where the student has a deep interest or confidence in the subject of the book.

INSTRUCTIONAL READING

LEXILE READING RANGE	PURPOSE	RECOMMENDED CONTEXT	STUDENT EXPERIENCE
50 to 250 Lexiles above the student's Lexile measure	• Skill instruction that exposes student to new vocabulary, difficult syntax, and challenging literary features. • Challenge student to grow as a reader, building new vocabulary and skills.	• Use text at this level when providing one-on-one support to the student, in small-group instruction, or during read aloud.	**Challenging** • Student will not be able to read the text independently, but with the right amount of support, the student will build skills.
50 Lexiles above to 100 Lexiles below the student's Lexile measure	• Skill instruction that focuses on teaching new or difficult skills and subjects.	• Use text at this level when asking students to read independently as you instruct. One-on-one support is not needed.	**On Level** • Student will read with confidence and control, as well as with the appropriate level of challenge to grow as a reader.
100 to 250 Lexiles below the student's Lexile measure	• Skill instruction for remedial or reluctant readers.	• Use text at this level with reluctant or remedial students and to help students master a challenging subject or skill.	**Easy** • Student will experience fluency.

Using Lexile Measures in Your Classroom

Within any one classroom, there will be a range of readers and a range of reading materials. For example, within a fifth-grade classroom, students may be reading from the third-grade to eighth-grade level. Therefore, in that fifth-grade classroom, there need to be reading materials representing the third- to eighth-grade levels. As long as students are reading materials at their Lexile measure or within their Lexile range, they will comprehend what they read and therefore will be able to practice the same skills as those reading above or below them.

Once you know the Lexile measures of your students, there are a number of ways you can use that knowledge to maximize reading instruction. Here are some tips to consider for successfully teaching in a classroom with a range of Lexile measures.

Whole Class Reading

- Consult the Proficiency Report, Reading Performance Report, or Targeted Reading Report (see pp. 166, 162, 172) to determine an appropriate level at which to select a book for whole class reading. Make sure to select a book that is no more than 250 Lexiles above the lowest measure in your class. Provide extra instructional support to students who are reading text that is more than 50 Lexiles above their measure.
- Use the Book Expert (see p. 119) to select books that represent the different Lexile measures in your class and that connect to the themes and topics you are studying, as well as the core reading programs you are using. For example, if you are studying the Civil War, select five different books on that topic that correspond to the different Lexile measures in your class.
- Select books at a higher Lexile measure if you are reading books aloud to the whole class or are using audiobooks. Students listen at a higher comprehension rate than that at which they read. Discuss the books and model reading strategies, such as summarizing text to personal experience and knowledge.

Using Lexile Measures in Your Classroom

Whole Class Reading *continued*

- Model reading strategies regularly, including making inferences, drawing conclusions, summarizing and visualizing text, identifying the main idea, and asking questions while reading, to make sure that all students receive the support that they need.
- Provide a variety of assignments for students to respond to text in different ways through writing, drawing, speaking, acting, etc.

Group Reading

- Assemble students into small reading groups according to their Lexile measures and interests. Ask each group to select common books on their Recommended Reading Reports to read and discuss. Assign group projects that provide responses to the books that have been read.
- Provide a sequenced approach when selecting reading materials for reading groups that are within each group's Lexile reading range. (Consult the Targeted Reading Report to identify the group's Lexile reading range.) Start with easier texts at the beginning of the year and then move to more challenging texts.

Independent Reading

- Select books that match each student's current reading level. Include books that are within the student's fluent (100–250 Lexiles below level) and challenging (100 Lexiles below to 50 Lexiles above level) ranges. Allow students to select their own books as well.
- Encourage students to read books on their Recommended Reading Reports.
- Encourage students to read above their Lexile measures when the book is on a topic in which they are very interested. Their familiarity with the topic, as well as their background and vocabulary knowledge, allow them to read at a more challenging level.
- Guide students who are reading about an unfamiliar or difficult topic to choose books at the lower end of, or below, their Lexile range. Reading lower-level books can help them gain the necessary background information to continue reading and understanding the material.

Instructional Reading

- When instructing students one-on-one or in small groups, choose books with a Lexile measure that is higher than the student's current measure (up to 250 Lexiles above). With the proper guidance, scaffolding, and support, the reader is capable of comprehending more challenging materials.
- When using guided reading, select texts that students can read independently—100 Lexiles below to 50 Lexiles above their Lexile measures.
- When teaching a new and challenging subject, or working with students on a difficult reading skill, select books that are on or below the students' Lexile measures so that their comprehension level is high.

Using Lexile Measures in Your Classroom to Motivate Readers

Reading books on appropriate levels and about interesting topics is an excellent way to motivate students to read more; and by reading more, students can ultimately achieve more. Use Lexile measures and students' Recommended Reading Reports to generate excitement about reading in your classroom.

- Choose high-interest books on a lower Lexile measure (up to 250 Lexiles below measure) to motivate readers to succeed.
- Use the Book Expert (p. 119) to find books on topics of interest to students. Consult their Recommended Reading Reports (generated according to their interests and Lexile measures), to find similar types of books to recommend.
- Set personal goals with students to read a set number of books within their Lexile reading ranges. (See My Personal Goal, Reproducible 14.) Reward students if they reach their goals by posting their names and goals on the bulletin board, or by any other means you choose.
- Encourage students to select their own books within their Lexile reading ranges on topics that interest them.
- Have students recommend their favorite books by completing the Book Recommendation Reproducibles 16–17.
- Group students (in small groups) and assign them books according to their Lexile measures so that they can read and discuss books that are on their level in a comfortable and small environment. Encourage each student to add to the discussion.
- Use the Book Expert to assign different books (reflecting your class's Lexile measures) on the same topic, so that all students can successfully understand the topic or theme you are studying.
- Chart students' reading growth on the Lexile Framework for Reading Map (Reproducible 18) and let them see their progress.

- Give students extra credit if they write book reviews on books from their Recommended Reading Reports.
- Create a book corner in your classroom or library media center to highlight books that are on students' Recommended Reading Reports.
- Provide awards for students who read every book on their Recommended Reading Reports.
- Send the Recommended Reading Reports home to encourage families to help children select appropriate reading material.
- Ask students to respond to books on their Recommended Reading Reports, both orally and in writing. For ideas, see p. 194.

Using Lexile Measures in Your Classroom to Motivate Readers *continued*

Respond to Books on Reading Lists

- Compare and contrast genres, themes, characters, and settings.
- Write alternate endings to a book.
- Analyze an author's style and point of view and how they affect the text.
- Hold a debate with one side of the class agreeing with the author's or main character's point of view and the other side opposing it.
- Act out a chapter in a book, as a class.
- Draw a new cover for a book, based on the student's interpretation of the book.
- Write book reviews, using details from the books to support the ideas and opinions stated.
- Write newspaper articles about topics explored in nonfiction books. Compile all the articles into a class newspaper.
- Pretend to interview a historic figure or leader read about in a biography, autobiography, or nonfiction book. Write questions and then answer them, pretending to be that person.
- Give an oral book review to the class.
- Create a book advertisement—it can have pictures, text, or can be a radio or video ad.
- Create a "story quilt" as a class, with each person illustrating a picture of his/her favorite scene from the book.

SRI Reproducibles

Use the reproducibles that follow to help foster the school-to-home relationship, to help you and your students keep track of their reading progress, and to help students respond to what they read in a variety of ways.

Reproducible 1: Introductory Letter to Parents (English)

Reproducible 2: Introductory Letter to Parents (Spanish)

Reproducible 3: Introductory Letter to Parents (Hmong)

Reproducible 4: Introductory Letter to Parents (Traditional Chinese)

Reproducible 5: Introductory Letter to Parents (Vietnamese)

Reproducible 6: Introductory Letter to Parents (Haitian Creole)

Reproducible 7: Follow-Up Letter to Parents (English)

Reproducible 8: Follow-Up Letter to Parents (Spanish)

Reproducible 9: Follow-Up Letter to Parents (Hmong)

Reproducible 10: Follow-Up Letter to Parents (Traditional Chinese)

Reproducible 11: Follow-Up Letter to Parents (Vietnamese)

Reproducible 12: Follow-Up Letter to Parents (Haitian Creole)

Reproducible 13: Conference Record

Reproducible 14: My Personal Goal

Reproducible 15: Reading Log

Reproducible 16: Book Recommendation (Grades K–4)

Reproducible 17: Book Recommendation (Grades 5 and up)

Reproducible 18: Lexile Framework for Reading Map

Dear Parent or Caregiver:

This year your child will be completing the *Scholastic Reading Inventory™ (SRI)*, a classroom-based reading test. *SRI* is designed to evaluate students' reading abilities, monitor student reading progress, set goals for reading growth, and match students to books at appropriate reading levels.

In *SRI*, the student reads a series of short passages taken from fiction and nonfiction books and articles. After each passage, the student completes a fill-in-the-blank sentence. The test is taken on a computer, and lasts about 20 minutes. Test results are reported using a readability measurement called the Lexile®. Think of the Lexile score as you would the reading from an outdoor thermometer. Just as you can use the temperature on a thermometer to decide what kind of jacket to wear, a Lexile score can be used to decide how difficult a book to read!

After each *SRI* administration during the year, I will send home a letter with your child's results. In addition, because the Lexile system is also used to assign reading measurements to books, your child will receive a personalized book list that reflects your child's Lexile score and reading interests. Encourage your child to read books on that list and discuss them with you. If you'd like, I can recommend additional books within your child's Lexile reading range.

Please make sure that your child comes to school ready to take the test on ______________. Remind your child that *SRI* is an assessment that will help your child grow as a reader and find pleasure in reading.

Feel free to contact me with any questions. Thank you for your support.

Sincerely,

Estimado padre o tutor:

Este año su hijo completará el *Scholastic Reading Inventory™ (SRI)*, una prueba de lectura que se realiza en el salón de clases. La prueba *SRI* está diseñada para evaluar las destrezas de lectura de los estudiantes, controlar los avances en esta área, establecer los objetivos para el crecimiento en esta disciplina y determinar los libros apropiados para cada estudiante según los niveles de lectura.

En *SRI,* el estudiante lee una serie de pasajes cortos de libros o artículos de ficción y no ficción. Luego, debe completar una oración llenando los espacios en blanco. La prueba se realiza en computadora y dura aproximadamente 20 minutos. Los resultados se informan a través de una medición de legibilidad llamada Lexile®. Podemos comparar la calificación de Lexile con la lectura de un termómetro exterior. De la misma manera que usted utiliza la temperatura que le marca el termómetro para decidir qué tipo de abrigo usar, la calificación de Lexile pude usarse para decidir el grado de dificultad de un libro.

Durante el año después de cada *SRI*, le enviaré una nota con los resultados obtenidos por su hijo. Dado que el sistema Lexile también puede usarse para asignar niveles de dificultad de lectura a los libros, su hijo también recibirá una lista personalizada de libros adecuados a sus intereses de lectura y a la calificación de Lexile que él obtenga. Anime a su hijo para que lea los libros que están en esa lista y coméntelos con él. Si lo desea, puedo recomendarle libros adicionales dentro del rango de lectura Lexile de su hijo.

Asegúrese de que su hijo asista a la escuela preparado para tomar la prueba el día ________________. Recuérdele que el *SRI* es una evaluación que le ayudará a crecer como lector y a descubrir el placer de la lectura.

Si tiene alguna pregunta, no dude en comunicarse conmigo. Le agradezco por brindar su apoyo a esta actividad.

Atentamente,

Nyob Zoo Tsoom Niamtxiv lossis tus Saib Xyuas:

Xyoo nov nej tus menyuam yuav tau ntxiv tswvyim rau Zaj kev Txheeb kev Nyeem Ntawv *Scholastic Reading Inventory™ (SRI),* ib zaj xeem kev nyeem ntawv hauv chav kawm. *SRI* raug tsim los ntsuas menyuam kawmntawv cov peevxwm, soj ntsuam kev vammeej ntawm lawv txoj kev nyeem ntawv, teeb homphiaj rau kev vamhuam ntawm kev nyeem ntawv, thiab khi menyuam kawmntawv rau cov phau ntawv kawm raws qib nyeem ntawv.

Hauv *SRI,* tus menyuam nyeem ib cov zaj lus raws seem kws muab los ntawm cov phau ntawv thiab phau xovxwm teev tej yam muaj tiag thiab tej yam kwvyees. Tomqab nyeem tej zaj lus tas, tus menyuam yuav ntxiv ib kab lus rau cov kab dawb. Zaj ntawv xeem muaj ua hauv ib lub kooputaw, thiab siv sijhawm li 20 feeb. Cov lus teb tshwmsim thaum siv ib hom twj ntsuas kev nyeem ntawv hu ua Lexile®. Xav txog hom twj ntsuas nov tibyam li thaum nej nyeem ib tus thermometer los xaiv saib yuav hnav lub tsho tiv no twg mus nraum zoov, ib hom twj ntsuas cov lus teb Lexile muab tau los siv teev tias ib phau ntawv nyeem nyuaj npaum licas!

Tomqab siv txhua zaj *SRI* tiav hauv xyoo ntawd, kuv yuav xa ib daim ntawv los tom nej tsev nrog nej tus menyuam cov lus teb. Ntxiv ntawd, vim hom txheejtxheem ntsuas Lexile siv tau los ntsuas kev nyeem cov phau ntawv, nej tus menyuam yuav tau txais ib daim ntawv rau nws tus kheej teev cov phau ntawv nyeem raws nws cov lus teb ntsuas tau raws hom twj ntsuas Lexile thiab hom txuj nws nyiam tsum. Txhawb nej tus menyuam nyeem cov phau ntawv raws daim ntawv teev ntawd thiab tham nrog nws txog cov phau ntawv ntawd. Yog nej nyiam tsum, kuv yuav muab tau tswvyim txog lwm phau ntawv raws nej tus menyuam qib nyeem ntawv tuaj ntxiv thiab.

Thov nej pab kom nej tus menyuam npaj txhij tuaj xeem tom tsev kawm ntawv rau hnub tim __________________. Hais kom nej tus menyuam nco ntsoov tias SRI yog ib hom xeem luj ntsuas uas yuav pab nthuav kom nws loj hlob mus ua ib tus kws nyeem ntawv thiab ntsib kev zoo siab txog kev nyeem ntawv.

Thov txhob ua siab deb yog nej muaj lus nug dabtsi. Ua tsuag ntau rau nej txoj kev txhawb nqa.

Ua tsaug ntau ntau,

親愛的家長或監護人：

您的子女將在今年參加以課堂為基礎的*Scholastic Reading Inventory™ (SRI)*閱讀測驗。*SRI*的設計旨在評估學生的閱讀能力，監督學生的閱讀進度，設定閱讀成長的目標，並且為學生介紹適當閱讀程度的書籍。

學生在接受*SRI*測驗時，必須閱讀一連串取自小說類和非小說類的書籍和文章的短文。學生必須在讀完每一段短文之後填空造句。我們利用電腦來進行測驗，測驗時間大約是20分鐘。測驗成績將由一種稱為Lexile®的閱讀能力衡量標準來評分。請將Lexile分數想像為室外溫度計上的讀數。正如我們可以察看溫度計上的溫度來判斷要穿厚薄夾克一樣，Lexile分數可用來決定一本書的閱讀難度高低！

在這一年中，每一次舉行*SRI*測驗之後，我都會將您孩子的測驗成績單寄給您。此外，由於Lexile系統也被用來指定書本的閱讀衡量標準，因此您的孩子將會收到一份反映出他們Lexile分數和閱讀興趣的個人專用書單。請鼓勵您的孩子閱讀書單上的書，並與您一起討論書中的內容。我也可以在您的要求下推薦其他適合您孩子Lexile閱讀程度的書。

請務必讓您的孩子在 ______________ 日到校準備接受測驗。提醒您的孩子*SRI*是一種評估工具，可以幫助他們在成長的過程中養成喜歡讀書的習慣。

如果您有任何疑問，歡迎隨時與我聯絡。謝謝您的支持和協助。

謹致

Kính Gởi Quý Phụ Huynh hay Người Giám Hộ:

Năm nay con quý vị sẽ làm bài thi *Scholastic ReadingInventory™(SRI)*, là một bài kiểm tra khả năng đọc làm tại lớp học. Bài thi SRI nhằm mục đích đánh giá khả năng đọc hiểu của học sinh cũng như theo dõi sự tiến bộ, xác định các mục tiêu trau dồi kỹ năng đọc, và giúp học sinh chọn sách đọc có trình độ ngôn ngữ phù hợp.

Khi làm bài thi *SRI*, học sinh sẽ đọc một loạt những đoạn văn ngắn (truyện hư cấu cũng như truyện có thật) được trích từ sách báo. Sau khi đọc mỗi đoạn văn, học sinh phải điền vào chỗ trống để hoàn tất một câu. Bài thi được làm trên máy tính và kéo dài khoảng 20 phút. Kết quả thi được báo dưới dạng một điểm số đánh giá khả năng đọc được gọi là điểm Lexile®. Quý vị có thể coi điểm Lexile này là một số đo chẳng khác gì số đo nhiệt độ trên một nhiệt kế để ngoài trời — quý vị có thể xem số đo nhiệt độ để biết mình nên mang áo ấm như thế nào, cũng như vậy, quý vị có thể xem điểm Lexile của con mình để biết cháu nên đọc sách có trình độ ngôn ngữ như thế nào!

Sau kỳ thi *SRI* hằng năm, tôi sẽ gởi thư về cho quý vị để báo kết quả. Không những thế, vì hệ thống Lexile cũng được sử dụng để đánh giá trình độ ngôn ngữ của nhiều sách khác nhau, nên chúng tôi cũng có thể cung cấp cho con quý vị một danh sách được soạn riêng cho cháu liệt kê tên của những sách truyện phù hợp với trình độ Lexile cũng như những chủ đề mà cháu ưa thích. Quý vị hãy khuyến khích con mình đọc các sách được đề nghị rồi thảo luận với quý vị sau khi đọc xong. Nếu quý vị muốn, tôi có thể đề nghị thêm những sách hay khác phù hợp với trình độ Lexile của cháu.

Xin quý vị hãy bảo đảm rằng con mình được chuẩn bị đầy đủ để làm bài thi vào ngày ______________. Nhắc cháu nhớ rằng bài thi *SRI* đánh giá trình độ đọc nhằm mục đích giúp cho cháu phát triển khả năng đọc và càng ngày càng thấy thích thú đọc sách hơn.

Nếu có thắc mắc xin đừng ngần ngại liên lạc với tôi. Xin cám ơn sự hỗ trợ của quý vị.

Chân Thành Cảm Tạ,

Chè paran oswa gadyen :

Ane sa a pitit ou an pral fini *Scholastic Reading Inventory™ (SRI),* yon egzamen sou lekti nan klas la. *SRI* fèt yon fason pou l evalye aptitid elèv yo nan lekti, siveye pwogrè elèv la fè nan lekti, fikse objektif pou kwasans nan lekti, epi matche elèv yo ak nivo lekti ki apwopriye.

Nan *SRI,* elèv la li yon seri ti pasaj ki soti nan liv ak atik imajinè ak non imajinè. Aprè chak pasaj, elèv la ranpli espas vid nan yon fraz. Elèv la pran egzamen an sou yon òdinatè, epi li dire apeprè 20 minit. Yo rapòte rezilta egzamen yo avèk yon endis liziblite ki rele Lexile®. Panse ak nòt Lexile la kòm si ou ta va li yon tèmomèt eksteryè. Menm jan ou ka sèvi ak tanperati ki nan yon tèmomèt pou deside ki kalite chanday pou mete, ou ka sèvi ak yon nòt Lexile pou deside nivo difikilte yon liv ou ka li !

Aprè administrasyon chak *SRI* pandan ane a, mwen pral voye yon lèt lakay ou ak rezilta pitit ou an. Anplis de sa, paske yo itilize sistèm Lexile la tou pou asiyen liv yo nivo lekti yo, pitit ou an pral resevwa yon lis liv pèsonalize ki reflete nòt Lexile pitit ou an ansanm ak liv li enterese li. Ankouraje pitit ou an li liv ki sou lis sa a epi pou l diskite yo avèk ou. Si w ta renmen sa, mwen ka rekòmande liv siplemantè ki nan nivo lekti Lexile pitit ou an.

Tanpri asire w pitit ou an vini lekòl tou pare pou l fè egzamen an le ________________. Raple pitit ou an *SRI* se yon evalyasyon ki pral ede li grandi kòm yon lektè epi ki pral fè l pran plezi nan fè lekti.

Pa ezite kontakte m si w gen nenpòt kesyon. Mèsi pou sipò w.

Sensèman,

Dear Parent or Caregiver:

This year your child is completing the *Scholastic Reading Inventory*™ *(SRI)*, a classroom-based reading test. *SRI* is designed to evaluate students' reading abilities, monitor student reading progress, set goals for reading growth, and match students to books at appropriate reading levels.

In *SRI*, the student reads a series of short passages taken from fiction and nonfiction books and articles. After each passage, the student completes a fill-in-the-blank sentence. The test is taken on a computer, and lasts about 20 minutes. Test results are reported using a readability measurement called the Lexile®. Think of the Lexile score as you would the reading from an outdoor thermometer. Just as you can use the temperature on a thermometer to decide what kind of jacket to wear, a Lexile score can be used to decide how difficult a book to read!

SRI Results:

Test Date:
Test Results:
Comments:

There are a number of ways you can help your child's reading progress at home. Here are some suggestions:

- Set a goal for your child of at least 20 minutes of reading per day.
- Because the Lexile system is also used to assign reading measurements to books, you can use your child's Lexile score to find books that are at an appropriate reading level. Your child received a personalized book list that reflects his or her current Lexile score and reading interests. Encourage your child to read the books on that list and discuss them with you.
- Share with your child the kinds of things *you* are reading. Tell about interesting things you read in the newspaper, or about a magazine article that taught you something new.

Thank you for taking the time to help improve your child's reading skills. If you have any questions, please feel free to contact me.

Sincerely,

Estimado padre o tutor:

Este año su hijo completará el *Scholastic Reading Inventory*™ *(SRI)*, una prueba de lectura que se realiza en el salón de clases. La prueba *SRI* está diseñada para evaluar las destrezas de lectura de los estudiantes, controlar los avances en esta área, establecer los objetivos para el crecimiento en esta disciplina y determinar los libros apropiados para cada estudiante según los niveles de lectura.

En *SRI,* el estudiante lee una serie de pasajes cortos de libros o artículos de ficción y no ficción. Luego, debe completar una oración llenando los espacios en blanco. La prueba se realiza en computadora y dura aproximadamente 20 minutos. Los resultados se informan a través de una medición de legibilidad llamada Lexile®. Podemos comparar la calificación de Lexile con la lectura de un termómetro exterior. De la misma manera que usted utiliza la temperatura que le marca el termómetro para decidir qué tipo de abrigo usar, la calificación de Lexile puede usarse para decidir el grado de dificultad de un libro.

Resultados de *SRI*:

Fecha de la prueba:
Resultados de la prueba:
Comentarios:

Existen diferentes formas en las que usted puede ayudar en casa a su hijo para que progrese en la lectura. Éstas son algunas sugerencias:

- Establezca un objetivo mínimo para su hijo de 20 minutos de lectura diaria.

- Dado que el sistema Lexile también puede usarse para asignar niveles de dificultad de lectura a los libros, usted puede usar la calificación de Lexile de su hijo para buscar libros que estén acordes al nivel de lectura obtenido. Su hijo recibió una lista personalizada de libros adecuados a sus intereses de lectura y a la calificación de Lexile que obtuvo. Anime a su hijo para que lea los libros que están en esa lista y coméntelos con él.

- Comparta con su hijo los distintos tipos de lectura que *usted* lee. Coméntele artículos interesantes que haya leído en el periódico o en una revista y que le hayan enseñado algo nuevo.

Le agradezco por el tiempo que dedica a mejorar las destrezas de lectura de su hijo. Si tiene preguntas, no dude en comunicarse conmigo.

Atentamente,

Nyob Zoo Tsoom Niamtxiv lossis tus Saib Xyuas:

Xyoo nov nej tus menyuam yuav tau ntxiv tswvyim rau Zaj kev Txheeb kev Nyeem Ntawv *Scholastic Reading Inventory™ (SRI),* ib zaj xeem kev nyeem ntawv hauv chav kawm. *SRI* raug tsim los ntsuas menyuam kawmntawv cov peevxwm, soj ntsuam kev vammeej ntawm lawv txoj kev nyeem ntawv, teeb homphiaj rau kev vamhuam ntawm kev nyeem ntawv, thiab khi menyuam kawmntawv rau cov phau ntawv kawm raws qib nyeem ntawv.

Hauv *SRI,* tus menyuam nyeem ib cov zaj lus raws seem kws muab los ntawm cov phau ntawv thiab phau xovxwm teev tej yam muaj tiag thiab tej yam kwvyees. Tomqab nyeem tej zaj lus tas, tus menyuam yuav ntxiv ib kab lus rau cov kab dawb. Zaj ntawv xeem muaj ua hauv ib lub kooputaw, thiab siv sijhawm li 20 feeb. Cov lus teb tshwmsim thaum siv ib hom twj ntsuas kev nyeem ntawv hu ua Lexile®. Xav txog hom twj ntsuas nov tibyam li thaum nej nyeem ib tus thermometer los xaiv saib yuav hnav lub tsho tiv no twg mus nraum zoov, ib hom twj ntsuas cov lus teb Lexile muab tau los siv teev tias ib phau ntawv nyeem nyuaj npaum licas!

Cov Lus Teb *SRI*:

Hnub Tuaj Xeem:
Cov Lus Teb Tawm:
Zaj Lus Ntxiv:

Muaj ntau txoj kev rau nej los pab nej tus menyuam kev nyeem ntawv kom vamhuam nyob tom tsev. Nov yog ib cov tswvyim pab:

- Teeb ib lub homphiaj rau nej tus menyuam los nyeem ntawv tsawg kawg nkaus yog 20 feeb hauv txhua txhua hnub..

- Vim hom txheejtxheem ntsuas Lexile siv tau los ntsuas kev nyeem cov phau ntawv, nej siv tau nej tus menyuam cov lus teb tawm raws kev ntsuas Lexile los nrhiav cov phau ntawv uas tsim nyog raws nws qib nyeem ntawv. Nej tus menyuam yuav tau txais ib daim ntawv rau nws tus kheej teev cov phau ntawv nyeem raws nws cov lus teb ntsuas tau raws hom twj ntsuas Lexile thiab hom txuj nws nyiam tsum. Txhawb nej tus menyuam nyeem cov phau ntawv raws daim ntawv teev ntawd thiab tham nrog nws txog cov phau ntawv ntawd.

- Muab tham nrog nej tus menyuam tej yam uas *nej* tabtom nyeem. Tham txog tej yam rub siab uas nej tau nyeem hauv tsab ntawv xovxwm, lossis tham txog ib zaj lus hauv ib phau xovxwm uas tau qhia tej yam tshiab rau nej.

Ua tsaug ntau ntau tias nej yuav siv sijhawm los pab kom nej tus menyuam cov txuj nyeem ntawv zoo tshaj qub. Thov txhob ua siab deb yog nej muaj lus nug dabtsi.

Ua tsaug ntau ntau,

親愛的家長或監護人:

您的子女將在今年參加以課堂為基礎的*Scholastic Reading Inventory™ (SRI)*閱讀測驗。*SRI*的設計旨在評估學生的閱讀能力，監督學生的閱讀進度，設定閱讀成長的目標，並且為學生介紹適當閱讀程度的書籍。

學生在接受*SRI*測驗時，必須閱讀一連串取自小說類和非小說類的書籍和文章的短文。學生必須在讀完每一段短文之後填空造句。我們利用電腦來進行測驗，測驗時間大約是20分鐘。測驗成績將由一種稱為Lexile®的閱讀能力衡量標準來評分。請將Lexile分數想像為室外溫度計上的讀數。正如我們可以察看溫度計上的溫度來判斷要穿厚薄夾克一樣，Lexile分數可用來決定一本書的閱讀難度高低！

*SRI*測驗成績:

測驗日期:
測驗成績:
評語:

您有很多方法可以在家中幫助您的孩子改善閱讀進度。請參考下列建議:

• 為您的孩子設定每天至少閱讀20分鐘的目標。

• 因為Lexile系統也可用來指定書本的閱讀衡量標準，因此您可以運用孩子的Lexile分數來找出適合孩子閱讀程度的書本。您的孩子收到了一份個人專用書單，其中反映出他們目前的Lexile分數和閱讀興趣。請鼓勵您的孩子閱讀書單上的書，並與您一起討論書中的內容。

• 與您的孩子一起分享*您自己*閱讀的書本內容。談一談您從報紙上讀到的一些有趣的事物，或是雜誌上的一篇文章教導了您哪些新知。

謝謝您抽空協助您的孩子增進閱讀能力。如果您有任何疑問，歡迎隨時與我聯絡。

謹致

Kính Gởi Quý Phụ Huynh hay Người Giám Hộ:

Năm nay con quý vị sẽ làm bài thi *Scholastic Reading Inventory™ (SRI)*, là một bài kiểm tra khả năng đọc làm tại lớp học. Bài thi *SRI* nhằm mục đích đánh giá khả năng đọc hiểu của học sinh cũng như theo dõi sự tiến bộ, xác định các mục tiêu trau dồi kỹ năng đọc, và giúp học sinh chọn sách đọc có trình độ ngôn ngữ phù hợp.

Khi làm bài thi *SRI*, học sinh sẽ đọc một loạt những đoạn văn ngắn (truyện hư cấu cũng như truyện có thật) được trích từ sách báo. Sau khi đọc mỗi đoạn văn, học sinh phải điền vào chỗ trống để hoàn tất một câu. Bài thi được làm trên máy tính và kéo dài khoảng 20 phút. Kết quả thi được báo dưới dạng một điểm số đánh giá khả năng đọc được gọi là điểm Lexile®. Quý vị có thể coi điểm Lexile này là một số đo chẳng khác gì số đo nhiệt độ trên một nhiệt kế để ngoài trời — quý vị có thể xem số đo nhiệt độ để biết mình nên mang áo ấm như thế nào, cũng như vậy, quý vị có thể xem điểm Lexile của con mình để biết cháu nên đọc sách có trình độ ngôn ngữ như thế nào!

Kết quả thi *SRI*:

Ngày Thi:
Kết Quả Thi:
Nhận Xét:

Có một số cách để giúp con quý vị trau dồi kỹ năng đọc ở nhà. Sau đây là một số đề nghị:

- Đặt mục tiêu cho con quý vị là phải đọc ít nhất 20 phút mỗi ngày.

- Vì hệ thống Lexile cũng được sử dụng để đánh giá trình độ ngôn ngữ của nhiều sách khác nhau, nên quý vị có thể căn cứ vào số điểm Lexile của cháu để tìm những cuốn sách có trình độ ngôn ngữ phù hợp. Con quý vị đã nhận một danh sách được soạn riêng cho cháu liệt kê tên của những sách truyện phù hợp với trình độ Lexile cũng như những chủ đề mà cháu ưa thích. Quý vị hãy khuyến khích con mình đọc các sách được đề nghị rồi thảo luận với quý vị sau khi đọc xong.

- Tâm sự với con quý vị về những sách báo chính quý vị đang đọc. Kể cháu nghe về những thông tin thú vị mà quý vị đã đọc trên báo, hoặc về một bài viết trên tạp chí đã cho quý vị biết một điều gì mới.

Xin cám ơn quý vị đã dành thời giờ để giúp con quý vị trau dồi khả năng đọc. Nếu có bắt cứ thắc mắc gì, xin đừng ngần ngại liên lạc với tôi.

Chân Thành Cảm Tạ,

Chè paran oswa gadyen :

Ane sa a pitit ou an ap fini *Scholastic Reading Inventory™ (SRI),* yon egzamen sou lekti nan klas la. *SRI™* fèt yon fason pou l evalye aptitid elèv yo nan lekti, siveye pwogrè elèv la fè nan lekti, fikse objektif pou kwasans nan lekti, epi matche elèv yo ak nivo lekti ki apwopriye.

Nan *SRI,* elèv la li yon seri ti pasaj ki soti nan liv ak atik imajinè ak non imajinè. Aprè chak pasaj, elèv la ranpli espas vid nan yon fraz. Elèv la pran egzamen an sou yon òdinatè, epi li dire apeprè 20 minit. Yo rapòte rezilta egzamen yo avèk yon endis liziblite ki rele Lexile®. Panse ak nòt Lexile la kòm si ou ta va li yon tèmomèt eksteryè. Menm jan ou ka sèvi ak tanperati ki nan yon tèmomèt pou deside ki kalite chanday pou mete, ou ka sèvi ak yon nòt Lexile pou deside nivo difikilte yon liv ou ka li !

Rezilta *SRI* yo :

Dat egzamen an :
Rezilta egzamen an :
Kòmantè :

Genyen plizyè fason ou ka ede pwogrè pitit ou an ap fè nan lekti nan kay la. Men kèk sijesyon :

- Fikse yon objektif pou pitit ou an pou l fè lekti omwen 20 minit pa jou.

- Paske yo itilize sistèm Lexile lan tou pou asiyen liv yo endis liziblite, ou ka sèvi ak nòt Lexile pitit ou an pou jwenn liv ki nan nivo lekti ki apwopriye pou li. Pitit ou an te resevwa yon lis liv pèsonalize ki reflete nòt Lexile li ansanm ak liv ki enterese li. Ankouraje pitit ou an li liv ki sou lis sa a epi pou l diskite yo avèk ou.

- Pataje ak pitit ou an kalite bagay *w ap* li. Pale l konsènan bagay enteresan ou li nan jounal, oswa konsènan yon atik nan yon revi ki te aprann ou yon bagay ou pa t konnen.

Mèsi dèske w pran yon ti moman pou ede amelyore aptitid pou lekti pitit ou an. Si w genyen nenpòt kesyon, tanpri pa ezite kontakte m.

Sensèman,

Conference Record

Student's Name ______________________ Date __________

Lexile® Measure ______________ Subject of Conference __________

In our conference we talked about: ______________________

____

____

Areas of improvement are: ______________________

____

____

Areas of strength are:

___ phonics/phonemic awareness
___ vocabulary
___ word attack/structural analysis
___ drawing conclusions/making inferences
___ summarizing text
___ separating fact from opinion
___ identifying cause and effect
___ recognizing the story sequence
___ understanding literary elements such as theme, main idea, setting, point of view
___ integrating new knowledge with prior knowledge
___ critical thinking
___ responding to text, orally and in writing

Areas that need work are:

___ phonics/phonemic awareness
___ vocabulary
___ word attack/structural analysis
___ drawing conclusions/making inferences
___ summarizing text
___ separating fact from opinion
___ identifying cause and effect
___ recognizing the story sequence
___ understanding literary elements such as theme, main idea, setting, point of view
___ integrating new knowledge with prior knowledge
___ critical thinking
___ responding to text, orally and in writing

Number of books read on Reading Report: ______________________

Favorite books on Reading Report (include author, genre, topic, theme):

____

____

Comments: ______________________________________

____

____

Date to check progress: __________

Student ______________________ Teacher ______________________
Signature *Signature*

My Personal Goal

Name ______________________________

Grade ______________________________

Teacher/Class ______________________________

My Goal is to read __________ **books.** **Fiction:** _____ **Nonfiction:** _____

Goal Starting Date: ______________ **Goal End Date:** ______________

Some of the books I will read: *(Place a check next to those that are on your Reading Report.)*

____

____

____

____

____

____

____

____

____

I will try my best to reach this goal.

Student ______________________________
Signature *Date*

We will help to reach this goal.

Teacher ______________________________
Signature *Date*

Parent ______________________________
Signature *Date*

Reading Log

Name ______________________________

I have read these books:

Title	Author	Date Finished
1.		
2.		
3.		
4.		
5.		
6.		
7.		
8.		
9.		
10.		
11.		
12.		
13.		
14.		
15.		
16.		
17.		
18.		

Student/Teacher Conference Dates:

______________ ______________ ______________ ______________

Book Recommendation (Grades K–4)

Recommend a Book to Your Classmates

Student's Name: ______________________________

I recommend ______________________________
title of book

by ______________________________
author

What is the book about? ______________________________

____

____

____

Why do you like this book? ______________________________

____

____

____

Describe the characters and setting or tell about the main idea. ______________________________

____

____

____

Draw your own cover for the book (on the back of this page):

Book Recommendation (Grade 5 and up)

Recommend a Book to Your Classmates

Student's Name: ______________________________

Book Title: ______________________________

Author: ______________________________

Book Summary: ______________________________

____

____

____

Why do you recommend this book? ______________________________

____

____

____

Describe the characters and setting, or main idea: ______________________________

____

____

____

What is the theme or main idea? What message does it communicate?

____

____

____

What do you like about the author's style (use of metaphor, figurative language, tone, voice, use of details, etc.)? ______________________________

____

____

____

____

____

Lexile Framework® for Reading Map

Chart Your Student's Reading Growth Student's Name ______________________________

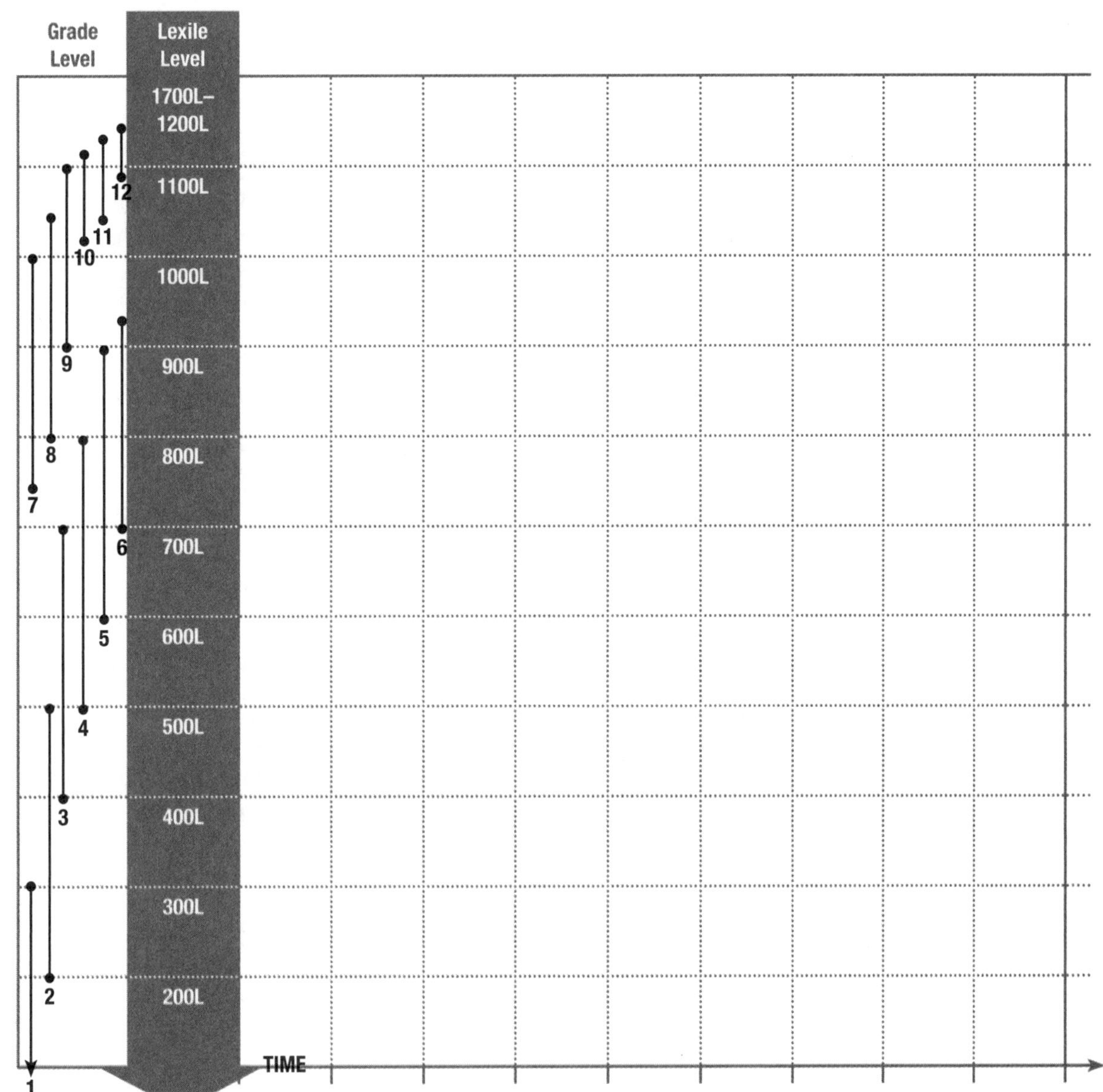

Chart a student's reading growth on the Lexile map. Place a dot on the map at the appropriate level indicating the student's current Lexile measure that corresponds to the date you fill in on the x-axis (time). Write the exact Lexile measure in parenthesis (e.g. 880) next to the dot. Record the student's past Lexile measure(s), as well as future ones (each time the student takes *SRI™*) to see the student's reading growth.

You can also list a few of the books the student has read, at each of the recorded Lexile levels to create a more comprehensive picture of the student's reading growth. If you wish, keep a portfolio of the student's written responses to literature at each of the levels to complement what you've recorded on the map.

Glossary

Adaptive Test: An adaptive test, such as *SRI*, is one that is targeted to each individual examinee. As the student takes the test, the questions step up or down in difficulty, with the aid of a computer algorithm, according to the student's performance. Each examinee takes a unique appropriately-leveled test designed based on abilities. In order to further reduce testing time while still producing precise results, information about the examinee's prior level of proficiency (based on other standardized test results) can be used to determine the optimal starting point for the test.

Beginning Reader (BR): A text or student with a Lexile measure of 99 or below. BR designation is an indication that the student cannot yet comprehend continuous text.

Criterion-referenced Test: A criterion-referenced test is one that provides results which indicate the knowledge or skills possessed by a student. Scores from these tests have meaning in terms of what the student knows or can do, rather than in relation to the scores of an external reference (or norm) group. *SRI* is a criterion-referenced test, that also provides norm-referenced results.

Grade Equivalent: A grade equivalent (GE) is a score that represents the typical (mean or median) performance of students tested in a given month of the school year. It is a decimal number that shows performance in terms of Grade Level (to the left of the decimal) and months (to the right of the decimal). It is not an equal interval scale and should not be used to measure growth. *SRI* does not report in GE.

Grade Level: Indicates whether the student is reading on, above, or below grade as determined by the place on the norm scale. Grade Level also corresponds to the student's Performance Standard. (See *Performance Standard*.)

Lexile: A Lexile is a unit of measurement that is used to determine the difficulty of text and the reading level of readers. It is an equal interval scale and can be used to measure growth.

Lexile Framework: The Lexile Framework is a system that can help determine the reading level of any written material—from a book to a test item. The Framework can also be used to assess a reader's reading comprehension level. After test results are converted into Lexile® measures, readers can be matched to reading materials on their own level. The Lexile Framework enables teachers to forecast what material each student can read with the desired level of comprehension.

Lexile Reading Range: The number of Lexiles above and below the student's Lexile measure at which the student can be successful when reading for different purposes—independent reading, instructional reading, and fluent reading. Generally, the ranges for each of these are:

- **Independent:** 250 Lexiles below the student's Lexile measure to 50 Lexiles above the student's Lexile measure.
- **Instructional:** 250 Lexiles above the student's Lexile measure to 100 Lexiles below the student's Lexile measure.

See pp. 187–188 for more information.

Lexile Reader Measure: The Lexile measure of a student's reading level is determined by the results of a test such as the *SRI*. A student whose reading skills have been measured at 500 Lexiles (500L) can confidently read a book that is also measured at 500L.

Lexile Text Measure: A Lexile text measure is the specific number assigned to any text. A computer program called the Lexile Analyzer computes this. The Analyzer carefully examines the whole text to measure such characteristics as sentence length and word frequency—characteristics that are highly related to overall reading comprehension. The Analyzer then reports a Lexile measure for the text.

NCE: A normal curve equivalent (NCE) is a normalized student score with a mean of 50 and a standard deviation of 21.06. NCEs range from 1 to 99. NCEs allow comparison between different tests for the same student or group of students, and between different students on the same test. NCEs have many of the same characteristics as percentile ranks, but have the additional advantage of being based on an interval scale. That is, the difference between two consecutive scores on the scale has the same meaning throughout the scale. NCEs are often required by many categorical funding agencies (for example, Title I). See also stanines and percentiles.

Grade	Below Basic	Basic	Proficient	Advanced
1	—	99 & Below	100 to 400	401 & Above
2	99 & Below	100 to 299	300 to 600	601 & Above
3	249 & Below	250 to 499	500 to 800	801 & Above
4	349 & Below	350 to 599	600 to 900	901 & Above
5	449 & Below	450 to 699	700 to 1000	1001 & Above
6	499 & Below	500 to 799	800 to 1050	1051 & Above
7	549 & Below	550 to 849	850 to 1100	1101 & Above
8	599 & Below	600 to 899	900 to 1150	1151 & Above
9	649 & Below	650 to 999	1000 to 1200	1201 & Above
10	699 & Below	700 to 1024	1025 to 1250	1251 & Above
11	799 & Below	800 to 1049	1050 to 1300	1301 & Above

** Reported in Lexiles*

Diagram of a normal curve with stanines, NCEs, and percentiles.

Non-adaptive Test: A non-adaptive test is one that is not customized. Each student is administered the same test questions regardless of her prior level of proficiency on the skills and knowledge being assessed. Each test includes a wide range of questions to cover the needs of both the low-achieving students and the high-achieving students. However, while some questions may be appropriate, the overall test may not be at the appropriate level for each student.

Norm-referenced Test: A norm-referenced test is one which produces results that relate to the performance of a comparison group. Norm-referenced interpretations tell how the scores of each student or group of students compares to the scores of the original (norm) group that took the test. The scores of the students do not necessarily produce the same distribution of scores as the scores of the norm group. *SRI* provides norm-referenced as well as criterion-referenced results.

Percentile Rank: The percentile rank of a score indicates the percentage of scores less than or equal to that score. Percentile ranks range from 1 to 99. For example, if a student scores at the 65th percentile rank, it means that he performed as well as or better on the assessment than 65 percent of the norm group.

Note: Percentile rank does not refer to the percentage of items answered correctly.

Performance Standard: A descriptor of student performance that describes what students must do to demonstrate various levels of proficiency with respect to the specific content (for example, reading comprehension). Four default levels have been identified to describe student performance on the *SRI* at each grade. The levels are based on end-of-year test results.

- **Advanced:** Students scoring in this range exhibit superior performance when reading grade-level appropriate text and can be considered as reading "above Grade Level."
- **Proficient:** Students scoring in this range exhibit competent performance when reading grade-level appropriate text and can be considered as reading "on Grade Level." Students performing at this level should be able to identify details, draw conclusions, and make comparisons and generalizations when reading materials developmentally appropriate for the Grade Level.
- **Basic:** Students scoring in this range exhibit minimally competent performance when reading grade-level appropriate text and can be considered as reading "below Grade Level."
- **Below Basic:** Students scoring in this range do not exhibit minimally competent performance when reading grade-level appropriate text and can be considered as reading significantly "below Grade Level." Intervention is recommended.

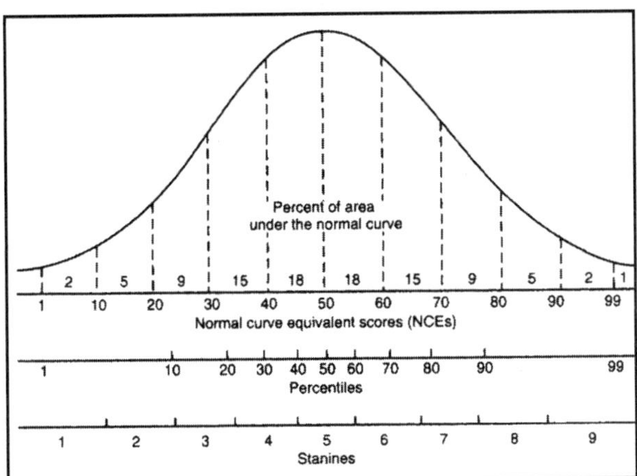

Raw Score: The number of correct responses by a student to a set of test items. Raw scores cannot be compared across tests, nor are they equal interval. Generally, raw scores are converted to a scale score or—as with *SRI*—to a Lexile measure.

Scale Score: A non-linear transformation of the raw score to make the scale units equal interval, and thus useful for measuring growth.

Stanine: Stanine is a standardized student score with a mean of 5 and a standard deviation of 2. Stanines range from 1 to 9. In general for all grades, stanines of 1 to 3 are considered below average, stanines of 4 to 6 are considered average, and stanines of 7 to 9 are considered above average. A difference of 2 between the stanines for two measures indicates that the two measures are significantly different. Stanines, like percentiles, indicate a student's relative standing in a norm group.

Note: Page numbers preceded by "R" refer to Reproducibles at the end of the manual.